The United States and China
in World Affairs

Published volumes in the series,
"THE UNITED STATES AND CHINA IN WORLD AFFAIRS"

A. M. HALPERN (EDITOR)
Policies toward China:
Views from Six Continents

A. T. STEELE
The American People
and China

ALEXANDER ECKSTEIN
Communist China's Economic
Growth and Foreign Trade:
Implications for U.S. Policy

LEA E. WILLIAMS
The Future
of the Overseas Chinese
in Southeast Asia

R. BLUM
—EDITED BY A. D. BARNETT
The United States
and China
in World Affairs

The United States and China in World Affairs

ROBERT BLUM

Edited by A. Doak Barnett

A VOLUME IN THE SERIES,
"THE UNITED STATES AND CHINA IN WORLD AFFAIRS"

PUBLISHED FOR THE COUNCIL ON FOREIGN RELATIONS BY THE

McGRAW-HILL BOOK COMPANY

New York · Toronto · London · Sydney

THE UNITED STATES AND CHINA IN WORLD AFFAIRS

Copyright © 1966 by Council on Foreign Relations, Inc. All Rights Reserved. Printed in the United States of America. This book, or parts thereof, may not be reproduced in any form without permission of the publishers.

Library of Congress Catalog Card Number: 66-26490

First Edition

06183

To Isabelle, Rolland, and Antoinette Blum

Foreword by Allen W. Dulles

This is the fifth volume in the series on The United States and China in World Affairs, the outcome of studies sponsored by the Council on Foreign Relations with the aid of a generous grant from The Ford Foundation. Through this program the Council seeks to encourage more active and better informed consideration of what is obviously a crucial area of United States foreign policy.

The aim has not been to produce any single set of conclusions on a subject so complex as that of America's relations with China. Each study in the series therefore constitutes a separate and self-contained inquiry written on the responsibility of the author, who has reached his own judgments and conclusions regarding the subject of his investigations and its implications for United States policy. The authors of the various volumes include persons with a variety of backgrounds in Chinese affairs and foreign policy. Some have had long personal experience in China. Others have studied China and Far Eastern problems during recent years or dealt with them as officials and administrators. In each case they have been able to consult with a group of qualified persons invited by the Council on Foreign Relations to meet periodically with them. The project has been guided by a Steering Committee which includes Hamilton Fish Armstrong, A. Doak Barnett, Arthur H. Dean, George S. Franklin, Jr., Sidney F. Giffin, Joseph E. Johnson, Grayson Kirk, John J. McCloy, and Lucian W. Pye, in addition to myself.

The present volume has a special significance in the series because Robert Blum, until his untimely death in July 1965, was the able and imaginative director of the project as a whole. He envisaged the total enterprise, arranged for the authors of the separate studies, and counseled them during the formative stages of their work.* In addition to all these duties, he completed the first draft of this book and had outlined his revisions before his death.

The Steering Committee asked A. Doak Barnett to complete and edit the book, which he undertook to do in spite of his already extensive obligations. Although in structure and organization this book is fully the work of Robert Blum, special recognition must be given to the skill and sensitivity with which Professor Barnett, guided by his deep respect for Mr. Blum and his knowledge of Mr. Blum's thinking, fulfilled his difficult assignment.

The spirit in which this book was completed underlines the Council's basic policy that all opinions and conclusions in the studies it sponsors are those of individual authors and that the Council itself does not endorse or advance any specific policy recommendations. Neither Mr. Barnett nor any member of the Steering Committee necessarily subscribes to all the opinions and arguments in this study; we have individually and collectively sought only to carry out our sober responsibility to Robert Blum and his work.

Before Mr. Blum's death he had discussed the entire manuscript with the Steering Committee, which was joined by members from the Steering Committee of the Atlantic Policy Studies, a companion project of similar scope. Since Mr. Blum was striving to develop a new understanding of an immensely troubled area of American policy, his ideas inevitably provoked sharp debate and at times vigorous dissent. It could not have been otherwise so long as he would not content himself with platitudes or bland generalities. While it recognizes that no one can fully know how events and additional discussion might have further affected his views, the Steering Committee believes that this study merits publication. In its opinion, the long-range considerations on which he based his views remain valid today.

* After Robert Blum's death, Lucian W. Pye, professor of political science at the Massachusetts Institute of Technology, agreed, without hesitation and despite heavy commitments, to assume the responsibilities as director of the project because of his respect for Mr. Blum and his sense of the importance of the effort.

The spirit in which Mr. Blum approached his task combined an historical and philosophical perspective with a sense of urgency about immediate and concrete policy choices. Above all, he wanted his country to avail itself of all possibilities for contributing to a more stable and peaceful Asia. He was also, however, an enemy of wishful thinking, and his philosophical reflections had no room for romanticism—he knew the central place of realism and firmness in the actions of great powers.

In a very personal manner, Mr. Blum felt the anguish and frustrations inherent in America's relations with China. He was eager to hold out the possibility of friendship to the Chinese people even though their government now chooses to be our enemy; he was sensitive alike to the desirability of flexibility in detailed actions and the necessity of strength and steadfastness in fundamental policy.

When Mr. Blum wrote his volume the mood in this country was not as receptive as it possibly is now to the discussion of new approaches to the problem of China. All he would ask today is that those inclined to advance differing conclusions should examine alternatives as realistically as he has tried to do. It is the Council's hope that this book will contribute to the vigor of the American public's thinking about relations with the world's most populous country.

Editor's Preface

When the Council on Foreign Relations initiated its research project on The United States and China in World Affairs, it decided that as director of the project it should find a man with wide international and Asian experience. The aim was to find someone competent to examine the positions and relations of the United States and China in the broad context of the great political, economic, and social changes now under way throughout Asia and the world. The person chosen was Robert Blum, former president of The Asia Foundation, a man of high intelligence, deep humanity, and great understanding, who had long been concerned with the problems of United States relations not only with China but with Asia as a whole.

Mr. Blum, working under the general guidance of a Steering Committee chaired by Allen W. Dulles, developed the research plans for the project, defined the studies to be made, recruited the men to write them, helped organize the study groups which assist all authors working on Council projects, and encouraged, advised, criticized, and guided everyone connected with the project.

The resulting studies * serve as a permanent testimonial to the

* The studies published at this writing include: A. M. Halpern, ed., *Policies Toward China: Views from Six Continents* (New York: McGraw-Hill for the Council on Foreign Relations, 1966); A. T. Steele, *The American People and China* (New York: McGraw-Hill for the Council on Foreign Relations, 1966); and Alexander Eckstein, *Communist China's Economic Growth and Foreign Trade: Implications for U.S. Policy* (New York: McGraw-Hill for the Council on Foreign Relations, 1966). Still in preparation are studies of the overseas Chinese, Communist China's military forces and power, Asian security and American policy, U.S. negotiations with the Chinese Communists, Taiwan and the Nationalist government,

effective way in which he performed his task. I am sure that he would have wished to express here his special gratitude for advice and assistance from a number of individuals, including Allen W. Dulles, Lucian W. Pye, and the other members of the Steering Committee. David Albright, his Research Associate and close colleague, and Ruth Drilling Pashman, his devoted Administrative Assistant, aided him in innumerable ways. To both, he would have expressed his deep appreciation. George S. Franklin, Jr., David MacEachron, Lorna Brennan, and other members of the Council's staff and Donald Wasson, Janet Rigney, and other members of the Council's library staff also rendered special help.

In addition to directing the project, Mr. Blum himself undertook to write a volume analyzing United States relations with China. He conceived of it as a general discussion of both the forces and the attitudes affecting American policy and of the policy alternatives deserving consideration, a book that would draw upon the more detailed and documented studies written by other members of the project but would not duplicate their detail. Somehow, despite his manifold duties as director of the entire project, he found time to write the book in rough, draft form and to discuss it at length with the Steering Committee as well as with many other knowledgeable individuals. By the summer of 1965, he had gathered numerous comments on his first draft and was preparing to start work on the final version of the volume when he was suddenly and tragically struck down by a fatal heart attack.

Robert Blum's death was not only a great personal blow to the many people who had felt warm admiration, affection, and respect for him as a person. It was also a tragic loss in a broader sense, for there are few with his experience and perception who have been willing to devote themselves so wholeheartedly and completely to the task of understanding the problems of American relations with Asia—and, most particularly, with China.

The Council decided that it was important for his book to be completed, and it asked me to edit the volume and prepare it for publication. I agreed because I too felt that the results of

Communist China's foreign policy, and the political development of Communist China.

his work and thought should be made widely available, but I did so with serious misgivings. Editing someone else's book is a delicate task under any circumstances, and it becomes infinitely more so when it is impossible to obtain the author's stamp of approval on the final edited volume.

I decided that the only thing I could legitimately do was to take his rough draft, study the notes he had made on planned revisions and the recorded suggestions and comments that had been presented to him by members of his Steering Committee and others, and then try, as best I could, to determine what he himself would have wished to do in preparing the final version for publication. It would be presumptuous to claim that I have totally succeeded. However, shortly before his death he did discuss with several members of the Council and the project staff the general nature of the changes and revisions that he planned to make, and these have provided essential guidelines for what I have done. I can only hope that he would have approved the result.*

I have resisted the temptation of trying to impose my own views, or style, on his. The fact that earlier I myself had written a book for the Council on United States policy toward China was perhaps an advantage in that I had already stated my own views in detail.** I felt no compulsion to try to convert his volume into mine. Perhaps if he had lived to complete his book himself, he might have decided to do more revision and rewriting than I have actually done. Since, however, there is no way of knowing, I have felt it both necessary and desirable to leave as much as possible of his original draft intact. In short, I have tried to take my responsibility as an editor seriously, but the book remains Robert Blum's. And despite the fact that he was receptive to others' suggestions and criticisms, in many respects the book is a very personal document, reflecting his own views of problems and prospects at the time of his death in 1965.

Mr. Blum's hope was that the book would help to stimulate

* In performing my task, I have been greatly assisted by many of the people whose contributions to the project as a whole have already been noted. In addition, B. Lynn Pascoe checked all the citations and footnotes, and Marina Finklestein gave editorial advice.
** *Communist China and Asia: Challenge to American Policy* (New York: Harper and Brothers for the Council on Foreign Relations, 1960).

"a sustained high level of orderly responsible discourse" in the
United States on various alternative policies toward China. If
it contributes to this end, I am sure he would have felt that his
effort had been worthwhile and his main goal achieved.

It was also his own personal belief, however, that new approaches and initiatives in United States policy toward China
are urgently needed. As he put it at the close of the book:

We cannot be sure that efforts to reach a reasonable understanding
with the Chinese Communists will succeed. The current prospects
are not good. The present commitment of the Chinese leaders to a
hostile attitude toward the United States is strong and will not be
easily changed. But we must try. Until we take the initiative, affirm
our leadership, and pursue our goals more vigorously but with greater
prudence, patience, and understanding, we cannot know whether or
not, over time, a better basis of relations, or at least a reduction in the
present level of tension and hostility, can be achieved.

This was his essential concern and his fundamental prescription.

A. DOAK BARNETT
April 1966

Contents

Introduction

Seventeen years have passed since the Chinese Communists completed their victory on the mainland of China. The United States tried in vain to prevent this victory, both by aiding the Nationalist Government against the Communist challenge and by attempting to promote a political settlement that would end the Chinese civil war. Whether one judges these American efforts to have been decisive or peripheral, well-intentioned or misguided, one fact is clear. They failed.

Bitterness and hostility were the product of the failure, and these emotions were soon intensified by the policies of the new government in Peking and by the Korean War. Relations between the United States and the Chinese Communists continue to have a special emotional quality about them, and there is a widespread feeling among critics both in the United States and abroad that American policy is shaped too much by past history rather than by the requirements of the present. Debate over the past can be useful, but the past should not be exhumed and exhibited as a present reality. What is urgently needed now is an examination of the situation as it exists today and is likely to evolve in the future.

The situation in 1966 is very different from that in 1949. The government of the People's Republic of China today exercises effective control of the China mainland with a disciplined totalitarian apparatus unprecedented in Chinese history. While economically weak and militarily circumscribed, it is diplomatically assertive and ideologically aggressive, and it challenges American interests in such widely scattered areas of the world as Asia, Africa, and Latin America. Its entrance into the nuclear club is a portent of a much enlarged capability for making its influence felt.

The entire balance in Asia has been changed. In the areas neighboring China the former colonial powers have disappeared, and in their place are now a variety of new states, most of them weak, inexperienced, unstable, and divided by complex rivalries. Japan, which two decades ago achieved a temporary dominance in Asia, is today disarmed, restricted to its home islands, and pre-occupied above all with its own affairs. The Soviet Union, which immediately after World War II reasserted its interests in Asia and then became the new Chinese Communist government's strongest sponsor and ally, is today openly challenged by Peking for leadership throughout the Communist bloc and world movement.

These varied elements—the defeat of Japan, the decline of European influence, the new dynamism of China, the weakness and disunity of most of the Asian successor states, and the formation of the Sino-Soviet alliance followed by the development of Sino-Soviet conflict—together have basically altered the situation in Asia, and the new situation is one in which the United States has become a major and essential element in the Asian balance. Since the war in the Pacific, the United States has become the strongest military power in the area, the principal source of outside help to the new countries, and the main counterbalance to the influence of the Chinese Communists.

The China policy of the United States obviously does not concern China alone or simply the recognition of a particular government and that government's claim to be seated in the United Nations. Moreover, diplomatic maneuvering alone will not unravel the tangled web of the China problem. Our policy must take account of the complex ideological and political currents that are sweeping the world and the varied interests and policies of many peoples other than the Chinese. In the background of the present power struggle are the diffusion of technology to China and other areas, hitherto underdeveloped, and the fashioning of modern nations with their own political institutions out of tradition-rooted societies. And underlying the struggle is the search for security and a viable world order. In shaping its China policy, the United States must be sensitive to all these factors and problems.

There is, however, the immediate problem of how best to deal with a militant, resurgent China, how to define our own long-term purposes, and how to take effective steps designed to achieve them. There are many volunteers for this task, and most of them, despite their many differences, claim that they are being "realistic." The trouble with such a simple test of policy is that reality, like Pascal's view of faith, "embraces many truths which appear to contradict each other." [1] For example, the continued existence of the Communist regime on the mainland is certainly a reality; so too are the 700,000,000 Chinese, whom we are being constantly reminded we cannot ignore. But there are other realities as well. The harsh and unabated hostility of the Peking government and its militant doctrine of world revolution are quite real. So is the Nationalist government on Taiwan.

It is important to avoid the facile but sterile course of making policy by coining slogans. Being "tough," "reasonable," or "realistic" are all necessary and desirable at the right time and place. The difficulty lies in defining specific goals and interests at any particular time and in selecting policies that correspond to the needs of the occasion in light of both short-term advantages and long-term objectives. It is essential to combat the spread of communism, but communism itself is changing and has different forms. And in the complexities of Asia, there is no simple formula for how best to check it.

At various times since 1949, the China question has been discussed primarily in terms of "Who lost China?" This was the nature of the debate after General MacArthur's recall from Korea and during many of our subsequent election campaigns, when pledges "to have nothing to do with Communist China" were sometimes considered prime symbols of patriotism and loyalty. Debate on this level, however, has not been very fruitful.

More recently, the dispute between Communist China and the Soviet Union, China's progress toward acquisition of a nuclear capability, and the crisis in Southeast Asia have provoked more active discussion with fewer restraints, but there has not yet been a responsible "great debate" on China policy. Because of the hurly-burly of American political life, is it too much to expect a sustained high level of orderly, responsible discourse on a subject

[1] Blaise Pascal, *Pensées,* no. 862.

as complicated and controversial as China policy? One hopes not.

Has the relative lack of discussion meant that a firm consensus has existed in support of our present China policy? This seems doubtful. There has been too much evidence of underlying uneasiness, both inside and outside the government. It is more probable that the continued influence of past inhibitions, the preoccupation with immediate rather than long-term problems, and the very complexity of the problems have all contributed to the lack of lively examination of our China policy. It has seemed safer as well as more urgent to deal with problems which have a greater apparent priority, such as, for example, the closely related problem of Vietnam.

The argument is sometimes made, both inside and outside the government—although with less conviction now than a few years ago—that we should not give the Chinese Communists any comfort by airing our differences. It is also argued that debate on our China policy may disturb our friends and weaken confidence in us on the part of those who rely on our protection. These arguments do highlight real problems, but they should not prevent us from discussing frankly, fully, and openly what it is we want to achieve and how best to achieve it.

It is certainly both hazardous and unwise to subject important aspects of foreign policy to capricious and petulant examination and debate. China policy, however, has received little broad, sustained, responsible attention, and discussion of it is probably plagued by more stereotyped thinking than any other issue of our foreign policy. Moreover, the vast changes that have occurred in the world, including what has happened in China since 1949, suggest that a re-examination is now very much in order. We need to have a better understanding of the alternatives in order either to confirm the validity of our present course of action or to move in new directions.

More than anything else we should try to see the problem in its full perspective, to avoid over-simplification, and to get a better understanding of a country whose strangeness is compounded by its isolation and hostility.

CHAPTER ONE

The Confrontation between Communist China and the United States

On July 3, 1844, Caleb Cushing signed on behalf of the United States government the Treaty of Wanghia, the first treaty between the United States and China. The Preamble of that document affirmed the desire "to establish firm, lasting, and sincere friendship between the two Nations," and Article I stipulated that

There shall be a perfect, permanent, universal peace, and a sincere and cordial amity, between the United States of America on the one part, and the Ta Tsing Empire on the other part, and between their people respectively, without exception of persons or places.[1]

A century later, China and the United States brought to a victorious close their war against Japan. They had fought together as allies, and although the alliance had at times been troubled, it achieved its objective. China was indebted to the United States for its primary role in the defeat of Japan, with which China had been at war since 1937, and the United States, on its part, regarded a friendly China as the mainstay of a newly emerging balance of power in the Far East.

Today, more than twenty years later, the peace that was to have been "perfect, permanent, universal" has vanished, and the United

[1] Hunter Miller, ed., *Treaties and Other International Acts of the United States of America* (Washington: GPO, 1934), v. 4, p. 559.

5

States and mainland China are now antagonists, not allies. A Chinese government hostile to the United States controls the mainland, and those Chinese with whom the United States fought the victorious war are confined to their island stronghold on Taiwan. The romanticized friendship of a generation ago and the glamour of East meeting West are gone, and today the United States and Communist China are bitter competitors. In mainland China, the United States is viewed as the most powerful bourgeois and "imperialist" nation and the principal obstacle to the achievement of China's ambitions, a capitalist country that is not only wealthy and powerful but makes its influence felt in all of Asia and could cause enormous damage to China itself. China is unable to threaten the United States directly, but it uses its diplomatic and ideological resources to challenge and undermine the American position wherever it can and seeks in other ways to escape from the restraints imposed by American power. In many respects, what exists is not a straightforward power conflict or military confrontation resulting solely from the clash of tangible and comparable interests. The situation is far more complicated than that. Ideologies and national emotions have been propelled into the currents of international controversy in a way that reflects the passions of a period of revolutionary turmoil.

The Development of the Conflict

Although we know for certain that our relations with China have gone badly, it is not easy to affirm with confidence what we should have done differently. Even during the Sino-Japanese War in the 1930s, we did not have a clear picture of China's role in the world balance or of the responsibilities that we would be called upon to assume. The United States was still relatively isolated and could, as far as China was concerned, enjoy the advantages of the cultural and economic relations that had been developed during the previous century. We did not fully understand the disruptive effect that the West had had on Chinese society and gave little thought to the relationship this might have to the growth of communism, which was then having its first practical test in neighboring Russia. It must have seemed as if the then-existing relationship between the Western world and China would go on forever. We were not alone, one should note, in being mistaken. The judgment of the European countries was no better, and the Japanese made far more serious misestimates than we did.

The consequences were serious for us not because of worse judgment on our part but because World War II and its wake left the United States heavily involved in situations and events that neither we nor others could control.

During the war years we subordinated our concerns in China to the overriding purpose of winning the war against Japan. The quarrels between the Nationalists and the Communists were troubling because they impeded the effectiveness of the Chinese war effort, but the likelihood that the Communists would emerge as the dominant force on the mainland seemed remote until later years. Virtually everyone except Mao and his closest colleagues underestimated the Chinese Communists' prospects for success; this included the Soviet Union as well as ourselves.

For a brief period, in 1945, when the war in Europe ended and the shape of things to come in the Far East was not yet clear, the United States sought, notably at Yalta, to enlist the support of the Soviet Union against Japan by promising Stalin concessions at China's expense. Subsequently, the Russians signed a treaty with the Chinese Nationalist government, on August 14, 1945, in which they obtained advantages in both Mongolia and Manchuria. The ink was hardly dry on this treaty when the situation began changing in spectacular fashion. The Japanese surrendered, and the Americans acquired the predominant role in administering occupied Japan. In Europe the confrontation between the Western powers and the Soviet Union rapidly developed. In China, the Communist-Nationalist civil war exploded into open conflict, and the United States undertook the fruitless task of trying to bring about a peaceful settlement between the two major Chinese parties.

The situation in China deteriorated rapidly during the ensuing years, and it is unlikely that anything the United States could have done, short of major military intervention, would have prevented the Nationalists' ultimate defeat. The United States was clearly not willing to intervene with large-scale military power,

8

and there was, in fact, no substantial body of opinion in the United States that recommended we do so. With the United States at the height of its power and China weakened by years of cruel and costly foreign and civil wars, it hardly seemed conceivable to most Americans that out of the China which we had befriended and which we had backed for an important role in the new balance of power in Asia there would soon emerge a unified, hostile, and dangerous antagonist.

This was, moreover, a time when the main danger to American interests appeared to be developing in Europe rather than in Asia. The awakening to Soviet ambitions, the growing strength of the Communist parties in the Western European countries, the Communist threat to Greece and pressures on Turkey, and the Communist coup in Czechoslovakia—in response to which there emerged the Truman Doctrine, the Marshall Plan, and NATO— all took place during the final years of the civil war in China.

By mid-1949 the lines were drawn. On July 1, Mao Tse-tung issued his statement "On the People's Democratic Dictatorship," [2] defining a policy of "leaning to one side." "Not only in China but throughout the world," he said, "one must lean either to imperialism or to socialism. There is no exception. Neutrality is merely a camouflage; a third road does not exist." A month later the Department of State issued its White Paper,[3] which sought to explain, interpret, and defend American policy toward China and to demonstrate to domestic critics of the administration that the U.S. government could not have prevented the downfall of the Nationalists. On October 1, 1949, the People's Republic of China was proclaimed.

The Chinese Communists lost no time in demonstrating their hostility to the United States and their ties with the Soviet Union, and on February 14, 1950, the Sino-Soviet Treaty of Friendship, Alliance, and Mutual Security was signed. At this time, however, Washington was not disposed to intervene further in the Chinese civil war, even to prevent the Communists from completing their victory by an invasion of Taiwan. As was

[2] Mao Tse-tung, *On the People's Democratic Dictatorship* (Peking: Foreign Languages Press, 1950).
[3] U.S. Department of State, *United States Relations with China* (Washington, D.C.: GPO, 1949).

just stated, our attention was focused on Europe. In Asia, our position as the major occupying power in Japan and Okinawa and our special ties with the Philippines seemed adequate to guard against further trouble. Moreover, the Communists were expected to have their hands full on the China mainland for a long time.

It is clear in retrospect that while we "let the dust settle" and attempted to limit our commitments in Asia, we did not accurately foresee the consequences of what had happened in China and underestimated the ability of the Chinese Communists to unify and mobilize the country and infuse its people and policies with hostility to the United States. We vaguely hoped that the Chinese people would in time part ways with international communism, which was then seen as being tightly controlled and directed from Moscow, but not many Americans foresaw the important and distinctive role that Communist China itself would soon play in Asia and the world.

The Korean War, which began less than a year after the Communists' victory on the China mainland, contributed greatly to the shaping of subsequent American attitudes and policies toward China. The frustrations of fighting a war without hitting the main adversary's centers of power and of not winning a decisive victory against an enemy whose military prowess we had originally failed to take very seriously left us bitter and divided. Many United States actions taken during the war influenced American policy in the Far East for years to come. The decision first to protect Taiwan from Communist attack and then later to sign a security treaty with the Chinese Nationalists, the conclusion of a peace treaty with Japan without Chinese participation, and the steps taken by Washington to play a more active role in Southeast Asia all stemmed in large part from the Korean War.

Communist China, which intervened in Korea after the crossing of the 38th parallel by United Nations troops and which subsequently refused to accept any United Nations proposals for settlement of the war, was condemned by the United Nations as an aggressor and soon came to be viewed as a dangerously aggressive power with almost unlimited ambitions throughout the area. The U.S. policy of containment, which had been formulated primarily in relation to the Soviet Union in Europe, was now applied in Asia against China, and thus the pattern of confrontation was set.

The Pattern of Confrontation

When the Communists first achieved victory on the Chinese mainland and the antagonism between the new regime and the United States gradually became apparent, it seemed to many Americans as if the threat from China should be looked upon simply as a part of an overall Communist assault directed by the Soviet Union. International communism appeared to be one and indivisible. Only subsequently, after the Sino-Soviet conflict emerged, was China fully recognized to be an independent challenge.

While, over time, a variety of international and domestic factors appear to have had a moderating influence on the Soviet regime, whose present leaders generally pursue a less militant policy than in years past, it is obvious that this has not yet happened to the Chinese Communists. The present Chinese leaders still face grave problems at home as well as severe obstacles to fulfillment of their ambitions abroad. They are, moreover, first-generation revolutionaries who have attempted to grasp from the Russians the torch of militant international communism and to carry it throughout Asia, Africa, and Latin America in search of new audiences for their anti-imperialist exhortations and of fertile ground in which to propagate the Chinese revolutionary experience. Unlike the current Russian leaders, Mao and his colleagues show little disposition to date to adapt to a world which they find ill suited to their ambitions. Instead, through both conventional diplomacy and Communist subversion they try everywhere possible to extend China's influence, undermine Western positions, and promote Communist doctrine as interpreted by Mao Tsetung. In the neighboring areas of North Vietnam and North Korea, geography and history obviously give China some special advantages, but elsewhere they have to deal with situations where it is more difficult for China to wield a decisive influence. However, the ideological and revolutionary components of their policy are always at hand and are often used in the service of Chinese national interests.

From Peking's viewpoint, the United States today is clearly the main barrier to China's aspirations in the world and the main potential threat to China itself. American bases and allies are situated on most of China's periphery and serve as tangible evidence of American opposition to Peking's policies and goals. American and Chinese troops fought in Korea, and wherever crises involving China have occurred, in Korea, Vietnam, Laos, or India, the United States has stepped in to oppose the extension of Chinese influence. Where military measures have not been required, American diplomacy, propaganda, and foreign-aid programs have competed against Chinese influence. It is the United States which stands between mainland China and "liberation" of the island of Taiwan, where American aid supports the rival government of the Republic of China. On a broader world scale, the United States is the mainstay of the international system that the Chinese Communists are attempting to change, and it has consistently used its influence to prevent full Chinese membership in the international community. And last but not least, the United States has the power to destroy China physically or at least to cause it incalculable damage, and the leaders in Peking are aware of this fact.

The Asian setting for our confrontation with China is very different from that in Europe where our principal encounters with the Soviet Union have taken place. In much of Asia, and, in fact, most of the underdeveloped areas of the world, we are faced by societies and peoples with whom we as Americans have little common tradition. By contrast, some of China's closest Asian neighbors have drawn heavily on Chinese civilization and have experienced varying degrees of Chinese influence in the past; both cultural attraction and fear characterize their traditional attitudes toward China. In more distant areas, the Chinese have searched for common ties in societies which have shared similar anti-colonial or anti-imperialist attitudes, low standards of living, and unsatisfied aspirations for modernization. It is not surprising, therefore, that it is in these areas where the Chinese apparently hope to make their strongest appeal and where they seem most optimistic about the possibility of undermining American influence.

In contrast to Europe, where the United States is joined by strong, friendly allies in facing the Soviet Union and where important steps toward regional unification have occurred, the alliance system that the United States has tried to develop in Asia has relatively little strong support from local resources. Most Asian nations are weak, and some of the strongest ones, although friendly to the United States, have been reluctant to join any regional security organizations. The confrontation, thus, does not involve massive opposing forces backed by the threat of mutual nuclear destruction, as in Europe, but occurs in many different forms and in many different situations of political unrest.

Despite Communist China's inability to threaten the United States directly in military terms and despite the weakness of the Chinese economy, there is now a feeling in some quarters in the United States that China may constitute a greater long-run threat to this country than does the Soviet Union. Undoubtedly, this feeling has arisen because Communist China has openly and defiantly challenged the basic principles of society and world order on which American policies and hopes rest and because to date Peking's leaders have shown little inclination to try to accommodate conflicting interests. Moreover, China's development of nuclear weapons and its huge population's determined development of its resources give cause for concern about the future.

An ominous picture of China's future threat has in many respects been reinforced by the recent improvement in American relations with the Soviet Union and the growing seriousness of the controversy between the Soviet Union and Communist China, which have tended to highlight China's belligerence. In actual fact, of course, it is the Soviet Union and not Communist China which has the greatest capability of causing direct harm to the United States and its principal allies. Perhaps the very magnitude and directness of the Russian threat force us, however, into a relationship of continuing contact and negotiation with the Soviet Union which is quite unlike any relationship that we have developed to date, or even considered developing, with the Peking government. In the absence of normal diplomatic, commercial, and cultural contacts, Sino-American relations now consist in large part of verbal assaults and competition for influence in third countries. It is true that we confront each other directly in the Taiwan Strait and that our ambassadors meet periodically in Warsaw. But elsewhere we are dealing with subversion, propaganda, and political pressures exerted on other countries. And in this situation it has been difficult to determine what the most effective responses should be.

Even during the early years after the Russian revolution of 1917, there was considerably more contact between Americans and Russians than exists today between the United States and Communist China. For example, an American famine relief mission was dispatched to the Soviet Union in 1921 and 1922; there was a Soviet trade mission in this country; and there were many American engineers in Soviet plants. With Communist China today, even minimal relationships of this kind are lacking. And yet each country looks upon the other as a major threat. This is surely an incongruous situation in a world so closely interdependent and constantly poised on the edge of tragedy.

The way in which some people in the United States have conceived of the Communist threat has complicated the task of defining just what the danger is that faces us. As was stated before, there was a tendency initially to see the Peking regime almost as an appendage or vassal of the Soviet Union, in the service of the international Communist cause without regard to Chinese interests. The Chinese Communists in the early years did, it is true, collaborate closely with the Soviet Union, but their relationship was never one of complete subordination, as the picture painted by certain American leaders during the months after the Communist victory in China seemed to suggest. Soviet imperialism was seen at that time as extending eastward and southward into Mongolia, Manchuria, and Sinkiang as well as westward into Europe. Perhaps it was thought that emphasis on China's subordination to Moscow might help stir nationalistic Chinese resentment against the Soviet Union, and the fact that China was weak and appeared to have an uncertain future lent support to the notion that China's role in the new partnership was destined to be a subordinate one. Moreover, at the time the Soviet Union was indeed the unquestioned leader of the international Communist movement.

However, the Chinese were not simply acting as tools of the Russians when they threw their forces into the Korean War. They apparently felt that their own security was threatened and also wanted a voice of their own in the settlement of Far Eastern problems. This did not prevent many Americans from being caught up in a wave of indiscriminate anti-communism which made it difficult in the next few years to distinguish between Russians and Chinese, or even, at times, between Communists and "liberals" in our own country. Over time, however, our view of the Peking regime seems to have come into clearer focus as a result of China's increasingly prominent international role, the growing conflict and competition between Moscow and Peking, and our own increasing involvement in Southeast Asia, where China is the principal antagonist even though it still operates in the background.

It would certainly not be realistic or reasonable to expect China not to have any influence in Asian areas beyond its own borders. Throughout history, strong Chinese regimes have exerted a significant influence on China's neighbors, and one might expect any Chinese regime to try to do so today, whatever its ideological coloration. The United States would be engaged on a futile mission if it tried to ignore this fact. We need to be clear, therefore, on just what it is we are against when we oppose the policies and actions of the Peking government. Although it would be futile to try to prevent the extension of any and all Chinese influence, we must oppose Chinese threats to the independence of its neighbors, attempts to impose Communist ideology on other societies, and encouragement of violence and subversion; in short, we must oppose direct challenges to the kind of international order that we are trying to preserve and promote. For this reason, Taiwan, Vietnam, Laos, and Korea, for example, are particularly important today.

The current situation is not one, therefore, that can be appraised solely on the basis of traditional diplomatic and historical criteria. Under present circumstances, Chinese hegemony in Asia would bear little resemblance to the traditional and largely nomi-

nal relationship of suzerainty existing between past Chinese dy-
nasties and China's Asian neighbors. Today China's dynamic and
revolutionary appeal, directed not only to Asian countries but to
all those in Africa, Latin America, and the Middle East who have
cause to be dissatisfied with their present situation or who are still
preoccupied with "imperialism," is not simply an idealistic sum-
mons to emulate the Chinese model. It is an attempt to create and
guide the processes of social change in other countries, and it is
supported by a vast apparatus of political control, propaganda,
and subversion. This apparatus is controlled by men and governed by rules that were shaped during years of hard revolutionary struggle in China when the goal of conquering power and
establishing a Communist system overrode all other considerations.

Only if one overlooks the dynamic revolutionary quality of
Chinese policies can one view them simply in traditional diplomatic and power terms. And only those who ignore the interplay
of national goals and Communist doctrine in Peking's policy can
view China's behavior as no more than what might be expected of
a nation concerned for its own welfare and security and seeking
its rightful place among the nations. While it is true that to fix
one's attention too narrowly on the notion of universal "communism" may obscure the complexities of the dangers we face, it is
equally true that if we do not take the Chinese Communist leaders at their own word and credit them with a genuine ideological
fervor that has sustained them during their successful revolution
at home and now motivates their policies abroad, we will fail to
grasp the challenge that the Chinese pose.

The experience of the past decade and a half does not indicate,
however, that Communist ideology is an irresistible contagion
spreading rapidly and unaided throughout the world. Actually,
the Communists' successes have been relatively few in recent
years, and these have all required clandestine and armed support
as well as serious mistakes on the part of the non-Communist
countries. We should not exaggerate the power and influence of
the Communists by giving them all the credit or blame for the
turmoil and uncertainty that prevail in so many parts of the
world where great pressures caused by the problems of national
independence, social and economic modernization, political unifi-

cation, and ideological choice have converged. Widespread turmoil and uncertainty do, however, open up new possibilities for
all manner of outside influences. The Chinese Communists have
not been slow to exploit these fresh opportunities, and as a consequence, there is now, in much of the underdeveloped world, a
vast new testing ground for both the competition of ideologies
and the confrontation of national power.

It is not surprising that in a situation of such complexity there
is no easy way to disentangle the various strands of influence or
to identify the varied problems and threats that exist. And in the
search for causes, there is an almost inevitable tendency to over-
simplify. Whereas not long ago many Americans tended to think
of Communist China as a danger primarily because it was believed to serve Moscow's cause, today there is a tendency on the
part of some observers to ascribe primarily to Peking the responsibility for virtually all troubles in Korea, Vietnam, Laos, the
Congo, or elsewhere. Some people are too prompt to see the hand
of Peking—or, less frequently these days, Moscow—in every situation that displeases us and to overlook or ignore other problems
that demand solutions. It is true, of course, that in many situations Peking's hand is present, and wherever our interests or
those of our friends are threatened by Chinese Communist policies, we must accurately identify the specific threats and problems involved and determine how best to cope with them. It
would be dangerous, however, to have only an undifferentiated
image of the nature and scope of the Chinese threat in every situation where China is in any way involved and to fail to distinguish between those situations where the Chinese openly, actively, and dangerously challenge our interests, those where
Chinese involvement is more limited and restrained, those where
local leaders may believe that some of their national interests
parallel Chinese interests, and those where local events simply
seem to be moving in directions that may give the Chinese some
advantages, perhaps temporary in nature. In short, we need to be
discriminating not only in identifying the dangers to us from
communism in general but also in determining the precise roles of
China in particular situations.

One might ask why the United States, with its great wealth
and overwhelming military power, should be apprehensive of the

threat posed by a country that is overpopulated, is struggling to raise its standard of living above the bare minimum, and has only begun to build a nuclear capability. There are good reasons for concern, despite China's relative poverty and weakness. One is the fact that the present Chinese leaders have accepted and proclaimed as an article of faith their fundamental hostility to the United States, which, as they now see it, stands in the way of many of their national goals and of the world revolution that they espouse. Moreover, in the pursuit of their national and revolutionary goals, they have used their limited material resources with great energy and considerable flexibility and have been sustained by their revolutionary experience and their disciplined dedication to the Communist cause. They have shown unswerving determination in their attempts to weaken and undermine United States interests wherever possible. The state of upheaval which has characterized much of the world in recent years has offered many opportunities for Chinese manipulation and exploitation, and the Peking government's revolutionary leaders have sought to induce all the other revolutionary leaders to follow their example and cast aside the values and traditions of the West. Unlike many of those whom the Chinese have tried to influence, the leaders in Peking have as their base a great nation with a long cultural history and a hard-working, highly skilled population. Their ambitions in Asia may not call for the direct domination of the populous, wealthy, and strategically important areas adjacent to China, but even lesser degrees of Chinese Communist hegemony would challenge the independence of many newly independent countries, threaten the precarious political balance that now exists, and adversely affect American interests.

Despite the challenge presented by Chinese Communist goals and policies, however, the tangible results which they have achieved to date are not spectacular. In many situations, moreover, it is not easy to define the Chinese role or to determine its Communist as opposed to nationalist elements. A Communist government was installed, it is true, in North Korea, and although at first this regime was under Russian rather than Chinese influence, the Chinese have reasserted a major influence in this neighboring strategic area. However, communism as such seems to have had relatively little to do with the Chinese conquest of Tibet or the attack on the Indian border territories. In fact, when Peking's military actions occurred in these areas, the Chinese Nationalists were careful to condemn only the methods used and not the validity of the Chinese national claims involved. In both Vietnam and Laos, it is difficult to disentangle the respective roles and responsibilities of the local Communist forces, the North Vietnamese, the Chinese, and the Russians, and while in both situations the Chinese have strongly backed the local Communist-led insurrections in what they consider to be "people's wars," in neither have they yet intervened directly with Chinese forces. In the Taiwan Strait, so important to Peking, the Chinese Communists are militarily checked by United States forces. Elsewhere, their ability to achieve their goals is today even more restricted, and they no less than the United States find themselves being used in ways not always consistent with Chinese interests.

None of these limitations, however, has deterred the Chinese Communists from continuing to pursue militant policies wherever they see opportunities for exploiting local situations to their advantage and wherever they believe they can weaken the position of the United States.

Parallelism and Interaction

The dangers that the United States and China create for each other, the threats that each sees posed by the other, and the mutual fears and antagonisms that these nourish have encouraged attitudes that tend to feed on one another. In some instances, the two countries seem to have acquired outlooks which, while totally different in some respects, have been parallel in others— despite the fact that they are adversaries who think they now have little in common but their antagonism. Neither country finds it easy to disentangle real dangers from imaginary threats, and the reality of the one combines with the vision of the other to create a picture that is often less than accurate. While this sense of threat reinforces a state of vigilance, it can and sometimes does obscure, on both sides, a clear understanding of what to be vigilant about. Perhaps both psychological and domestic political needs are often fulfilled in the process, but at times this is at the expense of sound policy judgment.

The existence of this parallelism, although noteworthy, should not be overstated, however, since there is clearly a basic and extremely important difference between the influences that shape the national attitudes of the two countries. In China, a totalitarian dictatorship, drawing its inspiration from Marxism-Leninism, as interpreted by Mao Tse-tung, regulates all aspects of national life, controls the flow of all communications within the country, and mobilizes hate campaigns or love campaigns as it sees fit. A small group of leaders determines the course of foreign policy, and they then attempt to mold the public attitudes that seem required to support their policy. If significant differences of opinion exist, they are kept under control and generally do not reach the public's attention, and strict party discipline prevents any effective challenge to decisions once they have been reached.

It is hardly necessary to say that the situation in the United States is very different indeed. While the government obviously does try to mobilize public support on matters of foreign policy and while there is a tendency toward a national consensus under Washington's guidance, at the same time there is a free flow of public debate (even if it is sometimes motivated by partisan purposes), a public display of sharp disagreements with government policy, and a free play of emotionalism. The freedom of action of policy makers is limited by the pressures of public opinion and shifting tides of public debate. There is no trained chorus to echo government policy, and whether Washington seeks to fight an adversary or to move toward conciliation and accommodation, there are always dissenters who raise their voices. Neither hostility nor friendship can be mobilized with the seeming unanimity and enthusiasm that characterize a totalitarian system such as that of the Chinese Communists.

Some critics of American policy toward China stress "the heavy contributions made to the conflict by the stubborn pride, self-righteousness, and ignorance of the United States." [4] But while these qualities have not been lacking on the American side, they have been much more characteristic of the Chinese leader-

---

[4] See, for example, Edgar Snow, *The Other Side of the River* (New York: Random House, 1961) pp. 732–733.

ship in its attitudes toward the United States, and in China there has been no free play of political forces or public discussion to temper the attitudes of this leadership.

In many respects, nevertheless, the United States and China have been mutually inclined to look at each other with a mixture of concern and scorn. Each has seen the other as a major threat to its policies, institutions, and ideals, and both have at times tended to deprecate the other. Mao Tse-tung labels the United States as a "paper tiger," while some Americans see only a China characterized by poverty, weakness, and failures (which they nevertheless see as posing a growing threat). The Chinese Communists tend to look back over a century of relations with the West and feel that they were misused and victimized. For them, the United States has been and remains the leader of the "imperialist camp" and the principal enemy. Americans tend to look back and see a century of friendship and feel ill repaid with Peking's present hostility and abuse. Especially since the worsening of the Sino-Soviet split and the tentative steps toward limited agreement between the United States and the Soviet Union, as has previously been mentioned, Communist China has come to epitomize in the minds of many Americans the Communist threat in its most virulent, militant, and dangerous form. Peking has emerged from the shadows of subordination to Moscow and is now seen as a major opponent in its own right, particularly in Southeast Asia but also in the other less-developed areas of the world.

When propaganda and policy become entangled, countries risk falling victim to their own propaganda and being caught in the trap of their own oversimplifications and distortions.

While the fervor of widely held emotions stems in part from the ideological quality of the antagonism, both the United States and Communist China today reserve for each other a place of very special hostility. Thus, the United States pursues diplomatic, economic, and cultural policies toward Communist China that differ in important respects from its policies toward the European Communist countries. China, for its part, distinguishes between the United States, the "leader of the imperialist bloc," and the other Western nations, many of which Peking now tries actively to cultivate. Ideological dogmatism is accompanied, therefore, by political flexibility or expediency. However, in some respects it is easier for the "fanatical" Chinese Communists to be expedient than it is for the "practical" Americans because the Chinese are less sentimental and their control over public policy is much tighter.

On the surface, it might seem reassuring that despite the sharpness of the present confrontation, both the United States and China profess sincere friendship for the people, as distinct from the government, of the other country. Such sentiments, however, are not so undiluted as they might appear to be, and there is little resemblance between "the people" in the two pictures. Americans tend to think of the hard-working, thrifty, friendly Chinese peasant and of the educators, officials, and businessmen with whom the West had cordial dealings in the past. To the Chinese Communists, on the other hand, the image evoked by the term American "people" consists of militant, class-conscious proletarians and members of oppressed minorities, who are seen as striving to break the chains of the capitalist system and wishing to re-establish fraternal relations with their Chinese comrades. With such an obvious gap between the meanings of the term "people," the professions of friendship frequently made have been of limited significance.

It is essential to understand the underlying attitudes involved in the present confrontation between the United States and China. Not all decisions are calmly weighed and objectively arrived at on the basis of an analytical appraisal of the facts of each situation. Many are influenced by passions which can easily create a cycle of self-deception and self-righteousness and which serve neither the requirements of clear thinking nor the goals of national policy. The need is to escape from this cycle, but the task is not easy since hostility breeds hostility and it sometimes seems easier to obscure issues rather than to clarify them. While these comments are especially true today of the leaders in Peking, they unquestionably apply to some Americans as well. In re-examining our China policy, therefore, we must make a special effort to surmount the obstacles that past attitudes and emotions have created and analyze the problems we confront with dispassionate objectivity.

CHAPTER TWO

The Asian Setting

The policy of the United States toward the People's Republic of China is often analyzed as if it were a strictly bilateral matter involving only Washington and Peking. If this were the case, the problem would be complicated enough, but there is much more to it than that. What is called the "China problem" has ramifications that are very broad indeed. It must be considered in relation to the power balance in Asia and elsewhere, the world Communist movement, the Sino-Soviet dispute, overall relations between the West and the Communist bloc, the growth of new social forces in the underdeveloped world, the problems of coordination within the Western world, the problems of international arms control, and many other broad issues. It is essential, therefore, to analyze this overall setting—especially the Asian setting.

The New Balance of Power in Asia

World War II destroyed the former social order and balance of power in Asia. This fact and the establishment of a Communist regime on the mainland of China have created an entirely new set of problems for the United States.

During and after the war, the disintegration of the European colonial system in Asia and the defeat of Japan left a virtual power vacuum, which was filled at the end of the war mainly by United States military strength. Having borne the major burden in the Pacific war, the United States in 1945 found itself as the only strong power in an area where everything else was upheaval.

22

But with the establishment of the government of the People's Republic of China in Peking on October 1, 1949, mainland China was soon converted into another center of growing power and influence. Then with the Soviet-instigated outbreak of the Korean War, the United States took it upon itself to establish a new balance. Currently, the United States and Communist China are the two major components in the power equation in Asia.

The Soviet Union, with its arsenal of atomic weapons, has been the West's major world-wide opponent, but in Asia its involvement since World War II has been limited and often indirect. After the war ended, it sought to re-establish its influence in the region first through physical occupation of a sphere of influence in Manchuria, then, after the Chinese Communist victory, through alliance with the new Peking regime, and subsequently through instigation of the Korean War as a means of reducing the influence of the United States on the eastern rim of Asia. In practice, however, the Russians have been reluctant, since the Korean War at least, to be drawn into situations that might involve conflict with the United States in Asia, where, by and large, they see the risks as great and the stakes less important than the Chinese Communists believe them to be. The Soviet Union has nevertheless sought to establish and strengthen its presence in Asia through diplomacy, aid, and the support of local Communist parties, but since the late 1950s, it has had to compete with the ambitions and policies of China—a historical rival and now a competitor for leadership in the world Communist movement— as well as with the United States.

The nations of Western Europe no longer play a major role in the general Asian balance. The British have continued certain commitments to the Commonwealth countries and maintain a few remaining colonial outposts, but their power in the region is now very limited. The remaining French interests are principally commercial and cultural, and General de Gaulle's dream of creating a Europe from the Atlantic to the Urals, to enable a reconstituted Europe to face eastward toward China as well as across the Atlantic toward the United States, is still a remote dream.

Several decades ago, it was China's disunity and weakness which invited Western and Japanese expansionism in Asia, but today China has become a major actor in Asia, not an object of exploitation. Its relative importance is enhanced by the fact that the countries on most of its borders are not only smaller and weaker but also disunited. China's size, its geographical position, its historical role in Asia, the ability and determination of its leadership, its growing military strength, its revolutionary doctrine and tactics, and its active diplomacy have clearly established its importance in Asia and have carried its influence to Africa and Latin America as well.

The United States' military power is much greater than that of China, and its sense of the rightness of American purposes is strong. But it has not found it possible simply to make its will prevail in Asia. Despite its massive power, the United States has not always been able to apply that power effectively at particular times and places, and in practice its ability to intervene successfully in many sorts of conflict situations has been limited.

As was stated earlier, the situation faced by the United States in its relations with China and Asia is quite different from that faced in regard to the Soviet Union and Europe. Western Europe is itself a major power center which together with the United States confronts the Soviet Union. Moreover, Western Europe has a power of attraction for the Communist East, not the other way round.

The situation in Asia is very different. China is the most populous country in the world and the central country in Asia, and its shadow hangs over smaller and divided neighbors. But China's military power, even with the beginnings of a nuclear capability, is still sharply limited and cannot be effectively used far beyond its own territory. The Chinese see American power, deployed on most of their periphery, blocking what they call the "wheel of history," which should, as they see it, carry both Chinese and Communist influence forward.

Because of the existing strategic balance, American policy has been able to give a relatively low priority to direct relations with Communist China while it paid major attention to the problems, created in part by the existence of Communist China, in areas around China, such as Laos, Vietnam, Taiwan, and Korea. But while in Europe there are strong, like-minded nations to help share the military burden, in Asia we have had to carry it largely alone, and it is in Asia, not in Europe, that Americans have had to fight in recent years. In Asia, also, the political trends and problems present unprecedented challenges.

We may be entering the period which Adam Smith, two centuries ago, predicted might eventually evolve as a result of the European discoveries of the East and West Indies:

At the particular time when these discoveries were made, the superiority of force happened to be so great on the side of the Europeans, that they were enabled to commit with impunity every sort of injustice in those remote countries. Hereafter, perhaps, the natives of those countries may grow stronger, or those of Europe may grow weaker, and the inhabitants of all the different quarters of the world may arrive at that quality of courage and force which, by inspiring mutual fear, can alone overawe the injustice of independent nations into some sort of respect for the rights of one another. But nothing seems more likely to establish the equality of force than that mutual communication of knowledge and of all sorts of improvements which an extensive commerce from all countries to all countries naturally, or rather necessarily, carries along with it.[1]

Asian Preoccupations

George Washington, in his second inaugural address, set as a major goal for the newly independent United States that it should seek "command of its own fortunes." This is a goal that the new states of today have also set for themselves, but these new states face enormous problems. Colonialism had debilitating and divisive effects. Many of the new nations have lacked cultural homogeneity. Only a few have a tradition of political legitimacy or a large body of trained leaders devoted to the service of the nation. They face complex economic and social difficulties with which they must deal at the same time that a variety of outside influences press in on them, and they are bombarded with advice and propaganda as well as aid.

The most widely shared impulses in the new nations have been nationalism and the desire for economic progress. Even these, however, have sometimes been little more than slogans in coun-

[1] Adam Smith, *An Inquiry into the Nature and Causes of the Wealth of Nations,* ed. by Edwin Cannan (5th ed.; London: Methuen, 1930), v. 2, p. 125.

tries where poverty, illiteracy, and old cultural patterns have continued to prevail and where political leaders have often relied on demagogy rather than solid accomplishments to attract and hold their followings. In such circumstances, ideological symbols and slogans can sometimes create false hopes and lead to dead ends. This is true whatever the source of the ideologies—whether they are home grown or introduced from the outside.

The vulnerability of these countries to outside political and ideological influences is not always so great, though, as we are sometimes led to believe. Unfortunately, even though the banners of freedom and democracy are widely paraded, democratic values do not always prevail in countries where there was no adequate preparation for self-rule during the colonial period. On the other hand, the ideological attractiveness of communism has also been exaggerated and in not a few places its force already seems to have dissipated. In many countries, there now seems to be an inclination to borrow whatever ideas and institutions seem applicable, from whatever the source, and to experiment and search for new local solutions to problems.

Under the conditions that prevail in some Asian countries, nevertheless, it is not surprising that a doctrine which preaches class warfare, focuses on the problems of the peasantry and proletariat, and calls for discipline and collectivism may appeal to many individuals and groups and may seem more relevant to them than the American version of democracy with its emphasis on free enterprise and individual rights.

In fact, however, Asian countries reveal a wide variety of political systems and values, and no single pattern can be discerned. Certainly it is not a Communist pattern. Except in North Korea and North Vietnam, both adjacent to China, and until recently in Indonesia, where strong Communist parties have existed, communism has not represented the predominant force. Nor is the Western democratic pattern widely found, except perhaps in countries such as the Philippines and Malaysia and to a certain extent Japan. In practice, there is a great variety of political and economic forms, borrowed and adapted from many sources including traditional institutions, the colonial heritage, the democratic models of the West, and various systems fostering differing forms of socialism, state control, and political or military dictatorship. The present influence of foreign countries in many of these countries is less ideological, in a cold-war sense, than it is technological and political. Ideological forces are simply the handmaidens of more basic technological concepts and political pressures, and the latter are sometimes the initiators of historical changes that they cannot control.

The future evolution of most of the Asian countries can be perceived only dimly and probably inaccurately. The recent trend has been away from parliamentary democracy and toward more authoritarian regimes, and this trend may continue. Possibly, in an unpredictable next stage—once a measure of stability and modernization has been achieved—increased respect for individual freedom and regard for the rule of law may grow in some of the countries. Probably, however, the prerequisite for this development would be an extended period of peace and economic progress and the emergence of leaders who are dedicated primarily to the welfare of their countries rather than to personal power. Even a gradual evolution in this direction may not be possible if there is serious and continuous international upheaval—or if organized internal subversion spreads more widely. Constant external pressures from whatever source can seriously weaken the foundations of self-reliance and national development; however, the countries of Asia cannot expect to be wholly free of outside influences since they are no more divorced from the forces of history than are countries elsewhere.

In most of these countries, there are at least some political leaders and factions who try to manipulate international issues and use them to domestic advantage. Many Korean nationalists have resisted reconciliation with Japan; many Indian communalists denounce any proposals for reaching understanding with Pakistan; many Japanese intellectuals seem to owe their reputation for "progressivism" in part to their criticism of the Western powers and sympathy for mainland China; and many Indonesians have attempted persistently to stir up nationalistic passions against Malaysia as well as the United States. All such, whether consciously or unwillingly, tend to involve their countries more deeply in international struggles in ways which invite trouble from outside. Thus, American and Communist influences are by no means the only ones affecting the region.

28

The sensitivity to outside influences of all kinds may be greater in the newly independent countries, many of which have only recently undergone or are still undergoing major social upheavals, than in more stable societies. The new nations tend to be more vulnerable because of their weaknesses, including their lack of universally accepted institutions and patterns of political behavior. One explanation for the recent trend toward authoritarianism has been the feeling of leaders in these countries that they must somehow reduce their vulnerabilities and impose a greater measure of national discipline. When the government of Thailand takes restrictive measures against its overseas Chinese residents and when the government of Burma expels foreign cultural organizations, they are, in their own ways, trying to immunize the political life of their countries against foreign influences about which they are apprehensive.

The preoccupations of most Asian countries are not the same as ours, and their problems cannot be summed up as a simple matter of choice between competing Communist or anti-Communist influences from abroad. Moreover, the policies and outlooks which they do adopt are not merely reflections of outside influences. To think otherwise is not only self-deluding but also politically unwise, because if we do not understand their attitudes and preoccupations, we risk overestimating our own capacity as well as that of others for influencing them and determining their future.

Attitudes toward the United States

Asian nations have observed American activities in Asia with widely varying and often mixed feelings. Moreover, within particular countries there are often many different opinions, and governmental attitudes may change as leadership and circumstances change. All the Asian countries, whether friendly, hostile, or neutral, are aware of American strength, but most are also conscious of the difficulty which the United States encounters when trying to apply its power effectively to complex situations. It is widely recognized that while American interests are often complementary, or parallel, to those of specific Asian countries, they are rarely identical; and quite naturally, most Asians—including those most sympathetic to Americans—feel that what the United States has to offer by way of example, exhortation, leadership, and aid should be accepted selectively.

During the past two decades, a great many Asian nations have turned to the United States for assistance or protection or both. At the same time many others, and even some of these same nations, have, on occasion, criticized Americans for being meddlesome, uncomprehending, and even aggressive. The massive strength of the United States, the far-flung and very visible American presence in Asia, and the variety of American programs in the area have had a very great impact. The presence and influence of the United States are felt in innumerable direct ways—through American aid programs and the Peace Corps, tourists and motion pictures, military bases and private business. Actually, in most of the region American influence is much more pervasive and obtrusive than that of China, and even those who most welcome United States aid and protection have shown some concern about their possible effects, both on their internal affairs and on their relations with neighbors.

This intensive and far-reaching American involvement in the affairs of Asia is relatively new, and many Asian nations are still uncertain how to assess the prospects for and probable significance of long-term American involvement in their affairs. In contrast, certain Asian nations—especially those on China's immediate periphery—have an acute awareness of the permanence of the Chinese presence, whether that country is under Communist or some other rule and whether they view it with admiration or fear.

Not all Asian countries have looked upon China as an imminent threat to their national life, however, in the way that most Western European nations regarded the Soviet Union during the years following World War II, and this fact has naturally affected their attitudes toward the United States as well. The Western European nations, already allied to the United States during the war, turned to the United States for help in the postwar tasks of restoring their shattered economic life and were eager to ally themselves with the United States for defense against the apparent

Soviet threat. The postwar situation in Asia was not comparable. There were fewer traditional ties with the United States. The postwar world of Asia was a new one for everyone. And the new nations in the area were preoccupied with the tasks required to give substance to their independence.

Looking at the evolution of American involvement and influence in Asia in recent years, one finds it difficult to strike a general balance sheet of assets and liabilities or strengths and weaknesses. American military strength is greater than ever before, and the United States' deep involvement in South Vietnam has provided dramatic evidence of a determination to back up American policies and commitments and support friends and allies, even at great cost in money and lives. However, the struggle in Vietnam has also raised many questions about how the United States both can and should try to help Asian nations cope effectively with Communist subversion and insurrectionary violence.

Many Asian countries are ambivalent about the United States, as most also are about China. They want help and protection, but they also want to be left alone. And they insist on pursuing their own interests as they see them. Many that agree in broad terms with United States aims object when they see American policies conflict—as they inevitably do on occasion—with their particular interests. Illustrations of this phenomenon abound. Japan has wanted to increase its trade and other contacts with the China mainland, despite its close ties with the United States, which has frowned on such contacts. Thailand has at times shown concern that the United States might not take a strong enough stand in opposing the expansion of Communist influence on its borders. Pakistan has been alarmed by the fact that American opposition to Communist China has led to increased American support of India, and as a consequence, while still formally linked to the United States in a military alliance, Pakistan has steadily increased its ties with China. In short, each country, including the United States' friends or allies in Asia, interprets its own interests according to its own lights.

Even though many of the non-Communist nations of Asia regard the United States as their principal outside source of support against aggression and subversion, their desires for support are often based on special interests different from those of the United

States. In Asia, as in other major regions of the world, there are many imbalances and tensions in regional power relationships and serious conflicts between neighbors, such as those between India and Pakistan, Cambodia and Thailand, Vietnam and Cambodia, and Indonesia and Malaysia. At times the preoccupation of the United States with the problems posed by Communist China has been resented by these countries when they have felt that American policies have limited their own freedom of action or failed to provide support in conflicts with their immediate neighbors.

Actually, many Asian countries probably do not think of themselves as being either pro-American or anti-American in any total sense. They may recognize China's important position in the area and feel that Americans are slow to accept its reality, but they may also applaud United States help in opposing Chinese encroachments, even if they may in addition raise questions about the permanence and reliability of the American involvement. They may welcome many types of assistance; however, they are at the same time jealous of their independence. It is clear that such a complex mixture of attitudes leads to contradictions and ambiguities as each country tries to adjust to various external pressures while it simultaneously works to achieve its domestic goals.

Opinions of the United States also fluctuate and change in response to the particular ways in which the United States handles specific situations. In some situations, a show of American strength and determination may reassure America's friends, but in others it may cause concern—either because of a fear that it is unnecessarily provocative or because of a lack of confidence in its durability. American aid, which many Americans assume should always be welcomed with open arms and with no questions asked, is carefully scrutinized in terms of the motives that lie behind it, the strings that may be attached, the domestic complications that it may create, the competing external pressures which it may stimulate, and even the soundness of the proposed aid itself. Only the Communist nations in Asia have a clear-cut position with regard to the United States. They want us to get out and stay out.

Despite widespread respect and admiration in non-Communist Asia for American economic and other achievements, there is much in American life and culture that separates the United

States from Asia. The substance of American democracy is unfamiliar to most Asian countries, even those that have democratic institutions of their own. Many American national values seem alien to nations whose people have different religious, historical, and cultural roots. Despite the impressiveness of American competitiveness and of the spirit of free enterprise, in countries where the society is tightly knit, traditions are strong, and the margin of subsistence is narrow, these do not always seem either congenial or applicable. Homage to freedom and democracy is fairly general, in Asia as elsewhere. But freedom may mean simply nationalistic self-assertion rather than respect for the individual, and democracy may be equated with "people's democracy," "democratic centralism," or some other euphemism which in fact means the politicization of the masses under authoritarian rule. The technological achievements of the United States are almost universally admired; however, in some nations that have a burden of illiteracy and poverty and are still bound to old ways, people find it difficult to see the relevance of these achievements to them. America's planes, factories, and tractors may be envied, and efforts may be made to acquire them. But each country hopes to modernize in its own way. And finally, sentiments of racialism, anti-Westernism, and anti-imperialism exist throughout the region, even if only in latent form, and it is often not difficult for politicians to arouse them.

Domestic developments as well as foreign-policy considerations shape the attitudes in any particular Asian country at any given time. The recent history of many Asian countries has shown how the political leader, the intellectual, the military officer, the student, and the religious leader all play roles in determining attitudes toward the United States. Sometimes the United States—or for that matter China or other countries—may be used as a pawn in the competition between opposing domestic forces. If one could predict the likely evolution of internal forces in the various Asian countries, it would be possible to forsee more clearly the probable course of their future attitudes toward and future relations with both the United States and China.

In view of the complex factors influencing attitudes in Asian countries, the American public and government cannot and should not expect Asians always to be clear and unambiguous in their attitudes toward either the United States or China. Because these countries each have their own individual preoccupations, domestic and foreign, they cannot be expected simply to defer to the supposedly superior wisdom of outsiders. And they are not engaged in a simple exercise of choosing sides between China and the United States. Each is pursuing its own purposes and trying to shape its own future while attempting to respond and adapt to the forces around it and use them for its own benefit.

Attitudes toward China

Since the unification of China under the Ch'in dynasty in the third century B.C., the Chinese have played a major role in Asia. At the time of Christ, some neighboring countries were already paying tribute to China, and Chinese rule over what is now the northern part of Vietnam lasted for almost a thousand years. To see China's influence in Asia today only in terms of contemporary communism is to misunderstand the nature of the problem. Communist ideology and methods of organization have given the Chinese leaders new doctrines and new instruments with which to influence their neighbors and a revolutionary zeal that gives new forms to the extension of Chinese national influence. The present dynamism, moreover, has been all the more striking because it has come at the end of a period of Chinese weakness and disunity during which the historical record of China's past influence in Asia faded into the background. But China's influence in Asia is no new phenomenon.

When American contacts with China first developed in the nineteenth and early twentieth centuries, the country was weak, declining, and passive. It had lost much of its traditional influence in the neighboring countries of Asia, and most of its energy was directed to warding off the intrusions of foreign governments. Many Westerners tended to assume that this low point in China's effectiveness as a nation was the normal state of affairs, and it was easy to overlook the prominent and, indeed, central role that China had played during many periods in Asian history.

Most other Asian nations are aware of this history and do not need to look at China's new nuclear weapons or armies to understand China's importance. For the countries around China's rim to the east and south, just as for the countries of Eastern Europe, the big neighbor is not only a Communist country but a country which in terms of history, geography, and power has had a very special role in the region; and common frontiers, the impact in many places of Chinese culture, the intermingling of ethnic groups in the border areas, and the presence of large overseas Chinese communities in Southeast Asia create continuing sensitivity to China's challenging immediacy. China's performance in Korea against United Nations forces, its attack against India in 1962, and its detonation of nuclear devices in 1964 and 1965 have simply been reminders to China's neighbors that China is a country that must always be included in their calculations.

The ways in which the various nations regard China, however, depend on many factors. Fear of communism is one, but not the only one. A variety of motives impel some countries to take strong stands against Peking and others to make their peace with it.

Japan has followed Washington's lead in not recognizing the Peking government but nevertheless seeks to develop its trade and other contacts with the mainland as much as possible without jeopardizing its trade and political links with the United States and Taiwan. In addition to economic motives, domestic political pressures and a long history of cultural links with China impel the Japanese to try to "separate economics and politics" and to avoid every provocation of Peking at the same time that they rely on America's military protection and postpone consideration of diplomatic ties with mainland China.

Two countries that are allied to the United States and take a strong stand against Communist China are Thailand and the Philippines. Both have significant overseas Chinese populations, and both have been the targets of Communist-inspired subversion. Both are members of SEATO and have committed themselves to close military cooperation with the United States. Each is unique in some respects. The Philippines, because of its colonial history, has felt a special affinity toward the United States and has developed political and economic institutions which show a greater degree of American influence than those of any other

Southeast Asian nation. Thailand, as the only Southeast Asian country which was able to preserve its independence during the period of European colonialism, appears to have been less affected by anti-colonial sentiments, and therefore less inhibited about establishing close relationships with a Western power than the former colonies in the area.

Indonesia, in contrast, because of its colonial past, has been moved by virulent anti-colonialism. This, plus the flamboyance of President Sukarno's leadership and aspirations for Indonesia to play a major role in Asia, helps to explain its violent anti-Western outbursts and a variety of policies that have tended to disturb the peace and security of Southeast Asia. Until the fall of 1965 Sukarno exhibited increasingly friendly attitudes toward China, designed apparently to identify Indonesia with China as a major leader of the so-called "newly emerging forces." However, the abortive coup in 1965, followed by a violent clampdown on the Indonesian Communist party, greatly reduced both Communist and Chinese influence.

Cambodia has gone perhaps the furthest of any non-Communist Asian country in accommodating itself to Peking. It was one of the few, for example, which followed Peking's lead in refusing to sign the partial nuclear test-ban treaty of 1963. Yet its ruler, Prince Sihanouk, has continued to resist the growth of communism within his country. As a leader of a small country embroiled in quarrels with two of its neighbors—South Vietnam and Thailand—he has been remarkably frank in explaining that Cambodia must adjust to shifts in the overall power balance. Apparently, he hopes that his friendly posture toward China will deter Peking from exerting pressure on his country and that China will benevolently protect Cambodia against pressures from its neighbors.

Partly because of Burma's long common border with China and the embarrassing presence of remnant Chinese Nationalist forces on Burmese soil, the government of Burma has been extremely prudent in all its dealings with Peking. It, too, has gone quite far in accommodating to Peking. But cordiality has been mixed with caution, and Burma's desire to have peaceful relations with its big neighbor has not deterred its government from exercising tight control over the local overseas Chinese and trying to suppress the several Communist rebel factions in the country. Nevertheless, the Burmese leaders apparently feel that the precarious foundations of Burmese independence and unity require them to avoid doing anything that might antagonize their Chinese neighbor.

Indian and Pakistani attitudes toward China have changed greatly over time. For almost a decade, Prime Minister Nehru, speaking for India, was the voice of Sino-Indian brotherhood and peaceful coexistence, the friendly spokesman for China's aspirations to be recognized as an equal power in the world. Then in 1959, when China suppressed the Tibetan revolt and there were serious border incidents between India and China, the change set in. Prime Minister Nehru began wondering "if we, the government of India and the government of China, speak quite the same language . . . it seems sometimes as if China is acting like some nineteenth-century nation in their pride and arrogance, ignoring the rest of the world.[2] Three years later Prime Minister Nehru was to have even more cause to be troubled. Faced by alarming Chinese border attacks, he looked for assistance and support to both the United States and the Soviet Union. Since then, anti-Chinese feeling has steadily grown in India to the point where it is now a crucial influence on, and theme in, India's policies.

Pakistan, which recognized Peking in 1950, has never considered its membership in SEATO as a bar to cultivating friendly relations with China. Until fairly recently, however, their relations, though friendly, were not close. But since the deterioration in relations between India and Communist China and the increase in American military support of India, Pakistan has moved increasingly nearer Peking and has looked to it for support that would strengthen Pakistan's position vis-à-vis India. The signing of a border agreement with the Chinese, the establishment of regular airline service between the two countries, an increase in Chinese trade and aid, and a degree of military cooperation have marked the course of Pakistan's swing away from the United States toward increasingly collaborative relations with China.

The Communist nations of North Korea and North Vietnam have, of course, a very special relationship to Peking, deriving from geography as well as common ideology and political sys-

[2] Statement of September 10, 1959, *The New York Times*, September 11, 1959.

tems. However, even here one cannot accurately describe relationships with simple slogans such as "pro-Chinese." Few Vietnamese, particularly in Tonkin, are unmindful of the long history of Chinese domination in the past, and many Vietnamese heroes are revered because of their resistance to such domination. Both North Korea and North Vietnam have relied heavily on Chinese support, but they have been cautious about accepting too much Chinese military and political guidance. They have attempted, to a degree, to balance Soviet and Chinese influence and have sought to minimize the extent of direct Chinese involvement in the internal affairs of their countries.

From the above, it should be clear that there is a wide variety of Asian policies and attitudes toward China, and it is obviously hazardous to generalize. Nevertheless, some overall observations can be attempted. It is apparent that each country sees China as creating a set of distinctive problems in relation to that country's own interpretation of its own particular interests. For a host of reasons the perspectives tend to differ in many respects from those that underlie United States views of the problem, even though there may be agreement on many important things. Some Asian countries look on Communist China as an imminent threat, but others do not. All, however, are very much aware of its presence, of its vast potential as compared to their own, and of its doctrinal militancy. They see many dangers in the world, and Communist China is one of them, but not the only one.

Chinese Communist doctrine by no means spontaneously attracts the neighboring nations. Especially when it is recognized as a likely instrument for the advancement of China's interests, communism is feared. However, in some Asian countries where local Communist parties are legal and play significant roles, the tendency is to play down their international links, and sometimes for political reasons, Asian governments have chosen not to see any possible Chinese connection.

Asian nations frequently try to distinguish between China and communism. The former is viewed as a powerful nation, a towering fact of history and geography. Communism, on the other hand, is regarded as a doctrine and movement that each country should deal with in its own way. The fact that Communist political activity at home may be suppressed, or tolerated, is no automatic measure, therefore, of a country's attitude toward the Peking government.

There was a time when "the spirit of Bandung" reigned among many Asians, and communism gave off a glow of brotherhood and peaceful coexistence. This mood has largely receded, even though individual countries may on occasion stand with the Chinese in denouncing the "imperialists," the "neo-colonialists," and the "warmongers."

Many of China's neighbors are concerned in particular to minimize or eliminate potential causes of conflict or tension. Border agreements have been concluded between China and many of its neighbors (including Afghanistan, Nepal, Pakistan, and Burma, as well as Mongolia), and trade relations have been established between mainland China and a majority of the Asian countries. A steady stream of visitors goes to China from all the Asian countries which recognize the Peking government—as well as from Japan, which does not. (Actually, there are more Japanese involved in these exchange programs than visitors from any other country.)

Attitudes and policies toward China—as toward the United States—are in many cases intimately bound up with the forces in domestic politics. For example, in Malaysia, where there is a delicate balance of forces between the Malay and Chinese populations, it is official policy to have nothing to do with either Communist China or Nationalist China. It is feared that increased influence from either might upset the equilibrium on which the survival of Malaysia as a unified country depends.

The ethnic problem is less acute elsewhere, but the presence in many other countries of Southeast Asia of sizable Chinese minorities certainly affects both domestic politics and relations with China. These overseas Chinese have not been the principal vehicles of Chinese influence in most places, and the long-term trend appears to be toward increased local acculturation. Nevertheless, they are still, in many places, largely distinctive groups; the governments of Southeast Asia are mindful that integration is a slow process; and the desire everywhere is to prevent the overseas Chinese from being propagandized and manipulated by either Communist China or Taiwan. With the exception of Malaysia and Singapore, however, the overseas Chinese do not appear to be decisive in the calculations of either China or the governments in Southeast Asia.

There are other examples, too, where domestic influences greatly affect relations with the China mainland. For instance, many pressure groups in Japan urge closer relations with Peking, and the government is sensitive to their opinions. The United States is by no means the only country, therefore, where the question of relations with Communist China is tied up with domestic politics and passions. In many of the Asian countries, in fact, objective study and understanding of China have been limited, and the availability of information about the Chinese Communist regime is restricted because of factors affecting the domestic political climate—for example, either extreme governmental anti-communism, as in the case of the Philippines, or generally Marxist and pro-Chinese Communist feelings, as in the case of a large percentage of Japanese intellectuals.

Not the least of the influences on the policies of the other countries in Asia toward China is the attitude of China toward them. During the Bandung period, when China seemed friendly, India more than reciprocated, but after 1959 and the Chinese attacks, things changed. When China has meddled openly in the affairs of overseas Chinese communities, which it has done on occasion, or has overtly supported local Communist activities, it has aroused strong antagonism.

The issue of nonalignment and neutralism was a crucial one in the 1950s, but it has now lost much of its sharpness for a number of reasons. Many Asian nations have not been pressed so hard as they were in the early 1950s, either by the Communist nations or by the United States, to take a firm stand with one bloc or the other. Not only the United States, but China as well, has recognized the need to be more flexible, and in practice neither now insists on drawing as sharp a line as previously between "pro-Communists" and "anti-Communists." A recognition has grown that the Asian situation cannot be dealt with simply in the contrasting terms of cold-war confrontation. Moreover, the sharpness of the differences between the Soviet Union and Communist China and the competition between them in the Asian countries have given many countries more room for maneuver. Finally, when India, the principal apostle of nonalignment, found its policies so severely shaken that it looked for support from both Washington and Moscow, fresh light was thrown on the ambiguities of nonalignment.

The attitudes of Asian countries toward Taiwan have received little attention in this discussion because in most cases they are directly linked to—and really are simply the converse of—attitudes toward mainland China. The governments that are strongly opposed to Peking, such as South Korea, South Vietnam, the Philippines, and Thailand, recognize the Chinese Nationalist government as the government of China and are well disposed toward it. Japan, too, recognizes the Nationalist regime on Taiwan, with which it has important trade relations. Most of the other Asian nations ignore Taiwan. Taiwan is clearly a secondary consideration for the majority of them, and policy toward Taiwan is subordinated to the demands of their policies toward the China mainland or the United States. Specific questions may exist concerning trade or the allegiance of the overseas Chinese populations, but these, too, are subordinate to the bigger issues.

Asia in the Plans of International Communism

During the twenty-five years after World War I, when the Communists were struggling for power in China, related but far less significant developments were taking place in other Asian countries. However, the colonial governments and Japan were able in most places to prevent the Communist movements from making much headway. It was Japan's defeat and the dissolution of the colonial empires, followed by the Communist success in China, that gave many Asian Communist movements new opportunities.

Lenin, in *Imperialism, the Highest Stage of Capitalism*, written in 1916, had pointed to the "colonial and semi-colonial" countries as particularly vulnerable areas in the structure of imperialism and Western capitalism. Soon after the Russian revolution, representatives from sympathetic movements in Asia and the Middle East were brought together under Russian leadership, and in November 1918 the first Congress of Communist Organizations of the East convened in Moscow. This was followed a few months later, in March 1919, by the First World Congress of the Comintern.

In 1920, the Second Comintern Congress adopted Lenin's "Theses on the National and Colonial Questions," which called on all Communist parties to give active support to revolutionary liberation movements and, even in alliance with bourgeois parties, to fight against imperialism. The prospects for revolution in Europe receded as the postwar situation stabilized, and attention turned more hopefully to Asia. At the Baku Congress of the Peoples of the East convened in September 1920, Zinoviev called for the overthrow of British imperialism and proclaimed that "the real revolution will blaze up only when the 800 million people who live in Asia unite with us." [3] Stalin reiterated this theme in 1924 when he proclaimed that "the road to the victory of the revolution in the west lies through a revolutionary alliance with the liberation movement of the colonies and dependent countries against imperialism." And the following year Zinoviev told the executive committee of the Comintern: "There is no doubt that the road to world revolution lies through the east rather than through the west."

In the meantime, with Soviet and Comintern assistance, various Asian Communist parties were established, either clandestinely at home or in exile. The early 1920s saw the creation of Communist parties, for example, in Indonesia, China, Japan, India, and Vietnam. To provide encouragement and training for Asian Communists, the Communist University of the Toilers of the East was established in Moscow in April 1921. This was followed by the founding of the Lenin School in 1924 and Sun Yat-sen University in 1925. A Far Eastern Bureau of the Cominterm in Shanghai and a South Seas Communist group in Singapore were set up at about the same time.

As the Communist movement in China gathered momentum, it became a training ground for many Communist leaders from other Asian countries, and it is not surprising that its decisive im-

[3] The development of the Communist movements in Asia is described in J. H. Brimmel, *Communism in Southeast Asia: A Political Analysis* (London: Oxford University Press, 1959) and Captain Malcolm Kennedy, *A History of Communism in East Asia* (New York: Praeger, 1957). This and the following three quotations are taken from Kennedy, pp. 123, 134, 138, and 158.

42

portance was widely recognized. The Sixth Congress of the Chinese Communist Party, held in Moscow in July 1928 at a time when the party's fortunes were faring very badly, affirmed that "the Chinese revolution will affect neighboring countries, large colonies like India, Indo-China, Java, and Korea—arousing the teeming masses of those oppressed nations to political struggle; it will fundamentally shake the foundations of imperialist Japan and England and deal a heavy blow to capitalism in the U.S.A. Therefore, the completion of the Chinese revolution will be the prelude to the victory of the world proletariat dictatorship."

As the civil war in China approached its climax, the Chinese Communist leaders became increasingly conscious of the special place of their revolution in history. Thus, in the spring of 1947, more than two years before the formal establishment of the People's Republic of China, an article put out by the Yenan leaders explained that the Chinese Communists, adapting the teachings of the Europeans Marx and Lenin, had shown the way not only to the Chinese but "for the billion folk who live in the colonial countries of Southeast Asia." [4] As soon as the Communist victory was complete, Liu Shao-chi, addressing the Asian and Australasian Trade Union Conference in Peking in November 1949, re-emphasized this theme:

The road taken by the Chinese people in defeating imperialism and in founding the Chinese People's Republic is the road that should be taken by the people of many colonial and semi-colonial countries in their fight for national independence and people's democracy. . . . This is the essential road on which the Chinese people marched to achieve victory in their country. This road is the road of Mao Tse-tung. It can also be the basic road for liberation of peoples of other colonial and semi-colonial countries, where similar conditions exist.[5]

This conference reinforced the call to revolution in Asia that had been issued by the Communists' Calcutta Conference of February 1948. Liu stressed the importance of wars of national liberation based on Mao's guerrilla experience. He saw a major role for Communist leadership in national united fronts and emphasized the

[4] Anna Louise Strong, "The Thought of Mao Tse-tung," *Amerasia*, v. 11, no. 6, June 1947, p. 161.
[5] Quoted in Donald Zagoria, "Some Comparisons Between the Russian and Chinese Models," in A. Doak Barnett, ed., *Communist Strategies in Asia* (New York, London: Praeger, 1963), p. 17.

need for national liberation armies in order to achieve the success in the revolutionary movements already in progress in Asia, Africa, and the Middle East. "Armed struggle," he said, was "the sole path for many colonial and semi-colonial peoples in their struggle for independence and liberation." [6] His call was addressed not only to the remaining colonial areas but also to the newly independent countries. In Malaya, the Philippines, Indonesia, and Vietnam, violent Communist-led insurrections were already under way.

Two years later, Lu Ting-yi put the same theme more succinctly and directly. Referring to the Asian Communist struggles, then in their militant phase, he said:

China's example and experiences have strengthened the fighting will of the peoples of these countries and their confidence in victory.

The integration of the universal truth of Marxism-Leninism with the concrete practice of the Chinese revolution constitutes Mao Tsetung's theory of the Chinese revolution. . . .

The classic type of revolution in imperialist countries is the October Revolution.

The classic type of revolution in colonial and semi-colonial countries is the Chinese revolution.[7]

The Chinese were not content to use mere words in encouraging their neighbors, for in the late 1940s and early 1950s both they and the Russians, seeking to take advantage of the postwar turmoil, actively encouraged and supported insurrection in many Asian countries. Ho Chi Minh had already set the example by initiating armed action against the French in December 1946. The main signal, however, had been the one given under Russian leadership at the 1948 Calcutta Conference, which set the stage for the wave of Communist-inspired violence that was to be experienced in India, Burma, Malaya, Indonesia, and the Philippines.

It was only after these insurrections had largely failed that the Chinese decided it would be more profitable, at least for a period of time, to support other Asian Communist parties in less aggres-

---

[6] New China News Agency, November 23, 1949.
[7] Extracts from Lu Ting-yi's article "The World Significance of the Chinese United Democratic Front of China" (1951) are reprinted in DeVere E. Pentony, ed., *China, The Emerging Red Giant: Communist Foreign Policies* (San Francisco: Chandler Publishing Co., 1962), pp. 11-15.

sive ways so that it could at the same time, under the slogans of Bandung, attempt to cultivate friendly relations with existing Asian governments.

The renewal of Chinese militancy came in the late 1950s. In the same period, insurrection broke out again in Laos and Vietnam and received strong Chinese encouragement and support. As the Sino-Soviet dispute developed, moreover, the Chinese not only began to compete against the Soviets for influence over other Communist parties but also became increasingly strident in their insistence on the desirability of violent "people's wars."

When the struggle in Vietnam rose to new heights of intensity in 1965 and United States involvement greatly increased, Peking's Defense Minister Lin Piao on September 2 issued an article entitled "Long Live the Victory of the People's War," which elaborated in detail the Chinese model for revolutionary warfare. "In the last analysis," he stated, "the Marxist-Leninist theory of proletarian revolution is the theory of the seizure of state power by revolutionary violence, the theory of countering war against the people by people's war," and he declared that Mao's theory of revolutionary war is of "universal practical importance for the present revolutionary struggles of all the oppressed nations and peoples." [8]

Statements of this sort left no doubts about Peking's desire to promote revolutionary struggles in other countries where it could. But in practice its capacity to do so has been and remains limited. As of early 1966, its ability to influence and effectively support local Communist insurrections was most obvious in Vietnam and Laos. Elsewhere, neither Chinese influence nor the local strength of Communist forces has been sufficient to make Lin Piao's prescriptions practical.

Actually, as has already been suggested, the relationship in the Asian scene between China as a nation and communism as a doctrine and program is an intricate one. Each could exist without the other and still pose a problem for the other Asian nations. The Communist problem would be greatly reduced in the absence of the impetus, the example, the material support, and the ideological inspiration given by China. The converse is also true, for communism strengthens China's national ambitions by providing a

[8] *Peking Review*, no. 36, September 3, 1965, pp. 23-24.

doctrine, strategy, and tools to make them more effective. As the Chinese Communists themselves have emphasized, in certain circumstances they can provide a more relevant model than the Soviet Union can for underdeveloped countries. However, in a different sense China is an obstacle to the spread of communism in Asia, for the attractive aspects of Communist doctrine are sometimes offset by the fear that behind them lie Chinese power and influence. Conversely, fear of China is increased by the awareness that communism calls for international revolution and interference in other people's affairs. Most Asian countries which lean toward a socialist pattern of society prefer to go about it in their own way without accepting China's guidance or following a rigid Communist pattern, both of which would bring undesirable foreign influences with them.

The fact is that despite low living standards, resentments against the West, and political instability in many Asian countries, there has been no Communist ideological wave sweeping over the area. The inherent powers of national resistance have been strong. This does not mean, however, that communism does not pose major dangers to specific Asian nations. It clearly does.

As of late 1965, for example, Indonesia had the largest Communist party of any non-Communist country in the world. Still, its strength was due less to direct Chinese Communist influence than to the confused state of Indonesian politics under President Sukarno's leadership. The sympathy Sukarno had often exhibited toward Peking undoubtedly tended to reinforce the Indonesian party's influence and popularity, but its successes had been achieved by careful organizational work, appeals to nationalism, and avoidance of direct confrontation with Sukarno instead of by emphasis on allegiance to the international Communist movement. Nevertheless, when China was charged with involvement in the 1965 coup in Djakarta, Indonesian military leaders used this as a major weapon of attack against the Indonesian Communists, and the steps taken to suppress the party greatly reduced its strength. It no longer, in fact, seemed to pose any immediate threat.

Wherever the Communists have been able to move from general organizational and propaganda activity to active subversion and have fomented wars of "national liberation," the threat has been serious. As was stated above, several such Communist insurrections took place in Southeast Asia during the first decade after World War II. By the early 1950s, however, all these had been checked and brought under control.

Since the renewal of militant tactics in the late 1950s, insurrection has again become a major threat, but on a much less widespread scale than earlier. Today the danger is greatest in Vietnam and Laos. China's contiguity has been one important factor. Another has been the Communists' ability, more than elsewhere in Asia, to capture the appeals of nationalism. But perhaps most basic of all has been the failure, in the 1950s, of the non-Communist leaders in these areas to create viable governments, muster popular support, and carry out needed social and economic programs.

In both South Vietnam and Laos, it should be added, support from the contiguous area of North Vietnam has been of very great importance. Nevertheless, it would be incorrect and misleading to view this as the only explanation for the Communists' strength. As was just indicated, other factors, especially political instability and the absence of able leadership, have been at the root of the problem. Even though there is external support, communism in this area has strong local roots as well as international inspiration—as it did in China two and three decades ago.

Today all Communist governments and parties have to adapt not only to domestic conditions but to the circumstances of the split between the Soviet Union and the People's Republic of China. Both Moscow and Peking compete for influence among them, and they find themselves subjected to varying pressures. Attitudes and allegiances, as well as policies and leadership, vary a good deal from country to country, but the dispute between the two leading Communist powers has put new strains on most Asian Communist governments and parties. Some, such as the party in India, have been split and greatly weakened. Others have been impelled toward a sort of "Communist neutralism." Still others have felt compelled to "line up" with one of the two largest Communist nations. Almost everywhere, however, with the notable exception of Mongolia, Peking's influence appeared to grow in the early 1960s. But from late 1965 on, there was evidence that this trend might be receding.

The world Communist movement thus no longer enjoys any sort of effective central leadership, and despite shared long-term goals, the differences among the Communist parties are so sharp that it is really inaccurate now to speak of a single movement. Trends toward "national communism," once believed to be a contradiction in terms, have become a reality, and each Communist party must adjust in its own way to local conditions, to the Sino-Soviet dispute, and to the non-Communist forces that affect it.

Regional Relations in Asia

The necessary shorthand of normal discourse can be misleading. We have been discussing "Asia," but while this word is a fairly clear geographical term, it has many different political and cultural connotations. Some see Asia as a world of impressive old cultures in which the new states are toiling valiantly to cast off the remnants of colonialism, redefine their cultural identity, progress toward modernization, and assume a place of equality and dignity in the world. Others are more disposed to see it as a region of old societies which are little inclined to change their ways, are misruled by their leaders, are persistent in blackmailing the larger powers into helping them, and pretentiously claim rights and privileges beyond their due. Some view communism as a doctrine essentially alien to the area, while others see it as an ideology that has acquired indigenous roots in Mao Tse-tung's teachings and reflects the yearning of the Asian peoples for social reform and freedom from Western influence.

Furthermore, the symbolism of Asian unity is often employed in a variety of ways. The Communists, for example, try to exploit it as a banner around which to rally anti-colonialist, anti-imperialist, and anti-Western sentiment. Some anti-Communists, on the other hand, try to use it primarily as an aid to mobilizing and organizing resistance to Communist China.

Actually, as one writer once put it, perhaps "there is no Asia." If one compares Japan with Laos or Korea with India, it becomes clear that there are enormous differences in the situations and outlooks of Asian countries. Even where there are significant similarities, the contrasts may also be great. Thailand is a Theravada Buddhist country, a monarchy, and an agricultural society which lacks a common border with China but is strongly anti-Communist and is closely allied to the United States. Neighboring Cambodia, with many of these same characteristics, is at present highly critical of the United States—and also on bad terms with Thailand—but is friendly with Communist China. India and Pakistan, which share a subcontinent and have a common history, could hardly be more hostile to each other. Throughout Asia, there are striking differences and complicated national rivalries.

Since the collapse of Japan's imperial ambitions and the disintegration of the colonial empires in Asia, no close-knit, regional community of nations has emerged to give shape to the international politics of the area. Both the deep-rooted cultural diversity of the countries and their varied experiences during the colonial period help to explain this fact; so, too, do the new tendencies toward intense nationalism which tend to exacerbate the unavoidable clashes of interests.

The countries that one might think could take the lead in developing regional cooperation and fostering unity have not in fact done so to date. For a time under Nehru, India did try, it is true, to exert a significant measure of regional leadership under the banners of neutralism and nonalignment. Recently, however, India's influence and prestige have seriously declined, especially since the Chinese attack on the Indian border in 1962. Moreover, India's methods and manner of dealing with its Asian neighbors and its own bitter controversy with Pakistan appear to have tarnished its claims to leadership. In addition, it is absorbed with pressing internal problems. Today, therefore, it is difficult to foresee wide acceptance throughout Asia of India as a regional leader in the years immediately ahead.

Japan today is linked to the Western nations as much or more than it is to most Asian nations, and it has shown relatively little inclination to seek a clear position of recognized regional leadership in Asia. Concerned mainly with economic matters and its own domestic development, it has not attempted to assert a major political role throughout Asia—although it does have important relations with the Republic of China on Taiwan and with Korea, which have had special ties with Japan in the past. As its diplomacy becomes more active, Japan may come to play a more prominent part in Asian affairs, but to do so, it will have to overcome the fears and resentments left by World War II and will have to take into account many factors: its special relations with the United States, the implications of the closer contacts it hopes to establish with China, and its position as one of the principal trading nations of the world.

Indonesia, unlike Japan, expresses its regional aspirations vociferously, especially in Southeast Asia. Whether because of basic urges toward nationalist self-assertion, genuine fear of neocolonialism, or subtle fears of the Chinese, Indonesia has sought to achieve a predominant role for itself in Southeast Asia, and to pursue activist policies throughout the Afro-Asian world. But other Asian nations have not voluntarily endorsed its pretensions, and it is difficult to see how Indonesia can really play a leading regional role unless the British and Americans simply disengage entirely from the area and leave Indonesia's smaller neighbors completely vulnerable to pressures from Djakarta.

China, with its central geographical location and vast population, has both the strongest position and the most intense motivation to exercise regional Asian leadership, but the very pressures created by China's influence, as well as the threatening character of its policies, create counterforces. Moreover, China suffers, on a magnified scale, from many of the same growing pains of modernization as its smaller neighbors in Asia, and there is no indication that the majority of Asian nations is prepared to look to Peking for leadership, even though virtually all of them are constantly aware of China's presence and power.

The United States, exercising its influence from across the seas in an attempt to stabilize the regional power balance, has been determined to prevent regional domination by a single power, whether Japan, as in earlier years, or China, as today. At the same time it has tried, so far with very limited success, to stimulate the growth of regional arrangements which might be able to offset China's growing influence. But local resources have been too weak, and divisive elements too strong. In the one regional security arrangement in Asia which the United States helped to organize, the Southeast Asia Treaty Organization, Asian participation is even less significant today than when SEATO was first established in 1954. Despite the existence of some useful efforts involving technical and cultural cooperation, one cannot yet perceive a framework for significant regional institutions.

Some Asian initiatives to encourage closer regional ties have taken place, but only on a very limited scale. And the few tentative attempts to date—including the Association of Southeast Asian States, linking Thailand, the Philippines, and Malaysia, and Maphilindo, which was intended to bring together Malaya, the Philippines, and Indonesia—have not been notably successful. The former has marked time because of differences between the Philippines and Malaysia, and the latter was stillborn when Indonesia launched its campaign of "confrontation" against Malaysia. The meager results suggest that one should not look to any grand regional designs emerging in Asia in the near future. There are a few fragile buds that may deserve to be nurtured, but there is little basis for expectations of early or spectacular results.

The Bandung Conference of 1955 and subsequent moves to build Afro-Asian solidarity represent other approaches to regional collaboration. However, the unanimity with which the Asian and African countries that met at Bandung denounced colonialism and endorsed general principles of peaceful coexistence has worn thin as Asian nations have become increasingly aware of their differing interests as well as their areas of agreement. Since that time, Peking has sought to make varied types of Afro-Asian movements manipulable instruments to be used both in the struggle against the United States and in the competition with the Soviet Union. But other countries have not been willing to see the Afro-Asian movements become simply tools to serve Communist China, and the collapse in 1965 of what was to have been a "second Bandung" meeting in Algiers—a meeting which the Chinese Communists clearly hoped to dominate—was a major foreign-policy setback for Peking. Today the Afro-Asian movements provide little more than opportunities for like-minded nations to meet from time to time in order to proclaim common principles and probe opportunities to extend their influence. The non-Western, and even anti-Western, character of these movements has made Peking stress their importance in relation to Chinese interests. But neither China nor any other nation has been able to control or direct them, and each nation continues to pursue its own policies as it thinks best.

Thus, the political setting in Asia is predominantly one of proud, sensitive, and competing national states for whom proximity is as likely to breed suspicion or hostility as it is to promote mutual respect or solidarity. The sharing of common problems has not insured a common outlook. The great powers have all in their own ways sought, however, to persuade the countries of the area to collaborate in the pursuit of common purposes. The United States has put forward the vision of a region of independent states cooperating to achieve stability and prosperity with the help of American and other non-Communist aid and protected by the United States from Communist threats. Communist China, on the other hand, looks at the area not only as one with which it has many special geographical, historical, and cultural ties but also as one sharing with China a common past of victimization by imperialism, and its vision is of a unity created by revolution and cemented by the bonds of Communist ideology, under Chinese leadership. So far, though, the diversities of the area and the intractability of its problems have made both of these visions seem remote. If anything, as in the Balkans in the late nineteenth and early twentieth centuries, existing rivalries have been accentuated and new ones stimulated as external powers have exerted their competing influences.

This lack of a clear sense of regional unity is often a source of frustation and even despair to those who believe that American interests cannot be effectively pursued with anything less than a united regional bastion resisting Communist encroachment. Without in any sense underestimating the value of increased regional collaboration, however, one can perhaps derive some comfort from the fact that the national forces in the area cannot be easily regimented by the Communists any more than by others. When the United States encounters difficulties in the long, hard task of building strength in the area, it would be well to remember that at least some of the same factors that create problems are also ones that help to make the region stubbornly resistant to outside Communist influences as well. In short, a diversity of interests and outlook may in some respects be a protection as well as a weakness.

CHAPTER THREE

The Peking Regime
and Its Prospects

It is no easy task to understand what is going on in China or to fathom the motives and behavior of the government in Peking. In the search one should recall Pascal, who wrote more than three centuries ago: " 'But China obscures,' you say; and I reply: 'China obscures, but there is light to be found; look for it.' "[1]

Our good sense tells us that the Chinese people we liked and the traditional values we admired cannot have totally disappeared overnight, but the new leadership seems to stand between us and the Chinese. Because we dislike the regime so thoroughly, it is difficult to believe in its strength or durability, but we are forced to recognize its existence and influence in a world where we ourselves have had to change many old beliefs.

The Revolutionary Élan

The People's Republic of China is led by men who planned and conducted a civil war for more than twenty years and established a government and remodeled a society according to their political ideas. Their determination and skill cannot be denied. Most Americans deplore the fact that revolution, not peaceful change, was employed to remake the face of China. But the Communists were not content with gradualism.

[1] Blaise Pascal, *Pensées*, no. 593.

Under their rule, Communist goals, discipline, and organizing
methods have been united with traditional Chinese abilities and
national ambitions, and the combination is formidable. No aspect
of Chinese society has been untouched as traditional institutions
have been discredited, discarded, or remolded to serve the Communists' new revolutionary goals. China's authoritarian tradition
may have helped ease the way, but the new totalitarianism is no
mere continuation of the past. It is true, as one writer points out,
that "nowadays, as in imperial days, inexorable decrees emerge
out of similarly mysterious councils inside the same palace
walls." [2] But today the decrees deal with the massive mobilization
of the Chinese people and nuclear explosions, not with imperial
ritual, and the councils comprise zealous Communist party leaders, not tradition-bound courtiers. We do not have here simply
"a new dynasty that had succeeded the old," for the Communist
revolution involves a ruthless determination to reorganize Chinese society from top to bottom and to place China in the van-
guard of the twentieth century. The present Communist leaders
believe they have the doctrinal and administrative tools with
which to do the job.

It is misleading, however, to think that the Communist leaders
merely embarked on a cynical and selfish drive to power, although clearly the goal of achieving and maintaining power is a
primary one. They were aroused to action by China's unsolved
social problems and by the spectacle of China's humiliation at the
hands of foreign nations. Desperate conditions, they thought, required harsh measures; the standards of a peaceful democratic
society did not apply. Opposition had to be destroyed, dangers
faced, discipline imposed, and privations endured. "Struggle" became a way of life, a path to self-realization and national great-
ness. As Chen Yun, one of the party chiefs, put it in 1939, "one of
the characteristics of the Chinese Communist party is its in-
domitable spirit of sacrifice and struggle." [3] The Communist
leadership has tried to infuse the Chinese people with this same
spirit.

[2] Mu Fu-sheng, *The Wilting of the Hundred Flowers: The Chinese Intellectuals Under Mao* (New York: Praeger, 1963), p. 116.
[3] Chen Yun, *How to Be a Good Communist Party Member*, May 31, 1939,
quoted in same, p. 127.

54

Like the Jacobins 160 years earlier, the Communists established a dictatorship in the name of democracy, decreed opposition to be a mortal sin, reformed those who resisted, destroyed those who could not be reformed, and proclaimed a doctrine to regulate both private thinking and public behavior. The Chinese Communist leaders believe that the party holds the key to true knowledge and that its duty is not only to lead the way to salvation but to destroy—morally if not physically—those who stand in the way. Individual rights, personal liberties, compromise, and tolerance are not the values stressed in this order of things. Instead, privation, sacrifice, and obedience are glorified as privileges to be endured in a spirit of national dedication and ideological fervor.

Moved by their apocalyptic vision, the Communists aimed to renew national confidence, re-establish hope, and restore idealism. But communism in action demonstrates that however grand the vision, when men act in the belief that they have discovered the key to absolute and universal truth and subordinate an entire society to their vision of Utopia, the harsh realities of totalitarian rule are very different from the Utopianism of the original vision. High ideals, worthy ambitions, and self-sacrifice become submerged in manipulation, controls, and secrecy, where no truth is admitted but the "one great truth" and the means are subordinated to the ends.

Unlike Western liberal democratic societies, China today is not concerned with the ideal of reconciling individual freedom with the authority of the state. Although the Communist regime in China has known one temporary period of major political relaxation, during the "Hundred Flowers" campaign of 1957, this was merely the result of a tactical move. It did not fundamentally affect the principle of Communist dictatorship or, to use the Communist euphemism, "democratic centralism."

In China today, the enforcement of the party line as determined by the leadership takes precedence over all else. The party decides what changes in society must take place, and then it provides the necessary doctrinal rationalization.

In many respects it is futile, however, to regret that American values of freedom could not simply be transplanted to China. Hardship, discipline, and restraints appear to have been almost permanent themes of Chinese national life, and they are not likely soon to disappear, whatever government is in power. Democratic attitudes of "live and let live" are difficult to reconcile with urgent needs to solve encrusted social problems and to transform traditional, impoverished societies into strong modern states.

Nevertheless, we cannot help but be dismayed by a government that systematically employs unjust methods for political ends, is contemptuous of individual dignity, and treats dissent as a moral and political crime. Behind the terms "dictatorship of the proletariat," "people's democracy," and "democratic centralism" lies the hard fact of a self-selected and self-perpetuating dictatorship. The Communist party, controlled by a small handful of top leaders, sets the society's goals and controls the lives of China's millions. It tolerates no impartial thinking and no independent criticism, for these are regarded as bourgeois foibles to be scorned as irrelevant or suppressed as dangerous. Those who stray from the fold may be charged, as Galileo was in 1616, with being "foolish and absurd, philosophically and formally heretical" for having contradicted the sacred tests in both "liberal meaning and according to the general interpretation of the Fathers and Doctors." They are then subjected to various pressures, particularly "thought reform," until, like Galileo, they are made to recant and "abjure, cure, and detest the said errors and heresies." [4]

In China today, the Communist party leaders are primarily concerned not with the views of the dissenters but with the imperative necessity, as they see it, of guiding the thinking of an entire nation and uprooting ancient prejudices so that a conscripted nation may move forward toward the goals set for it. "Mass persuasion," "ideological reform," "struggle," and the training of "soldiers of socialism" are simply tools for inculcating the new morality. Patriotism and poetry, statistics and song, hard work and hero worship are mobilized as in a military campaign for the greater glory of Communist China and the maintenance in power of the party leadership. The same methods of mass persuasion can be concerted to kill flies, hate America, produce more steel, and revere Mao Tse-tung. Ideology itself has become the servant of those who are its prophets.

[4] See I. Bernard Cohen, "A Man Who Looked to the Stars," *New York Times Magazine*, February 9, 1964, pp. 19–26.

Past Performance and Outlook for the Future

It is too easy and misleading, however, to describe the system simply as one of terror and harsh dictatorship. Such a characterization ignores the regime's subtleties and purposes. Actually, the evidence suggests that the top leaders, while ruthless in the pursuit of their goals, are not wild fanatics but calculating men. They have made serious mistakes but have known how to retreat and adjust when these mistakes have become obvious. As a group, they have to date maintained remarkable unity. With a few notable exceptions, party, army, and administrative leaders have maintained continuity, without faltering, in the decade and a half since the achievement of power.[5] The system, moreover, is not merely one for the enforcement of a governmental dictatorship. Within its philosophical framework and motivated by its vision of the future, it purports to offer comprehensive and pervasive answers to all of man's problems, whether in art or education, politics or economics.

The task of interpreting and appraising a system such as this one is not easy. Western liberal standards cannot but judge harshly a regime that is based on political dictatorship and the suppression of personal liberties and which challenges values that have been cultivated over the centuries. Paradoxes, however, are inherent in political life. How, for example, does one balance the harshness of the Communist system, the cynicism of its leaders, and its failures against its accomplishments and successes? It is clear that the regime has not, as its leaders may earlier have thought, found easy answers for China's basic problems—problems such as food, population, and economic growth. But it is also true that internal order has been maintained, health conditions improved, the educational system expanded, and science and technology promoted. And China's voice is now heard loudly in world affairs. Clearly, many Chinese regard these as real achieve-

[5] The political character of the Chinese Communist regime is analyzed in detail in H. Franz Schurmann's forthcoming volume in the Council on Foreign Relations series, *The United States and China in World Affairs*.

ments, and we would be misguided if we underestimated them. Economic development, and industrialization in particular, has been a major Chinese Communist goal, and because of the regime's ability to mobilize both human and material resources, it has made some progress. During China's First Five-Year Plan, 1953–57, industrial growth was impressive, and then briefly during the Great Leap Forward of 1958 it appeared as if China might be moving ahead at an almost fantastic pace.

Today, though, the Chinese leaders no longer speak so boldly and optimistically about China's bright economic future as they did during the heady days of the Great Leap Forward. The slogan "politics takes command," which inspired that frantic campaign, proved to be an inadequate substitute for careful economic planning and the prudent use of limited resources. Indoctrination and institutional reforms could not by themselves enable China to leap over the obstacles to economic progress. The Great Leap Forward and the communes introduced at the same time, plus serious natural disasters, created an internal economic crisis of major proportions during 1959–61. To make matters worse, the growing quarrel with the Soviet Union had serious economic consequences. Moscow withdrew its technicians from China in 1960, and trade with the Soviet Union dropped sharply.

During 1961–62, however, the regime retreated from communization and scaled down its aspirations, and the economy has steadily recovered since then. Agriculture now receives first priority in the regime's plans, and ambitious goals of industrial expansion have been at least temporarily deferred. The process of growth has resumed, but at a moderate rate far below that hoped for in earlier years.

Peking has not published any overall economic statistics since 1960, but it is estimated that in 1965 agricultural production, including food crops, was close to that of 1957, the year before the Great Leap Forward, and that industrial production was approaching this level. During the years since 1957, however, the population had increased substantially; therefore, per-capita production had declined accordingly. It will take several years before the per-capita output of the peak year of 1958 can be reached again. Nevertheless, the severe crisis of the early 1960s has passed, and the Third Five-Year Plan, covering the years

1966–70, may bring significant growth again, even if at a slower rate than in the early 1950s.

By improvisation and adaptation, thus, the regime has been able to overcome its economic crisis, retain its political leadership and control largely unchanged, and move slowly toward recovery and renewed development. Nevertheless, the Chinese Communist government can now have few illusions that the economic development of the country will be rapid or easy, and it has had no alternative but to adopt a more gradualist approach.

It is a moot question, however, whether the Chinese Communist system can afford to relax its fervor indefinitely. Tactically, it was necessary to do so when morale was sagging after the failures of the Great Leap Forward. Even the cadres were demoralized, and Peking's propaganda had an empty ring. But the basic system remains unaltered, and regardless of tactical shifts, reliance on party discipline, exhortation, mobilization of the masses, and tight controls of necessity continue. Since late 1962, in fact, there has been a steady tightening of political controls, even though economic policies remain fairly pragmatic and "moderate" in Chinese Communist terms. In the Soviet Union, significant changes did not come until forty years after the revolution, when the standard of living had greatly improved and new leaders had appeared. Similar changes have yet to occur in China.

As a result of the internal economic crisis and the deterioration of relations with the Soviet Union, Communist China's foreign trade has undergone some important changes in both composition and direction since the late 1950s. Food grains have replaced producer goods as the principal import items, and these have come principally from the West, not from the Communist countries. China's need for food grains could not be met by the Soviet Union. Imports of industrial capital goods from Communist bloc countries have also declined precipitously, and the Chinese have purchased a growing number of complete industrial plants from non-Communist countries. As a result, close to two-thirds of Communist China's trade is now with the non-Communist rather than the Communist world. There are, however, obvious limits to China's ability to pay for needed imports to speed industrialization.

There has also been an important change in Peking's views on birth control. The Communist leadership has overcome its ideological scruples and introduced a campaign to limit the growth of China's population. There are few signs of spectacular results to date, however, and limiting population growth will at best take time.

In sum, the Chinese Communists in the past decade and a half have initiated a process of significant growth, but they have also undergone a major economic crisis which has forced them to place greater priority on solving basic agricultural and population problems. Nevertheless, the likelihood is that slowly but steadily they will push on toward their goal of building an industrial base for power and demand whatever sacrifices are necessary to achieve this end.[6]

The Leadership

One important question for the future is what will happen in China when the present generation of leaders passes from the scene. One of the most striking characteristics of the top leadership today is that it is rapidly aging—the average age of the party's Central Committee is well over sixty—and it will soon begin to change as a result of natural attrition.

The first generation of Chinese Communist leaders, which is still in power, has had long years of comradeship; in addition, the personal prestige and authority of Mao Tse-tung have helped hold them together. As Soviet experience indicates, this cohesion is not necessarily inherent in the Communist system, but it has served the Chinese Communists well.

The unity of the leadership, however, has not meant that there has been a lack of debate on difficult issues. There is evidence of significant differences on many political, economic, and military issues. Will these differences grow when Mao dies and a new generation of leaders emerges?

[6] China's economy and foreign economic relations are examined in detail in Alexander Eckstein, *Communist China's Economic Growth and Foreign Trade: Implications for U.S. Policy* (New York: McGraw-Hill for the Council on Foreign Relations, 1966). This volume is part of the Council on Foreign Relations series, *The United States and China in World Affairs*.

The Chinese themselves know that the transition to a new generation of leaders will raise many problems and questions about the future. It may be difficult to maintain the unity and discipline of recent years, and increasing diversity of opinion, both within the leadership and within the society as a whole, seems likely. Reporting from Peking in the summer of 1963, Anna Louise Strong, an American long sympathetic to the Chinese Communist regime, declared that: "If I asked Chinese friends today what is the chief problem, the chances are that they will not say 'agriculture' or 'industrialization' but 'Socialist education.' How to keep the revolutionary spirit alive when the men who made the revolution pass?" [7] The current deification of Mao Tse-tung, in which oracular qualities are attributed to his writings, is probably viewed as a means of indoctrinating and unifying a new generation around the symbol of Mao's reputed infallibility. More generally, the leaders have also been devoting increasing attention to the task of "Cultivating and Training Millions of Successors to the Proletarian Revolution," [8] and this problem, unlike the problem of succession to positions in the top leadership, has been dealt with publicly. The more society becomes modernized, the more important and difficult it becomes to prevent revolutionary enthusiasm from flagging. Consequently, to strengthen Communist orthodoxy and to fight "revisionism" as well as subversive "bourgeois" values, the "Thought of Mao Tse-tung" is being incessantly extolled, and any sign of relaxation is vigorously combated. Qualities of self-sacrifice, modesty, and self-criticism are held up for emulation within the political context of Marxism-Leninism, the teachings of Mao Tse-tung, a spirit of revolution, democratic centralism, and class struggle. In this way, the present leadership hopes to prevent "proletarian ardor" from flagging, especially when major shifts in political leadership take place. Still, there is good reason to expect that at least subtle changes in the society will take place despite all the regime's efforts to forestall them.

The men who immediately succeed the present leaders may well

[7] Letter No. 10, July 26, 1963, *Letters from Peking* (Peking: World Press, n.d.), quoted in *Problems of Communism*, May/June 1964, p. 43.
[8] See the editorial by this title in *People's Daily*, August 3, 1964, reprinted in *Peking Review*, no. 32, August 7, 1964, pp. 12-15.

have many of the same qualities as the current leaders. In time, however, there may be new leaders who lack the memory of years of common revolutionary struggle and who therefore may well have a variety of differing preoccupations and outlooks, reflecting their own backgrounds and careers. There is no reason to believe that they will be any less dedicated to maintaining themselves in power, strengthening the present political and economic system in China, and furthering China's interest abroad, but one may be hopeful that they could conceivably be easier to deal with than the present leadership and that they may be impelled to consider a greater variety of policy options. Like the men now in Peking, they can be expected to appraise their prospects quite coldly and do what they think best in order to advance their purposes, but there may be more differences among persons promoting varied policy approaches—from extreme radicalism on the one hand to relative pragmatism and moderation on the other—and a greater fluidity and competition among policy alternatives as a result.

A Summing Up

The present leaders in Communist China are doubtless troubled because progress at home has not been so rapid as they had hoped and because there is no easy formula in sight to speed it up suddenly. They are almost certainly aware of chronic dissidence, and they know that it could become more serious, as it did during 1957 and the difficult years of 1959–61. Nevertheless, there is no evidence of effective opposition that could pose any real challenge to the regime. There has been no dramatic or substantial improvement in the general standard of living, and the obstacles to faster progress persist. But for some the conditions are better than they were, and a process of economic growth has at least been initiated. The rigid discipline and the tight controls are undoubtedly considered oppressive by many, but there may be little real expectation of milder alternatives since the Chinese population has never enjoyed a government emphasizing individual rights.

The regime's balance sheet can be struck in different ways;

inevitably, appraisals will vary. It might be comforting for Americans to think that because the Communist regime is totalitarian and hostile it cannot last. The evidence indicates, however, that it is likely to exist for the indefinite future, and it is essential that we recognize this fact, even though it clashes with our own moral values and political wishes. As one wise Chinese observer, who himself chose to leave his homeland rather than live under Communist rule, declares: "History . . . does not encourage the optimists to hope that the Communist rule will end because it is a tyranny, nor the apologists to prove that it is not tyrannical on the ground that it has not ended yet." [9]

Other countries cannot, however, ignore the special characteristics of the Chinese Communist system, which shape Peking's foreign as well as domestic concerns. The present Chinese leaders themselves insist upon a revolutionary continuity between their foreign and domestic policies. The calculated, disciplined manipulation of Chinese society; the relentless pursuit of goals set by the Communist party, which has unbounded intellectual arrogance behind a demeanor of austerity and self-sacrifice; and the contempt with which the dignity of the individual is treated cannot be viewed complacently. This system has few self-correcting devices, except for those tolerated by the top leaders themselves. Propaganda campaigns can be mounted overnight; friendships that have been hailed as traditional can disappear without trace; deep-seated historical ties are discovered where none existed before; and the Chinese population has little to say in the matter and must simply echo the cheers or insults of its leaders. The conduct of foreign relations, like the management of affairs at home, resembles a series of campaigns in which all energies are mobilized to struggle toward the desired end, no tactics are barred, and no dissent permitted. No Chinese may stand aside from such campaigns. There is no right to remain silent. In support of their foreign policy, the Chinese Communist leaders insist upon a nation in a permanent state of mobilization.

At the same time, however, the leaders in Peking are not mere creatures of Marx and Lenin. Their conception of China's position in the world is reminiscent of the traditional Chinese assumption of superiority as the center of civilization. China's example as

[9] Mu Fu-sheng, cited, p. 295.

a model for others, its role as the expounder of correct doctrine, and its tradition of standing alone and superior are themes that have appeared many times in Chinese history, and they reappear today in a new form. But the unprecedented mobilization of national power in the service of a revolutionary ideology has profoundly affected this ancient society, and neither Chinese society nor Chinese relations with the outside world will ever be the same again.

CHAPTER FOUR

Communist China in World Affairs

China's relations with the outside world have almost never involved easy relations among equals. Its size and geographical position, its long and great cultural history, and its proud tradition of superiority all have contributed to a sense of isolation and wariness of foreigners. Compared with Japanese society, Chinese society was much less receptive to modern Western influences. Beginning in the middle of the nineteenth century, China, while resisting encroachments from the West, underwent a period of domestic decline. The forces of traditionalism tried to protect themselves against the impact of Western influences, but the attempt was in vain. For close to a century thereafter, the Chinese regarded themselves as victims first of Western imperialism and then, after Japan had learned its lessons from the West, of Japanese aggression. The convulsions of the Taiping rebellion in the mid-nineteenth century, the Boxer rebellion at the turn of the century, and the Republican revolution of 1911 were signs of China's travail and the mounting internal and external pressures. But the first two failed, and the leaders of the third were unable to create a stable system to replace the obsolete Manchu dynasty.

After the Republican revolution, which it was hoped would point the way to modernization, China instead entered a period of internal turmoil that did not end until four decades later, when the victory of the Chinese Communists established a new kind of totalitarian order. It was the Communists, assisted by Japan's defeat in World War II, who finally threw out the remaining Western interests, unified the country under a centralized administration, and instituted a forced-draft program to achieve the goal of modernization. The Communists proclaimed their victory as one that would end a century of Western influence and encroachments.

The Ideological Impetus

Against this historical background, it is not surprising that the new rulers, Chinese as well as Communists, soon showed their unwillingness to abandon the accumulated resentments of a century of real and imagined grievances or to adopt a cooperative attitude toward other nations. However, the Chinese Communists' years of revolutionary struggle and the ideology that inspired them have also shaped their regime's national goals and its approach to international problems. They have given China today a distinctive foreign policy that projects the country's national interests in international revolutionary terms far beyond China's borders. Had the country been unified under a strong non-Communist government, it might well have sought certain national-security and territorial goals similar to those Peking now pursues, and it would almost certainly have asserted claims to be heard as a great power. Nevertheless, it would in all probability have been less defiant of other countries and more amenable to establishing normal cooperative relationships with them, and it would probably have lacked the Communists' missionary zeal to promote their system elsewhere. It would not, in short, have willingly accepted second-class status in the world—certainly not in Asia—but it probably would have been less provocative, interfered less in the affairs of others, and aroused fewer fears.

The years of the civil war in China taught the Communist leaders the virtues of patience and unremitting struggle. Tactics combining peaceful coexistence, ruthless conflict, united-front alliances, and tactical retreats all had their place in domestic strategy during those years, and they still do today in China's international dealings. The war against Japan reinforced the lessons already learned. Mao Tse-tung, in his Yenan lectures of 1938 on "protracted war," gave this prescription for methods to fight the Japanese: "To fight resolutely a decisive engagement in every

66

campaign or battle when victory is certain; to avoid a decisive engagement in every campaign or battle when victory is uncertain; and to avoid absolutely a strategic decisive engagement which stakes the destiny of the nation." [1]

The theme of "struggle" is persistent and pervasive. In March 1926, during the early harsh years, Mao Tse-tung stressed that "the two big forces, revolution and counterrevolution, are engaged in the final struggle. . . . There is no room for any to remain 'independent.' " [2] Twenty-three years later, on the eve of victory, Mao reiterated this position. His article "On the People's Democratic Dictatorship," issued in 1949, gave the following prescription for China's international behavior:

Externally, unite in a common struggle with those nations of the world which treat us as equals and unite with the peoples of all countries. That is, ally ourselves with the Soviet Union, with the People's Democracies, and with the proletariat and the broad masses of the people in all other countries, and form an international united front.
. . . In the light of the experiences accumulated in these forty years and these twenty-eight years, all Chinese without exception must lean either to the side of imperialism or to the side of socialism. Sitting on the fence will not do, nor is there a third road. [3]

Liu Shao-chi, long a top-ranking leader in the Chinese hierarchy, had articulated the same theme the year before, after Tito's expulsion from the Cominform. He wrote that "if one is not in the imperialist camp . . . then one must be in the anti-imperialist camp. . . . To remain neutral or sitting on the fence is impossible . . . so-called neutrality . . . is nothing but deception, intentional or otherwise." [4]

In Chinese Communist thought, the elevation of "struggle" into a governing principle of society and international behavior rests on the premise that "fundamental antagonisms" exist between socialism and capitalism and between "oppressed" and "oppressor." Neither domestic exploitation nor foreign imperial-

[1] Selected Works, v. 2 (New York International Publishers, 1954), p. 233.
[2] "Analysis of the Classes in Chinese Society," March 1926, same, v. 1 (New York: International Publishers, 1954), pp. 14–15.
[3] Same, vol. 5 (New York: International Publishers, n.d.), p. 415.
[4] Liu Shao-chi, Internationalism and Nationalism (3d ed; Peking: Foreign Languages Press, 1952), pp. 32–33.

ism can be conciliated; both must be combated through revolutionary struggle. However, in a speech on April 22, 1960, commemorating Lenin's ninetieth anniversary, Lu Ting-yi, one of Peking's leading ideologists, asserted that the Chinese Communists have consistently upheld the use of "all the means of revolution and forms of struggle, including the 'illegal' and the 'legal,' extraparliamentary and parliamentary, sanguinary and bloodless, economic and political, military and ideological." [5] In short, while the broad goals are prescribed, the tactics vary. But to deny the need for continuing struggle is to emasculate the revolutionary essence of Marxism-Leninism and to be guilty, like the Soviets, of modern revisionism and influenced by bourgeois ideology. [6]

A doctrine of this sort can and is used to justify all action taken in the name of the revolution. The Chinese convictions about the need for relentless struggle have been highlighted in the enormous outpouring of doctrinal arguments in the controversy with the Soviet Union. One should not, therefore, minimize the effects of the revolutionary experience on the Chinese. In the eyes of Peking's leaders, "all revolutions against imperialism, colonialism, and neo-colonialism, in whatever form (political struggle, or armed struggle, or both combined), play a positive role in the struggle for world peace . . . revolutionary struggle is never in conflict with the struggle for world peace." [7] Taking into account these premises and Mao's Clausewitzian view that war is the continuation of politics by other means, one can see the roots of the Communists' view that:

All wars, whether world, local, or special, started by the imperialists in the interests of a handful of monopoly capitalists, are unjust. All

[5] "Unite Under Lenin's Revolutionary Banner," *Peking Review*, no. 17, April 26, 1960, p. 37.
[6] See, for example, the *Red Flag* article, "Long Live Leninism," in commemoration of the ninetieth anniversary of Lenin's birth in April 1960, reprinted in *Peking Review*, no. 17, April 26, 1960, pp. 6-23, and the editorial in the *People's Daily*, December 31, 1962, reprinted in *Peking Review*, no. 1, January 4, 1963, pp. 9-21.
[7] This quotation is taken from an article, "The Correct Way to Defend World Peace," in *Hoc Tap*, the theoretical journal of the Central Committee of the Vietnam Workers' party, which was reprinted with obvious approval in *Peking Review*, no. 15, April 10, 1964, pp. 13-16. The quotation is from p. 14.

wars are just which are fought by the oppressed nations, the working class and laboring people of various countries against imperialism and monopoly capitalism, and for national liberation, or by the socialist countries to defend their revolutionary gains against aggression by imperialism and the bourgeois reactionaries of other countries.[8]

The present Chinese leaders have made it clear that in their view revolutionary wars are not something to be avoided, nor, as they see it, is there an easier peaceful substitute. As Mao put it on June 21, 1963: "Revolutions are not possible without wars of national liberation or revolutionary civil war. To say otherwise is opposed to revolutionary wars and to revolution." [9] In Chinese Communist eyes, therefore, the "struggle for peace," "national liberation movements," and "revolutionary wars" cannot be separated because "peace" can be achieved, they argue, only after a relentless fight against the imperialists and colonialists, as well as against domestic reactionaries and counterrevolutionaries.

The unique experience of the Chinese civil war, the requirements of the competition with Moscow for leadership of the Communist movement, the continuous assaults against the non-Communist positions defended by the United States, and the search for efficient uses of China's limited resources to establish its leadership in the world have all helped to shape China's revolutionary strategy. Peking's present leaders appear to be convinced that both national interests and ideological conviction are served by China's putting itself in the forefront of the fight against colonialism and imperialism.

Doctrinaire boldness is not matched, however, by recklessness in action. Here, too, Mao Tse-tung has provided an aphorism that

---

[8] Same, p. 15. Almost thirty years earlier, in December 1936, Mao Tse-tung wrote in his article, "Strategic Problems of China's Revolutionary War": "There are only two kinds of wars in history, just and unjust. We support just wars and oppose unjust wars. All counter-revolutionary wars are unjust, all revolutionary wars are just." *Selected Works*, v. 1 (New York: International Publishers, 1954), p. 179.

[9] Quoted in Tang Tsou, "Mao Tse-tung and Peaceful Coexistence," *Orbis*, Spring 1964, vol. 8, no. 1, p. 43. Some twenty-five years previously, Mao, in commenting upon the situation in China in a speech at a plenary session of the Central Committee, had observed: "Some people have ridiculed us as advocates of the 'omnipotence of war'; yes, we are, we are the advocates of the omnipotence of the revolutionary war, which is not bad at all, but is good and is Marxist." See "Problems of War and Strategy," *Selected Works*, v. 2 (New York: International Publishers, 1954), p. 272.

succinctly states his views: "strategically we should slight all enemies, and tactically we should take full account of them." [10]
Confidence and resolution in the pursuit of long-term objectives
should be combined with prudence and flexibility in practice.
The Chinese leaders did not really need Khrushchev to remind
them that the "imperialists," whom they scornfully describe as
"paper tigers," have "atomic teeth"; on a tactical level, Peking
has been very aware of this fact. The struggle must not cease, but
circumstances will dictate how it should be carried on. "Peaceful
coexistence and revolutionary struggle are, therefore, not contra-
dictorary: the two help each other forward." [11]

However, conciliation and compromise are not themselves desirable objectives. They are to be used like any other weapons in
the continuing struggle. This viewpoint was not that of Nehru
and U Nu when in 1954 they each joined with Chou En-lai in
proclaiming the "Five Principles of Peaceful Coexistence" and
accepted his assurances that revolution was "not for export," but
it was clearly that of the Chinese.

The Chinese Communists persist in seeing their greatest opportunities for successful revolutionary struggle in the remaining colonial areas of the world and in those countries which have recently acquired their formal independence but which, as Peking
sees it, still have not fully achieved real independence. The Chinese believe that it is in these areas that Communist revolutionary
doctrine and the struggle against imperialism are most applicable.
It is also these colonies and newly independent countries that are
felt to be most likely to accept the model of the Chinese revolution, with its emphasis on peasant-based revolutionary war and on
the fight against Western "imperialism" or "neo-colonialism." Peking's goal, therefore, is to turn nationalist and zenophobic sentiment in these areas against the West, and especially against the
United States.

A captured secret Chinese army document, dated April 1961,
described, for the benefit of high military officers, the special im-

[10] This quotation is from his speech to the leaders of the Communist countries in Moscow on November 18, 1957. The full text of the speech has
never been published, but excerpts are included in the selections of his
writings on the subject "imperialism and all reactionaries are paper tigers"
in *Peking Review*, no. 37, November 11, 1958, pp. 6–11.
[11] "The Correct Way to Defend World Peace," cited, p. 15.

portance that Peking has increasingly placed on Africa in its hopes for expanded world-wide revolution. The document asserted that: "The center of anti-colonial struggle is Africa. The center of struggle between East and West is Africa. At present Africa is the central question of the world." It then referred to the many "rightists" still in power in Africa and continued: "The rightists must lose their prestige and position; then other people should come forward, people who will carry out the national revolution." The history and significance of the Chinese revolution should be explained to these new leaders, but "they must act for themselves, foreign assistance being secondary only. Small rivers flow long distances. We do not expect quick results. If there were one or two among the independent countries which would effect a real nationalist revolution their influence would be great and a revolutionary wave would roll up the African continent." [12] The general strategy for Africa outlined in 1961 was described as one designed "to oppose imperialism and colonialism, emphasizing national revolutions and broad united fronts." Confidence was expressed that the revolutionary movements are destined to gather momentum and sweep all before them: "When the opportunity is ripe, the wave of revolution will roll up the continent of Africa like a mat so that more than 200 million Africans will become world leaders. We must not be shortsighted on this question." [13] The record of Communist China's growing activities in Africa during the early 1960s, in such places as the Congo, Zanzibar, Mozambique, Zambia, and Burundi, shows that Peking was attempting to back up its ideological and revolutionary fervor with deeds, but the fact that in some places Chinese activities boomeranged suggests that Peking was far too optimistic in its assessment of the possibilities of stimulating revolutions and promoting the Chinese model throughout the underdeveloped world.

Indeed, recent events, such as the collapse of the planned Algiers Conference of Afro-Asian states in 1965 after unsuccessful

[12] *Work Bulletin* (*Kung Tso Tung Hsun*), no. 17, April 25, 1961, as quoted in *China News Analysis*, no. 501, January 24, 1964, p. 1.
[13] *Work Bulletin*, no. 17, cited, as quoted in John W. Lewis, *Communist China's Party Leadership and the Succession to Mao Tse-tung, An Appraisal of Tensions* (Washington: External Research Staff, Bureau of Intelligence and Research, U.S. Department of State, January 1964), p. 27.

Chinese attempts to manipulate it and a little later the resurgence of anti-Chinese feeling in Indonesia, Ghana, and elsewhere, indicate that most newly independent countries are wary of excessive intervention by China, as well as by the Western powers. It remains to be seen, however, what impact such events will have on Chinese Communist strategy and tactics.

Most revolutionaries, of course, have some sense of world mission. Both the need for self-justification and a desire for security in a congenial world environment tend to impel the revolutionary to broadcast his message and seek emulation. Vanity tells him that he has discovered a universal truth that he must share with others, perhaps even through force.

Influences such as these have from the beginning bolstered the sense of destiny of the Chinese Communists. Thus, as early as November 1931, only ten years after the founding of the Chinese Communist party, the first provisional Soviet government of China, which had just been established, proclaimed the need not only to drive out imperialist influence from China but to fight it on a world-wide scale:

Furthermore, the provisional government of the Soviet Republic of China declared that it will, on no condition, remain content with the overthrow of imperialism in China but, on the contrary, will aid as its ultimate objective in waging a war against world imperialism until the latter is all blown up.[14]

After many more years of Communist struggle, Liu Shao-chi claimed in 1943 that "within these twenty-two years our party has witnessed more important changes and accumulated more experiences of the revolutionary struggle in various complicated forms . . . than any other Communist party in the World." [15] He went one step further in 1946 when he told Anna Louise Strong that Mao Tse-tung had discovered an Asian form of Marxism, that he had adapted Marx and Lenin to China, and that his revolutionary theories charted a path to power not only for the Chinese people but for all the peoples of the colonial coun-

[14] *Central China Post* (Hankow), November 25, 1931, quoted by O. Edmund Clubb, in *The International Position of Communist China* (New York: Association of the Bar of the City of New York, the Hammarskjöld Forum, December 2, 1963).
[15] Quoted in Edgar Snow, *The Other Side of the River* (New York: Random House, 1961), p. 650.

tries of Southeast Asia. Three years later, just after the proclamation of the People's Republic of China, Liu reiterated this theme in a speech to a major trade union conference in Peking. The road of Mao Tse-tung, he then declared, "can also be the basic road for liberation of peoples of other colonial and semi-colonial countries, where similar conditions exist." [16] And in 1951, as was quoted above, Lu Ting-yi asserted that while the Russian revolution was "the classic type of revolution in imperialist countries," the Chinese revolution was "the classic type of revolution in colonial and semi-colonial countries." [17]

At the time, not many in the West took these professions of faith very seriously. It was hoped that the Chinese Communists would "settle down" once they were in power and had their hands full with domestic tasks. The scope of their revolution aimed at undermining imperial and colonial rule was only dimly appreciated. Besides, Peking was seen only in Moscow's shadow, and China's special claim to be the model for revolution against imperialism and colonialism did not seem terribly important.

After a lull in the latter 1950s, when it publicly de-emphasized its dedication to world-wide revolution through violent struggle, Peking in the early 1960s again issued strident calls to revolution and hailed the applicability of the Chinese model. In Chinese Communist eyes, the historic mission that the combination of Chinese experience and Communist doctrine had given China became a major weapon in competing with the Soviet Union as well as combating the United States.

Although the Chinese now acknowledged that "the material atomic bomb is important," they confidently proclaimed that "the spiritual atomic bomb is more important. It is the spiritual atomic bomb that we have the monopoly of. No imperialist or reactionary can compete with us in this respect." [18] This confidence in the power of revolutionary ideas and tactics to compensate for material weakness and overcome the adversary is undoubtedly a heritage of the Communist experience during the Chinese civil war. As the leaders in Peking see it, the problem now, as then, is how to conduct prolonged and relentless struggle

[16] See Chapter 2, note 5.
[17] See Chapter 2, note 7.
[18] *Work Bulletin*, no. 3, January 7, 1961, quoted in Lewis, cited, p. 24.

against adversaries who outwardly appear powerful but inwardly
are weak and rotten and who can ultimately be overcome despite
their seeming strength in terms of material power.

Abroad, it is the United States and other members of the "imperialist camp" that must be opposed, just as at home it is the
landlords and bureaucratic capitalists who must be either reformed or destroyed. At home, there is some hope that the national bourgeoisie may be won over, or at least neutralized, if
they will accept the leadership of the socialist camp. In foreign
policy, the aim is to weaken the ties binding other countries to
the United States and if possible to link these countries to a
Communist-led "united front." Thus, there is a parallelism between the concept, applied domestically, of a tactical "united
front" of workers, peasants, petty bourgeoisie, and "national
bourgeoisie" and the idea of forming an international grouping of
"all the peace-loving forces in the world, including the forces of
the socialist camp, the forces of the national-democratic revolutionary movement in Asia, Africa, and Latin America, the forces
of the working class and the revolutionary people in the world,
and the forces of all peace-loving countries and peoples." [19]

While the dispute between the People's Republic of China and
the Soviet Union involves both ideological issues and conflicts of
national interests, the Chinese in their exchanges with Moscow
have vigorously reiterated and articulated their ideological convictions in an effort to place themselves in the forefront of the
world Communist movement. While contesting with the Soviet
Union over specific issues of national policy, they have placed increasing stress, both at home and abroad, on "the thought of Mao
Tse-tung" and its applicability to the present phase of international struggle.

In their letter to the Soviet Union dated June 14, 1963,[20] for
example, the Chinese recapitulated and underlined the essential
unity that they sought to give Communist doctrine. Projecting
from their own experience, they proclaimed that the contradiction between the bourgeoisie and the proletariat in the capitalist
world could be settled only by proletarian revolution and that

[19] Speech by Premier Chou En-lai in Colombo, February 28, 1964, *Peking
Review*, no. 10, March 6, 1964, pp. 16–17.
[20] Reprinted in *Peking Review*, no. 25, June 21, 1963, pp. 6–22.

the contradiction between the oppressed nations and imperialism must be settled by revolution in the oppressed nations. They denied that there could be a "peaceful transition from capitalism to socialism," and declared that "peaceful coexistence cannot replace the revolutionary struggle of the people."

However, even though the "universal truth of Marxism-Leninism," as interpreted by Mao Tse-tung, provides a unified doctrine designed to guide all policy and action, the Chinese Communists believe that it should be adapted in practice to the requirements of each situation, with proper obeisance to doctrinal requirements. Mao has divided all social "contradictions" into "antagonistic" and "nonantagonistic" varieties, and by classifying situations in one category or the other, the Chinese leaders can decide whether to be firm or flexible, harsh or conciliatory while they still maintain an aura of doctrinal infallibility.

Diplomatic Strategy and Tactics

Despite the barrage of ideological thunderbolts launched from Peking, the Chinese Communists have shown considerable diplomatic flexibility and adaptability in pursuing their goals. In practice, they do not always cling to dogmatic purity at the expense of effective diplomacy.

The militancy of the early period immediately after 1949, when they tended to dismiss "bourgeois nationalist" regimes in Asia as lackeys of imperialism, was followed by the "Bandung period," from 1954 or 1955 to late 1957, which was marked by the friendly and fairly successful cultivation of closer contacts with many Asian and African countries. Then in late 1957, Peking again adopted a militant posture, in part because Mao concluded that the first of the Soviet sputniks and ICBMs gave the entire Communist bloc decisive strategic advantages. This posture contributed to the dispute with the Soviet Union and led to sharpened hostility toward the United States.

The recent period has been characterized by a mixture of elements, including not only ideological militancy and increased activity in Asia and Africa but also efforts to strengthen diplomatic and economic relations with the countries in the so-called "intermediate zone"—countries such as Japan, France, Australia, and Canada—a zone in which, theoretically, all non-Communist nations except the United States might be included. Using a combination of revolutionary pressures and normal diplomatic techniques, Peking now seeks to isolate the United States, weaken Soviet influence, and expand Chinese influence wherever possible. The clarion calls to revolutionary struggle have not deterred the Chinese from cultivating certain "bourgeois nationalist" leaders or establishing diplomatic relations with France, a step which Chou En-lai hailed as "not only in the interests of the Chinese and French peoples, but also helpful to the development of economic, trade, and cultural relations between the two countries, the realization of peaceful coexistence between countries with different social systems, and the cause of world peace." [21]

Some observers have asserted that the Chinese Communists are deliberately following a policy of self-isolation in the world, but the record of recent years does not bear out this assertion. Aside from the extension of Chinese influence among many Communist parties, Peking's diplomatic activity has in many areas been fairly impressive, and it has been expanding its contacts with many countries, especially since the worsening of relations with the Soviet Union. For example, during 1963 and 1964 there were marked increases in trade relations with Western countries and important wheat purchases from Australia and Canada, agreements with Japan for the exchange of trade delegations and newsmen, increased activity in Afro-Asian organizations, trips by both Liu Shao-chi and Chou En-lai to a sizable number of Asian and African countries, the conclusion of a border agreement with Pakistan, authorization for Pakistan International Airlines to operate to China, and an exchange of correspondents with Canada and the Federal Republic of Germany (neither of which recognizes Peking) as well as the exchange of ambassadors with France, which has previously been mentioned.

Peking's considerable diplomatic effort, dictated by China's immediate economic as well as political requirements, is rationalized ideologically by arguments that label the United States as the

[21] Press interview in Dacca, February 25, 1964, *Peking Review*, no. 10, March 6, 1964, p. 21.

enemy of the entire world. As early as 1946, in the interview that Mao Tse-tung gave Anna Louise Strong, Mao labeled the "U.S. reactionaries" as enemies not only of the socialist countries but also all of the capitalist as well as colonial and semi-colonial countries, which would in time come to realize that the United States was oppressing them. "The day will come," Mao declared, "when the U.S. reactionaries find themselves opposed by the people of the whole world." [22]

Building on this theme, the Chinese have attempted to define a so-called "intermediate zone" divided into two parts: "one part consists of the independent countries and those striving for independence in Asia, Africa, and Latin America; it may be called the first intermediate zone. The second part consists of the whole of Western Europe, Oceania, Canada, and other capitalist countries; it may be called the second intermediate zone." [23] In the latter countries, even though the ruling class exploits the people, the countries as a whole are oppressed by the United States, so Peking claims, and therefore hope to free themselves from U.S. control. "By making itself antagonistic to the whole world, U.S. imperialism inevitably finds itself tightly encircled." [24] Thus the Chinese seek to rationalize some of their diplomatic actions which can in fact be best explained by Peking's pragmatic attempts to solve certain pressing problems.

Undiluted dogmatism, in sum, could not be allowed to dictate diplomatic tactics in the mid-1960s when the real world of international politics was far more diverse and subtle than it had appeared to Peking's leaders fifteen years earlier. Speaking on May 3, 1964, to a group of foreign journalists visiting Peking, Foreign Minister Chen Yi said: "Some countries call themselves aligned, but aren't. Some call themselves nonaligned but are nothing of the kind." To complete the circle he added, "Some are both aligned and nonaligned at the same time. China is one of these." [25]

In other words, China was trying to be many different things to different countries—except to the United States, toward which Peking remained consistently hostile.

[22] *Selected Works*, v. 5, cited, pp. 99–100.
[23] Editorial published in *People's Daily*, January 21, 1964, reprinted in *Peking Review*, January 24, 1964, p. 7.
[24] Same.
[25] *The Economist* (London), May 9, 1964, p. 574.

This example is but one of many of Peking's manipulation of symbols and its flexibility in action. Focusing on China's long-term objectives, maintaining firm centralized control over the formulation and execution of policy, and yet showing tactical flexibility, the Chinese leaders pursue their goals with determination and considerable skill. Sometimes strong statements, as in the Vietnam and Taiwan crises, are accompanied by prudent actions that limit China's risks and commitments. Sweeping denunciations of imperialism are made, but these do not necessarily bar the cultivation of selected "imperialist" nations. The goal of supporting hard-core Communist strength in other countries is pursued, but at times this may involve encouragement of united-front tactics that are not narrowly sectarian. China is portrayed to the Communist parties and "people" of the world as a model of revolutionary dynamism and inspiration, yet at the same time many non-Communist governments are cultivated with friendly words about "peaceful coexistence" and world peace.

"Nonofficial people's diplomacy" aims at attracting and influencing sizable numbers of foreign students, women, lawyers, scientists, pacifists, doctors, and others. Whether Communist or not, they are encouraged to support policies compatible with Communist China's objectives. Such people are invited to visit China in large numbers. For example, during the two-month period of August–September 1964, twenty-eight such groups went to China from Africa alone. In appealing to them, the exponents of international Communist doctrine attempt to manipulate many sorts of nationalist and anti-colonialist appeals, sometimes with racialist undertones.

Mao Tse-tung once said that the Chinese Communists regarded concessions or retreats, when necessary, "as part of the entire revolutionary policy, as an indispensable link in the general revolutionary line, a segment in a curvilinear movement. In short, they are positive." [26] Although this statement was written during the civil war, the tactical approach that it reflects continues today. However, Peking's leaders are also capable of clinging stubbornly to stereotyped images of the world, and negotiations are often viewed as opportunities to stall and delay rather than as

[26] "The Question of Independence and Autonomy within the United Front," *Selected Works*, v. 2, cited, pp. 263–264.

occasions for flexible compromise. Diplomatic negotiations then become a test of conflicting wills, a particular form of struggle and not an opportunity to reach agreement for mutual advantage. Sir David Kelly, who had long experience dealing with Soviet diplomats during the more militant phases of Soviet diplomacy, has written that "the totalitarians regard peaceful negotiations as warfare carried on by other means—in fact 'cold war.' This is the exact reverse of the old diplomatic tradition, which assumed that negotiation must be a process of give and take, and that the only lasting agreements could be those which are genuinely accepted by both parties." The Communist view, he went on, was the application of Marxism-Leninism to negotiations, "the result of a system which regards mankind as irreconcilably divided into two hostile camps." [27] What Sir David Kelly wrote about the Soviet diplomats in the 1950s is still applicable to much of Chinese diplomacy of the 1960s.

In an authoritarian political system such as that in China, the government attempts to maintain absolute control over its foreign policy, with freedom to make major policy shifts at will. An internally imposed isolation, which prevents free contact between the Chinese people and outsiders, goes hand in hand with the attempt to control all information coming into and going out of China. Neither persons, goods, nor ideas are allowed to move freely. The internal political system and external diplomacy are viewed as intimately related. In this respect, the situation is almost reminiscent of that which Lord Macartney found when he arrived in China at the end of the eighteenth century to represent King George III as resident minister in Peking. Macartney's plans were cut short by an imperial edict to the King of England, promulgated in 1793 by the Emperor Chien Lung, in which the designation of a resident British minister at the Celestial Court was declared to be

not in harmony with the state system of our dynasty and [it] will definitely not be permitted. . . . There are well-established regulations governing tributary envoys from the outer states to Peking, giving them provisions (of food and travel expenses) by our posthouses and limiting their going and coming. There has never been a precedent for letting them do whatever they like.

[27] "The Lost Art of Diplomacy," *Foreign Service Journal*, v. 33, no. 1, January 1956, pp. 35, 40.

King George was thanked for the gifts he had sent, but little value was attached to such objects. And the Chinese Emperor declared:

As a matter of fact, the virtue and prestige of the Celestial Dynasty having spread far and wide, the kings of the myriad nations come by land and sea with all sorts of precious things. Consequently there is nothing we lack, as your principal envoy and others have themselves observed. We have never set much store on strange or ingenious objects, nor do we need any more of your country's manufactures.[28]

The Chinese Communists would hardly endorse Chien Lung's statements, but today they, too, reveal traits of extreme pride, insist on strict control of all foreigners' contacts with China, and stress the desirability of self-reliance.

Unquestionably, a combination of centralized direction, tight control, and tactical flexibility gives China certain advantages. Critical situations elsewhere can sometimes be quickly exploited; the vain can be flattered; the pace and tone of diplomacy can be readily adjusted to circumstances; and the drag of public debate and dissent can be avoided.

The record shows, however, that the Chinese, like the Americans, have had to contend with a great variety of recalcitrant international situations; that they have by no means had things their own way; and that in practice their successes to date have been limited. In many areas, Chinese motives have been suspect, and Chinese power and militancy feared. The Communist ideology that Peking has sought to spread has met with widely differing responses, and many have viewed with alarm the threat of Chinese national power behind the ideological drive. Now that the alliance with the Soviet Union has been severely weakened, China finds itself without a single major ally. Even where foreign Communist governments and parties are subject to strong Chinese influence, they are not mere tools of Peking but have wills of their own.

Like other countries, China has discovered no formula for quick success and no guarantee of ultimate victory, and many factors will continue either to help or to harass the Chinese leadership. The men in Peking have already had a significant impact

[28] Ssu-Yü Teng and John K. Fairbank, *China's Response to the West* (Cambridge: Harvard University Press, 1954), p. 19.

on the international enviroment, but to operate in this environment, they may well find it increasingly necessary in the long run
to adapt to it—and to the interests and attitudes of others.

China's Military Position and Policy

As in the case of all large powers, military strength plays an
important role in relation to Communist China's foreign policy.
The armed forces of the People's Republic of China, known as
the People's Liberation Army (PLA) and made up roughly of 2.7
million men, provide military support for the political purposes
of the regime.[29] Clearly, their prime missions are the defense of
the integrity of the nation against possible outside attack, the establishment of Peking's control over all territory claimed to be
part of China's domain, such as Tibet (and Taiwan, were it possible to "liberate" it), and support for Chinese national interests in
key neighboring countries, such as Korea and Vietnam. In addition, these military forces, including their prospective nuclear
capability, serve as symbols of China's status as a world power
and provide psychological support for the pursuit of most of Peking's foreign-policy objectives. Finally, but not necessarily least
important, they help to maintain domestic control and unity and
serve as a prop for preservation of the Communist system itself.

During the Chinese civil war it was the PLA that gave the
Communists their victory. Its political mission was inherent in its
task, and much of the present political leadership served in it.
There is now some concern in Peking lest military professionali-
zation lead to a reduction in the PLA's political ardor, and the
Chinese Communists reject the "purely military viewpoint" that
the task of the armed forces is merely to fight. The PLA is
charged with supporting all the political purposes of the revolution, not only by fighting when necessary but also by propagan-
dizing and in other ways defending communism's revolutionary
mission. The army, in fact, is now held up to the entire population

[29] For a detailed analysis of Communist China's military power, see Samuel
B. Griffith's forthcoming volume in the Council on Foreign Relations
series, *The United States and China in World Affairs*.

as a model of ideological rectitude, discipline, and Communist dedication. And the party insists on close political control over it, under the slogan "the party commands the gun."

The supremacy of political considerations comes naturally to a regime which used political indoctrination and other controls as major tools to achieve power and which continues to stress their indispensability to the Communist system. Peking's international message that people, not weapons, are the makers of history and that man, not technology, is the decisive factor in war reflect its insistence that while military power is essential, it must be subordinated to politics. This viewpoint is buttressed by the facts that China does not see its own international position resting on material wealth or military strength alone since Chinese power is still very limited, at least compared to that of the two "superpowers," and that its revolutionary appeals are addressed to those who, like China itself, are materially poor. Ideological conviction and the imperatives of China's material position combine to make a virtue of necessity.

Still, this general outlook has not prevented the People's Republic of China from stressing the establishment of industries relevant to military power and modernizing its armed forces with the means that it can command. In short, Mao Tse-tung's pride in China's "spiritual atomic bomb" does not preclude developing other kinds of power as well. It is significant, nonetheless, that when Peking announced its first nuclear explosion, its declaration suggested that Peking was still very much aware of the limitations on its military power and intended to continue, therefore, stressing its belief in the importance of the nonmaterial components of power. "The atom bomb is a paper tiger. . . . We believe in the people," the statement said. "It is the people who decide the outcome of a war, and not any weapon. The destiny of China is decided by the Chinese people, and the destiny of the world by the peoples of the world, and not by the nuclear weapon." [30]

The tempering of ideological bravado with an awareness of hard facts carries over into the assessment of broad strategic policy and of policy toward the United States. For example, Mao

[30] Chinese government statement, October 16, 1964, reprinted in *Peking Review*, no. 42, October 16, 1964, special supplement.

Tse-tung's scorn for the imperialists has not been put to practical tests except with great prudence, and while the imperialists may have been regarded as weak strategically, their power has been fully respected tactically. Moreover, although Peking apparently believes that selective and controlled military action—even up to the point where American intervention may at times have to be risked, as in the offshore island crises—can be used to advance Chinese interests, it has given every indication that it wishes to avoid any direct military confrontation with the United States because superior American strength could cause enormous destruction in China and because the United States itself is still virtually invulnerable to Chinese military attack.

While avoiding risks of major military involvement, China attempts to use its versatile armory of political weapons in ways that weaken American positions but restrict the ability of the United States to counter them by the use of superior American force. In other words, Peking, while steadily building up its military power, has to date placed primary emphasis on political means to achieve its international objectives—an emphasis which is consistent with both its revolutionary professions and the limits on its capabilities.

There is little reason to think that China's acquisition of a nuclear capability will basically alter these principles and methods, at least not until some remote day when China—in theory—might achieve military equality with the United States or at least an ability to establish a local superiority and apply it without fear of the consequences of escalation. Contrary to some popular misrepresentations of Chinese views, the leaders of China are not reckless fanatics actually seeking nuclear war, and today they cannot rely with any confidence on their Soviet allies to back them up by striking, regardless of the circumstances, against the United States—if, indeed, they ever could have.

The Soviet Union, assisted by Yugoslavia, has helped spread the charge of Chinese rashness. In fact, what the Chinese leaders have said is that they do not want nuclear war but that if war comes, China has a better chance than other countries of surviving it and there will be new gains for socialism in its aftermath.[31]

[31] See, for example, Chinese official statements in the *Peking Review*, no. 36, September 6, 1963 pp. 9–10, and no. 38, September 20, 1963, pp. 15–18.

In practice, the Chinese have avoided, not sought, military engagements with the United States, although apparently they feel that morale at home and prestige abroad are enhanced by the use of defiant language. The Chinese themselves do not claim that their possession of the beginnings of a nuclear capability has revolutionized their strategic position. They probably also realize that while they enhance their strength in some respects in developing a nuclear capacity, they also incur new liabilities and vulnerabilities—political liabilities, which no nuclear powers can fully escape, and military vulnerabilities, arising from the danger that in an escalating conflict the United States might be tempted to attack the plants which manufacture their atomic weapons. They may now feel that they have a new reason for prudence.

In the years immediately ahead, what seems most likely is that the Chinese will attempt to exploit their nuclear capability principally for political purposes to enhance China's prestige, strengthen its voice in the world, weaken the resolve of America's friends in Asia, and impose new restraints on the United States in order to deter it from considering any use of its nuclear weapons in Asia.

China's geography, population, and economic resources, as well as the revolutionary traditions of the regime, have helped to shape the character of its military forces and its strategic outlook. Apart from the beginning of a nuclear capability, its military forces today consist of a large but still only partially modernized army, an air force which, while sizable, has some serious vulnerabilities and has never been fully tested, a weak navy, and spotty air defenses. Improvement and further modernization of all these forces must overcome serious economic and technological handicaps. At present, they can only be effective in areas immediately adjacent to China and against an enemy or enemies that cannot deploy a large modernized force or bring massive air power to bear against the Chinese homeland.

Consequently, the Chinese leaders probably cannot see many opportunities at present for the direct use of China's military power to solve major problems or to achieve major goals. For example, they appear to be dissatisfied with the current frontiers with the Soviet Union, to the north and west, which were imposed on them by the czars but have been maintained by the present Russian regime; however, there is little they can do to change the situation without incurring intolerable risks. To the south, there are weaker neighbors, but there are also important geographic barriers and many political inhibitions—plus the major restraint imposed by the dangers of provoking larger American intervention or even retaliation against China. As was demonstrated in India, these handicaps may be overcome when military force is used for very limited purposes; still, the Chinese cannot be confident that even this type of action can be repeated with impunity very often.

For the present, American power prevents the Chinese Communists from using military means to destroy the rival Nationalist government on Taiwan and reincorporate Taiwan as a province of China. The military strength of the United States Seventh Fleet and the Nationalist forces could be overcome only if there was a political disintegration of the alliance between the United States and the Nationalist government or a radical change in the political situation on Taiwan itself. Peking's acquisition of a nuclear capability will not necessarily alter this military balance if United States commitments to defend Taiwan remain firm, for Peking could not possibly hope to profit from a nuclear exchange, with Taiwan as a hostage. The political impact on Taiwan of a growing nuclear capability on the mainland may be more serious, but its character will depend on a number of factors, including the balance of political views within the Nationalist government itself, the relationship of the Taiwanese on the island to the politically dominant mainlanders, and the policy and actions of the United States. The Chinese leaders in Peking clearly hope to end the political separation of Taiwan from the mainland eventually. Nevertheless, it is doubtful, despite the Nationalist and American military build-up in and around Taiwan, that the principal reason for this ambition is a military one. Peking's major preoccupation with Taiwan probably arises from political frustration at its inability to seize the island and end the rule of the Nationalists.

In Vietnam, Peking has strongly encouraged and supported the efforts of the Viet Cong, with North Vietnamese backing, to take over the south. To date, however, the Chinese have carefully limited their own involvement by providing equipment and supplies but not intervening with Chinese troops. Peking has, it is true, made strong threats not "to stand idly by," and in 1965 it took steps in South China—including partial evacuation of some cities—that looked like defensive actions against possible attack. Nevertheless, it has acted very cautiously. Even though the prospects for Viet Cong victory must seem less favorable now, as the Chinese Communists view the situation, than before the massive American involvement in 1965, Peking apparently still hopes for a long struggle—without direct involvement of Chinese troops —which would ultimately result in an American withdrawal. It has, in effect, stated that encroachments on Chinese borders would bring a violent response but that otherwise the Communists in Vietnam must carry out the struggle themselves—with Chinese material aid but without direct support by Chinese military forces.

As for Korea, present indications are that the Chinese seem prepared to accept the existing military balance there. Actually, there is very little they can do about changing it. American forces remain in Korea, a fact which Peking obviously dislikes, but the Chinese must know that the United States has no desire to become involved again in active hostilities. And even now the Communist government of North Korea serves as a buffer and gives a measure of protection to China itself. From the Chinese point of view, the current situation, while not ideal, may be acceptable and is certainly not threatening. Peking's perspective would almost certainly change, however, if the United States abandoned its commitments there. Under such circumstances, the Chinese would likely step up their support of Communist attempts to take over the south.

The strategic position of Japan, as viewed from Peking, presents the Chinese with problems of a different order. Here is a potentially strong power which, although still only weakly armed, is an ally of the United States; on its territory are American military bases which are invulnerable to existing Chinese military power. Although there is probably little that the Chinese see that they can do militarily to change the situation, China's possession of effective nuclear power can probably be expected to increase fears in Japan. The consequences of this are difficult to predict, but there might be increased hostility toward

China and a desire to build up Japan's own military strength. Japan's industrial and technological capabilities are not now mobilized against China; however, the possibility that they could be at some time in the future must be an important factor in the calculations of the Communist leaders in Peking as they scan the Asian horizon.

Because of the limits to their military power, the Chinese Communists will probably in the foreseeable future look upon diplomacy and support for revolutionary struggles elsewhere as their most effective means of trying to offset American military superiority and reduce American influence in the areas around China. Political warfare is something that the Chinese, even with their limited resources, can afford, and it has special appeals in some parts of the world.

The overall military position of the People's Republic of China is more uncertain now than in earlier years because, as has already been indicated, China is unable to count with certainty on Soviet support. Although the alliance still remains in force formally, its military significance has been significantly reduced. Moreover, Soviet military aid to China has ended, and the dependability of Soviet guarantees must now be in doubt. Even if the rift between the two Communist countries were somehow, to some degree, repaired, it seems unlikely that in the years immediately ahead Chinese strategists will be able to rely on Soviet military backing in the way they probably did before. It was not solely because of the Chinese leaders' independent spirit that Liu Shao-chi, in September 1963, stressed that "the revolutionary spirit of self-reliance represents both patriotism and proletarian internationalism." [32]

Attitudes toward Disarmament and Arms Control

The position of the People's Republic of China with regard to international disarmament and arms-control negotiations and agreements reflects its present military situation and its general

[32] See his speech in Pyongyang, North Korea, on September 18, 1963, reprinted in *Peking Review*, no. 39, September 27, 1963, pp. 8–14.

foreign-policy objectives. Until serious negotiations regarding a limited nuclear test ban took place, the Chinese seemed content to support from the side lines some of the most sweeping Soviet proposals for general disarmament and prohibition of the use of atomic weapons. They themselves, however, not only did not participate in international arms-control negotiations but seemed not to expect very much to come of them. Their main aim was propagandistic or, in their own words, "to arouse the people throughout the world to unite and oppose the imperialist scheme for arms drive and war preparations," for in their opinion "it is of course inconceivable that imperialism will accept proposals for general and complete disarmament . . . only when socialist revolution is victorious throughout the world, can there be a world free from war, a world without arms." [33]

As the Sino-Soviet dispute grew more acute and particularly when it looked as if a limited test-ban treaty might actually be signed, however, the Chinese made it increasingly clear that they would not be bound by any agreements negotiated without their participation. This position, adopted by the Standing Committee of the National People's Congress on January 21, 1960,[34] has been maintained ever since. To date, the Chinese Communists have shown no eagerness to join in international arms-control negotiations, and they have stated that they would take no part in disarmament talks conducted under United Nations auspices as long as the People's Republic was deprived of its "legitimate rights" in the organization.[35]

The Chinese Communists' bitter denunciation of the partial test-ban treaty of 1963 was particularly vehement, for instead of forbidding the use of nuclear weapons, the agreement seemed consciously designed to inhibit countries such as China from developing a nuclear capability. Moreover, Peking regarded the treaty as an American-Soviet entente directed against China. The Chinese rejection of the treaty, therefore, was total, and it was

---

[33] From a speech, "On the Question of War and Peace," by Liu Chang-sheng, Vice-President of the All-China Federation of Trade Unions, to the General Council of the World Federation of Trade Unions, June 8, 1960. *Peking Review*, no. 24, June 14, 1960, p. 14.

[34] Same, no. 4, January 26, 1960, p. 19.

[35] Editorial in *People's Daily*, November 22, 1964, reprinted in *Peking Review*, no. 48, November 27, 1964, p. 14.

accompanied by a demand for an end to all nuclear testing, the dismantling of military bases on foreign soil, and a ban on the use of nuclear weapons.[36] Sweeping proposals of this sort were clearly intended as propaganda rather than as subjects for serious negotiation.

Fifteen months later, when the Chinese exploded their first atomic device, they put forth new proposals for the prohibition of nuclear weapons and reiterated their past proposal for the creation of nuclear-free zones. (The latter had been advanced in various forms for a number of years. As early as 1955, Peking had suggested that a "peace zone" be established in the Asian and Pacific region through the conclusion of a "collective peace" pact, to include the United States. Then in February 1958, in response to an initiative by Prime Minister Nehru, Chou En-lai had supported the idea of "an area free of atomic weapons, an area of peace, throughout the whole of East Asia and the Pacific Region." Similar proposals had been put forward in August 1960 and subsequent to the conclusion of the nuclear test-ban treaty in 1963.) Peking also asserted that it would not itself engage in "first use" of nuclear weapons and went on to say that

no question of control is involved in undertaking first of all not to use nuclear weapons. So long as the countries concerned have peaceful intentions, agreement can be reached quickly. Therefore this is simple and can be easily carried out.

This statement must have startled the Soviet and American negotiators who, for years, had wrestled unsuccessfully with the important and intricate problem of controls.[37]

In summary, the Chinese Communists have not themselves taken part in arms-control discussions and have strongly objected to the 1963 test ban, but they have sought to gain propaganda advantage out of sweeping demands for general disarmament and for the abolition of nuclear weapons, which would most affect

[36] For a convenient summary of Chinese attitudes on this and other arms-control issues, see Hungdah Chiu, "Communist China's Attitude Towards Nuclear Tests," *China Quarterly*, no. 21, January/March 1965, pp. 96–107. Portions of the discussion have been drawn from this source.

[37] The statements issued after the first Chinese nuclear test may be found in *Peking Review*, no. 42, October 16, 1964, special supplement; no. 43, October 23, 1964, pp. 5–6; and no. 48, November 27, 1964, pp. 12–14. The quote is from no. 48, p. 13.

those countries which already have large nuclear arsenals. They appear determined to pursue an independent course in their own nuclear and other arms development and have given little indication of any concern about the possible dangers of nuclear proliferation. While they have not themselves indicated a desire to engage in serious arms-control negotiations, it should be added that they have never been invited to do so.

The Extension of China's Influence

As has previously been mentioned, any Chinese government able to establish its authority and unify the country in the mid-twentieth century would like to recover all national territory claimed by China,[38] demand recognition as a great power, try to assert its influence over areas close to China, and seek to make its influence felt in other parts of the world. Moreover, the People's Republic of China, like any other government, has a primary concern with the security of its frontiers, the integrity of the national territory, and the preservation of its political system. If big neighbors cannot be kept friendly, their encroachments should be resisted, and it is desirable that small neighbors should not be allowed to be used as bases by hostile powers.

Certain elements, at any rate, in Communist China's policies and behavior in the Asian area can be explained in these terms. Its entrance into the Korean War was at least in part Peking's response to its sense of danger at the prospect of having an unfriendly and strong power establish itself on China's northeastern border; it was also in part an emphatic assertion of Peking's claim to be heard in the settlement of major Far Eastern questions. The demand for the reunification of Taiwan with the mainland reflects long-standing Chinese territorial claims and is echoed by the Na-

---

[38] In a major work, first published in Chinese in 1943 and in English in 1947, Chiang Kai-shek stated that "Formosa, the Pescadores, the Four Northeastern Provinces, Inner and Outer Mongolia, Sinkiang, and Tibet are each a fortress essential for the nation's defense and security. The separation of any of these regions from the rest of the country means the disruption of our national defenses." See *China's Destiny* (New York: Roy Publishers, 1947), p. 36.

tionalist government. Peking and Taipei disagree mainly on the question of which government is to control the reunited China. Support for the Communists of North Vietnam has doubtless been partially motivated by a desire to insure the existence of a friendly government there—something that the Nationalists tried to do for a brief period in 1945 by their military occupation of portions of the area—although support for full-scale "people's war" there and in the rest of Vietnam has also involved revolutionary aims that go much further and are far from being defensive alone. Tibet was forcibly reincorporated as an integral part of China to assert traditional Chinese claims, and when dissidence in Tibet raised questions about the security of China's southwestern frontier, Peking did not hesitate to establish tight and harsh control in that region. The introduction of border issues into Communist China's dispute with the Soviet Union also derives from traditional claims. In short, national prestige and considerations of security as well as a revolutionary determination to advance the cause of communism impel China to strive for a position of major importance in Asia and to extend its influence beyond its borders.

This does not necessarily mean that the Chinese Communists are simply trying to restore the traditional shape of imperial China and re-establish the old system of tributaries and suzerain relationships with China's neighbors. The dynamic revolutionary force that infuses the policies and actions of the Chinese Communists is very new and makes China today quite different from the slow-moving traditional China of earlier centuries. Nevertheless, the pattern is not irrelevant to what we see happening today.

By calling upon all its assets—revolutionary as well as nationalistic—the People's Republic of China today strongly asserts its claims for recognition as a great power. No longer content with seeking a position of major influence in the Asian area alone, it now tries to extend its influence throughout the world, in competition with the Soviet Union as well as the United States and others. Peking's present leaders consider themselves to be not merely the inheritors of China's traditional international position but new world leaders in their own right.

The claim of the People's Republic of China to occupy the China seat in the United Nations rests on an assertion of legal succession and on Peking's political demands for full recognition as a great power. Since the beginning, the Chinese Communists have maintained that they are members of the United Nations by right but that this right has been denied them and must be restored. For example, Foreign Minister Chen Yi told a group of Japanese journalists in 1964 that "China is not only a member state of the United Nations but is one of its founding members. However, China is excluded from the United Nations today, and its seat in the United Nations is usurped by the Chiang Kai-shek clique which long ago was overthrown by the Chinese people." He further stated that

U.S. imperialism's manipulation of the United Nations will sooner or later break down and the Chiang Kai-shek gang will sooner or later be ousted from it. The lawful seat of the People's Republic of China in the United Nations will sooner or later be restored. This, of course, takes time. We are not in a hurry, we can wait. Under no circumstances will we barter away principles and sovereignty; any attempt to make the restoration of China's seat in the United Nations a bait for our acceptance of the "two-Chinas" scheme is doomed to failure.[39]

In other words, the Chinese Communists maintain that they are claiming a right, not requesting a favor, and since as early as November 28, 1950, they have asserted that "so long as the United Nations persists in denying admittance to a permanent member of the Security Council who represents 475,000,000 people [the population estimate then accepted] it cannot make lawful decisions on any major issue or solve any major problems—particularly those which concern Asia." [40]

The People's Republic of China has repeatedly charged that the United Nations is dominated by United States "imperialism" and serves as its tool.[41] Such charges reached a peak in January 1965, when Peking hailed Indonesia's withdrawal from the United Nations as a "just, correct, and revolutionary action." At that time, the Chinese Communists asserted that "the United Na-

[39] *Peking Review*, no. 26, June 26, 1964, p. 7.
[40] U.N. Security Council, *Official Records*, 527th Meeting, November 28, 1950, p. 4.
[41] See, for example, the editorial in the *People's Daily*, December 4, 1964, "Restoration of China's U.N. Seat: U.S. Obstruction Will Fail," written on the opening of the nineteenth session of the United Nations General Assembly. It is reprinted in *Peking Review*, no. 50, December 11, 1964, pp. 11–13.

tions has been increasingly reduced to a tool of imperialism and old and new colonialism headed by the United States." Criticism was supplemented by scorn: "The United Nations is by no means sacred and inviolable. We can live on very well without it." Premier Chou En-lai called for steps to reorganize the United Nations to "make it conform to the aspirations of the Asian and African countries." Then he went on to threaten that "another United Nations, a revolutionary one, may well be set up so that rival dramas may be staged in competition with that body which calls itself the United Nations but which is under the manipulation of U.S. imperialism and therefore can only make mischief and do nothing good." [42] There has been little indication, then or since, that there would be any significant support for such a move, even on the part of Afro-Asian nations, and it is difficult to know whether Chou made the threat simply to exert pressure on the United Nations to seat Peking on its own terms or to float a trial balloon in order to see what the reactions would be.

The Chinese Communists' attacks on the United Nations and their support of Indonesia's withdrawal have not advanced their own cause in the international organization; nevertheless, support for the seating of Peking has steadily grown. The Chinese Communists themselves, however, have seemed in no hurry to join the body, and they may actually have ambivalent feelings about joining. A secret document of 1961 stated, for example, that "if we join the United Nations, we will still not be in the majority. Although the situation may seem relaxed on the surface, conflict will be sharpened in actuality, and we shall lose freedom of action. . . ." [43] And in the fall of 1965 Foreign Minister Chen Yi laid down extreme conditions for Peking's entry, including a demand that the United Nations retract the resolution that branded Communist China an aggressor in Korea. Peking can, of course, decide to ignore such conditions in the future, but the fact that Chen Yi advanced them in 1965 indicated that Peking was certainly not impatient to assume China's seat and might actually refuse, at least for some time, to join except on terms Peking itself

[42] See the statements and articles reprinted in *Peking Review*, no. 3, January 15, 1965, pp. 5–6, and no. 5, January 29, 1965, p. 6.
[43] Quoted in J. Chester Cheng, "Problems of Chinese Communist Leadership as Seen in the Secret Military Papers," *Asian Survey*, v. 4, no. 6, June 1964, pp. 867–868.

defines. The Chinese Communists can hope to reap some benefits over a period of time outside the United Nations, and at present they do not seem to be unduly concerned about actions that might delay their chances to be seated in it. Most likely, Peking feels that membership in international bodies is ultimately desirable but only on terms which advance its interests and that for the present its lack of membership is not really a very serious liability.

Whether in the United Nations or not, the People's Republic of China can be expected to continue pursuing its broad foreign-policy objectives with energy and determination and to devote special attention to the newly emerging countries, especially those in the Asian area.

CHAPTER FIVE

Communist China's Policy
toward the United States

Mao Tse-tung would have applauded the leader of the French Revolution who is reported to have said that breaking the Bourbon alliance with Austria was as necessary for the revolution as the seizure of the Bastille. As early as 1923, Mao deplored the error some Chinese were making of "superstitiously believing in America." [1] Twenty-five years later, when the Communists were on the eve of victory, Liu Shao-chi warned the Chinese people that "it would be extremely erroneous and harmful to harbor illusions that American imperialism would in good faith help the Chinese people to achieve real independence, peace, and democracy." [2]

As the Chinese civil war approached its climax, Chinese Communist policy called not only for victory over the Nationalists but also for strong opposition to the United States, which at that time was attempting to encourage formation of a coalition government with the participation of both the Nationalists and Communists while it still continued its support of the Nationalists. In September 1946, Mao told an American newspaper correspondent that "the policy of the U.S. government is to use the so-called mediation as a smoke screen for strengthening Chiang Kai-shek in every way and suppressing the democratic forces in China

[1] "The Peking Coup d'Etat and the Merchants," *Hsing-tao*, no. 31–32, July 11, 1923, pp. 233–234. Quoted in Stuart R. Schram, *The Political Thought of Mao Tse-tung* (New York: Praeger, 1963), p. 266.
[2] *Internationalism and Nationalism* (3rd ed.: Peking: Foreign Languages Press, December 1952), p. 18. The pamphlet was written in 1948.

through Chiang Kai-shek's policy of slaughter so as to reduce China virtually to a U.S. colony." [3] By this time, Chiang Kai-shek had become, according to Mao Tse-tung, no more than "the running dog of U.S. imperialism," and the defeat of Chiang as well as the broader purposes of the Communist revolution required the expulsion of American influence from China.

This the Chinese Communists proceeded to carry out when they swept into power in 1949. The way in which they treated U.S. government property and consular and diplomatic officials reflected both a revolutionary disdain for accepted legal and diplomatic practices and a special hostility toward the United States.

While the failure of American policy in China was being denounced in the United States as resulting from a weak and woolyminded attitude toward communism, the Chinese Communists were at the same time castigating the United States for intervening in the Chinese civil war on the side of Chiang Kai-shek and for being the leaders of the "imperialist camp." In fact, the United States had not intervened effectively in the civil war and had not been successful in its attempts to mediate between the two sides while it supported one of them.

It would be difficult to argue convincingly that friendly relations could have been quickly established with the Chinese Communists if the United States had behaved differently during the early years. The Chinese would be the first to insist that they were guided by more than diplomatic expediency and that only complete American accommodation to the so-called "progressive forces" could have altered the view expressed by Liu Shao-chi in 1948 that "American imperialism has become the bastion of all the reactionary forces of the world." [4] The heady wine of victory, combined with ideological militancy, did not favor an attitude of moderation and reasonableness. Although the Chinese Communists claimed that the United States was acting as an incorrigible imperialist power, they were actually themselves the prisoners of their history and of an ideology that inhibited compromise.

[3] Interview with A. T. Steele, September 29, 1946, in *Selected Works,* v. 5 (New York: International Publishers, n.d.), p. 109.
[4] *Internationalism and Nationalism,* cited, p. 32.

The Record of Hostility

The list of grievances against the United States which the Chinese Communists have compiled is now a long one. It is nostalgic to recall that when China was looking for allies after its defeat by Japan in 1895, Chang Chih-tung, one of China's leading scholars and administrators, addressed a memorial to the Emperor rejecting the United States as a possibility because it "does not like to interfere in the military affairs of others." [5] Today, in contrast, Peking's leaders see the United States as continuing a long record of imperialism and exploitation by persistently interfering in the Chinese civil war, encircling "new China" with hostile bases, and doing its utmost to prevent China's membership in the community of nations. They see little reason to regard the United States with a friendly eye; rather, they feel American policy gives them an enemy against which they can attempt to arouse domestic emotions and evoke sympathy on the part of many people in Asian and African countries.

Communist doctrine goes hand in hand with China's international ambitions to give the United States a unique place among China's enemies. The United States is depicted not merely as China's principal antagonist in foreign affairs but also as the fountain of evil and the principal cause of the world's ills. This "devil image" seems to be even more pronounced today than it was in 1949 when the Communist government first came to power. The principal struggle in the world is still analyzed in terms of two major camps, the imperialist camp and the socialist camp, and the former, led by the United States, is seen to be steadily weakening as the United States is ever more isolated and as contradictions within the imperialist camp constantly grow. "It is possible," the Chinese state, "for all forces excluding U.S. imperialism and its lackeys to unite. Despite the different political beliefs among the peoples and the different social systems in various countries, there is not a single country or people in the world today which is not

[5] Evan Luard, *Britain and China* (Baltimore: Johns Hopkins, 1962), p. 36.

subject to the aggression and threats of U.S. imperialism." [6] Un-
ceasingly, the "imperialist," "aggressor," and "warmonger" is
condemned, vilified, and held up for scorn to the Chinese people
and all others who will listen.

The Chinese people have, in fact, no choice but to listen.
Hatred of the United States is deliberately aroused by a selective
reinterpretation of history and by a calculated effort to muster all
possible evidence to support official policy. There is no dissent,
and no public conscience, to deflect the tide or mitigate its
force.

It would be comforting, but probably illusory, to believe that
all the efforts devoted to denunciation of the United States by the
Chinese Communists today demonstrate that a good deal of pro-
American sentiment still has to be overcome. It seems unlikely
that this is the case. Too much has happened in the past twenty
years, and it would hardly be reasonable to expect that the Chinese people, whose favorable attitudes toward the United States
even in earlier years may well have been exaggerated, have been
able to withstand the incessant barrage of anti-American propaganda over the past decade and a half.

The absence of almost all communication and contact between
Americans and mainland Chinese makes the task of the Chinese
leadership easier. Whatever understanding of the United States
the leaders may now have, it is clear that the mass of the Chinese
people cannot have anything but the most distorted picture of
this country.

There have been times since 1949 when the Chinese appeared
to be somewhat more flexible in their attitudes toward the United
States than at present, although this flexibility may have been
only for tactical reasons. After the 1954 settlements in Korea and
Indo-China and during the "coexistence" phase of their strategy
and diplomacy from 1955 to 1957, for example, they advanced
some proposals for "relaxing tensions" between China and the
United States. The bilateral, ambassadorial-level talks initiated at
that time in Geneva even produced an agreement which led to
the release of some of the Americans held in China and freedom

[6] Editorial in *People's Daily*, January 21, 1964, reprinted in *Peking Review*,
no. 4, January 24, 1964, p. 8.

for all Chinese in the United States who wished to return to the mainland to do so. At the talks, the Chinese also proposed an exchange of newsmen and increased contacts which might possibly lead to an eventual meeting of foreign ministers. The United States rejected these suggestions, however, because it tended to view them as little more than tactical devices designed to gain international recognition for the Peking government and to undermine the Chiang Kai-shek regime. By the time the American position regarding an exchange of newsmen had changed, so had that of the Chinese. Thus, one opportunity to test Peking's intentions and possibly even to establish limited contacts was lost.

Nevertheless, at the end of 1957, as was stated above, the general diplomatic outlook of the Chinese changed, and Peking entered a new phase of sharp militancy. And since then there has been no significant change in Peking's attitude toward the United States. The degree of ideological flexibility which the Chinese Communists have recently shown toward almost all non-Communist countries other than the United States suggests that ideological reasons alone do not explain their seemingly implacable hostility to this country. It is primarily attributable to the fact that they see the United States as the major obstacle to the achievement of most of their basic objectives. Only a fundamental shift in the attitudes of the Chinese leadership or a fundamental change of the international environment would alter this fact.

In short, the hostility toward the United States that now permeates Peking's domestic propaganda and international behavior appears to run too deep to be changed easily, simply by the settlement of minor or secondary issues—even if such issues could be settled. And Peking's present stand is that secondary issues cannot be negotiated until after the question of Taiwan is settled.

For the present, the Chinese Communists appear content to allow their bilateral relationship with the United States to continue as it is, in the hope that over time China will gain from a gradual attrition of American positions, a growth of dissension among the Western nations, and a steady emergence in the underdeveloped world of forces friendly to China and hostile to the United States. In 1961, for example, the secret army *Work Bulletin*, already mentioned, advised military and political cadres that "it is better to keep Sino-American relations frozen and stalemated for many years. All differences must be settled at the same time, if a settlement is expected; that is, the U.S. withdrawal from Taiwan, formal recognition of New China, the exchange of reporters, and so on must be settled together." [7] (This position is not dissimilar to the one which has been urged by some Americans who hope that firmness, patience, and the steadfast maintenance of present policies will eventually bring about an erosion of China's positions and thus create a situation where settlements favorable to the United States can be achieved without the risks involved in piecemeal negotiations. Those who hold such views seem to believe that any negotiations for the settlement of differences could be a dangerous trap and could weaken the will to oppose the enemy.)

As has been noted, Taiwan obviously occupies a special place in this picture. Ever since 1950, the Peking government has incessantly demanded the "liberation" of Taiwan from American "occupation." Until this has been accomplished, the civil war, in Chinese Communist eyes, will not be ended, and the Chinese Nationalists will continue to pose a challenge to the legitimacy of the Peking regime. This challenge, however, is really more legal, moral, and political than military. It should now be quite evident that the Nationalists cannot themselves pose a serious military threat to Peking, and the United States has made it clear that it does not plan to support a Nationalist attack on the mainland.

Peking maintains that "for the Chinese people to liberate their own territory of Taiwan is China's internal affair in which nobody can interfere." At the same time, it concedes that "there is an international aspect to the Taiwan question," but it defines this as "the question of U.S. armed occupation of Chinese territory, the Province of Taiwan." [8] Peking, as well as Taipei, rejects the argument that the legal status of Taiwan is undecided and can be settled at some time in the future by international action.

[7] *Work Bulletin (Kung Tso Tung Hsun)*, no. 17, April 25, 1961, quoted by John W. Lewis, *Chinese Communist Party Leadership and the Succession to Mao Tse-tung: An Appraisal of Tensions* (Washington: External Research Staff, Bureau of Intelligence and Research, U.S. Department of State, January 1964), p. 27.
[8] "China's Sovereignty Over Taiwan Brooks No Intervention," editorial in the *People's Daily*, May 12, 1964, reprinted in *Peking Review,* no. 20, May 15, 1964, pp. 6–8. The quotations are from p. 8.

100

The Chinese Communists persistently maintain that the present unfriendly relationship between China and the United States "is entirely the result of U.S. government policy of hostility to China and occupation of the Chinese territory of Taiwan." [9] This is not true, for there is little reason to believe that the settlement of the Taiwan issue alone, even if the issue were resolved to Peking's satisfaction, would end the contest of power and purposes between Communist China and the United States. Nevertheless, Peking, like Taipei, now chooses to treat the matter as a major and crucial question of principle. Part of the explanation for this position lies in the fact that the Taiwan question is intimately related to Peking's conception of a world-wide revolutionary struggle, with the United States as the primary enemy. In November 1960 Chou En-lai told Edgar Snow that "even if the United States does not withdraw from the Taiwan region and no breakthrough occurs there, breakthroughs will occur elsewhere. . . . As to where the breakthrough occurs first, this depends on the development of the struggle." [10] And the secret Chinese military documents already cited, after designating the United States to be Communist China's "major enemy," described Taiwan as the "central pawn" in a game of chess where one bad move could cause loss of the game.[11]

The Chinese Communists appear to recognize that they have no foreseeable prospect of gaining control of Taiwan by force. They probably do not expect the United States to withdraw its protection from the island soon, and they may suspect that there is a growing body of world opinion which, while critical of the present state of affairs, would be reluctant to see Taiwan simply turned over to Peking's control without reference to the wishes of the inhabitants. Nevertheless, they appear to feel bound to maintain the inviolability of their claim to the island and to resist all suggestions that would result in compromising what they regard as their historical and legal rights. Peking has vehemently opposed all proposals for a "two-China" or a "one-China-one-

[9] Same, p. 8.
[10] See Edgar Snow, *The Other Side of the River* (New York: Random House, 1961), p. 759.
[11] *Work Bulletin*, no. 26, July 13, 1961, quoted in Lewis, cited, p. 26.

Taiwan" solution, as well as the proposition, put forward by the United States and some other nations, that the future legal status of Taiwan is still undetermined.

When they have felt it tactically necessary, however, the Chinese have shown a certain flexibility even on issues relating to Taiwan. In April 1964, for example, they remained silent when M. Georges Pompidou, the French Prime Minister, suggested publicly that the fate of Taiwan could not be decided without taking into consideration the wishes of the inhabitants.[12] The Chinese did not argue with the French, with whom relations were then in the process of being established, but preferred to continue focusing their hostility on the United States.

While the People's Republic of China is not likely to abandon in principle its claim that Taiwan and the mainland are one and indivisible, it is conceivable that at some time in the future its leaders may decide that even the Taiwan issue should not be permitted to impair Peking's flexibility and freedom of diplomatic maneuver. If Peking were to decide at some point that for tactical reasons it stood to gain by changing its present rigid posture or by negotiating with the United States on certain issues other than Taiwan, it is not certain that the question of Taiwan would alone stand in the way. A change in tactics could be made without renouncing either the principle involved in Peking's claim to Taiwan or lessening the fervor in its overall struggle against the United States. We cannot, in short, count on Peking's continued rigidity and stubbornness to relieve us of the necessity of exercising flexibility and imagination ourselves.[13]

In recent years China's relations with the Soviet Union have also become a major conditioning factor in Chinese attitudes toward the United States. As has already been noted, differences on how to deal with the United States have figured prominently in the Sino-Soviet debate, and Peking has accused Moscow of having a faint-hearted attitude toward Washington. On February 4, 1964, *Red Flag*, the leading Chinese theoretical journal, charged that the Soviet Union was not only committing the sins of "splittism," "revisionism," and "opportunism" and thus departing from true

[12] See the statement quoted in *The New York Times*, April 24, 1964.
[13] For a further discussion of Taiwan, see Chapter 12.

Marxism-Leninism but was also substituting "class collaboration or class capitulation for class struggle, and social reformism or social pacifism for proletarian revolution."

They should draw a sharp line of demarcation between enemies and comrades and should unite with all socialist countries, all fraternal Marxist-Leninist parties, the proletariat of the whole world, all oppressed peoples and nations and all peace-loving countries and peoples in order to oppose U.S. imperialism, the arch-enemy of the people of the world and its lackeys. It is absolutely impossible for them to treat enemies as friends and friends as enemies, and to ally themselves with the U.S. imperialists, the reactionaries of various countries, and the renegade Tito clique against fraternal countries and parties and all revolutionary peoples in the vain pursuit of world domination through U.S.-Soviet collaboration.[14]

Behind the ideological verbiage the Chinese employed in this editorial lay the conviction that the Soviet Union was sacrificing China's national interests in the quest for peaceful coexistence with the United States. The list of Chinese grievances on this count alone was a long one: the failure of the Soviet Union to give China strong enough support during the Taiwan crisis of 1958, the neutral position the Soviet Union adopted regarding the Sino-Indian border dispute, the exercises in two-power summitry between Moscow and Washington to the exclusion of Peking, the reneging of the Soviet Union on commitments to aid China in the nuclear-weapons field, the failure of Moscow to stand up to the United States during the Cuban missile crisis, the conclusion with the United States and Britain of the partial nuclear test-ban treaty, and in general terms the apparent caution of the Soviet Union in promoting and supporting anti-imperialist revolutionary movements. In each of these instances, Peking saw attempts to undermine Chinese efforts to weaken the influence of the United States, limitations on China's freedom of action, sacrifices of Chinese interests for the sake of agreements with the United States, or abandonment of Communist militancy in the struggle against American imperialism.

Apparently, Peking has feared that the Soviet Union's alleged abandonment of true Marxist principles in favor of cooperation with the United States will perpetuate China's position of inferiority and help the United States to frustrate China's ambitions.

[14] See *Current Background* (Hong Kong), no. 728, February 19, 1964, p. 27.

To try to forestall this possibility, the Chinese have pressed forward with the development of their own nuclear weapons, extended their own revolutionary activity abroad, and expanded their contacts as much as possible with countries other than the United States and the Soviet Union. At the same time, they have continued unabated their hostility toward the United States and have persisted in opposing—as has the United States as well—serious negotiation of outstanding issues between themselves and the United States, although they have continued to participate in the Sino-American ambassadorial talks in Warsaw (where the talks were moved in 1958).

Future Prospects

At present, the Chinese Communists seem to feel that any accommodation with the United States would require unacceptable concessions and would deprive them of whatever advantages they may have acquired by "standing up to" the strongest "imperialist" power. Even if a less militant posture might yield some short-term benefits, at least many of today's Chinese leaders probably fear that it could risk long-term costs, including perhaps the renunciation or at least deferment of their claim to Taiwan, the necessity of accepting a less important position in Asia, and the abandonment of the principal means of extending Chinese influence throughout much of the Afro-Asian world. Conceivably, some Chinese leaders may also fear that a relaxation of tensions with the United States might have an adverse effect on the strength of political control at home.

It is difficult, therefore, to see major changes in Chinese policies and actions toward the United States on the immediate horizon. Peking will certainly continue to seek recognition as a great power as a matter of right, and it will continue to resist the alleged attempt of the other great powers to dominate the international scene. It will try to reduce the drawbacks of its liabilities and weaknesses, but it will at the same time continue to make maximum use of its limited resources because it will not wait patiently until it becomes a military and economic power of the first rank before it strives to achieve its goals abroad. That is, it will try with the tools at hand to protect its interests, as it sees them, and to overcome the obstacles caused by American opposition to its goals.

In short, China will continue to attempt to erode the United States position in Asia and elsewhere by political pressures, subversive activities, and promises of friendship to those who will oppose the United States. It will try to exploit the disagreements among the non-Communist nations on how to deal with China and with crises in which China is involved. And, more generally, it will continue to issue appeals to all those who for a variety of reasons are critical of the West, resentful of the United States, or desirous of Chinese support.

No one can say with confidence under what circumstances this outlook and these policies might change. The present leadership in Peking still appears to be stable and united, and the militant spirit, solidarity, and shrewdness that have carried it through years of revolutionary struggle have persisted. However, many of the successors to the present generation of leaders will have different backgrounds and training, and they may have different outlooks and perspectives. One cannot rule out, therefore, the possibility of future changes. Even if revolutionary zeal diminishes, however, it seems certain that any future Chinese leaders will seek to establish China's status as a major power by whatever means are availble. Economic difficulties may be a handicap, but short of miraculous successes or catastrophic setbacks—neither of which can be predicted—one can only say that progress is likely to be slow but steady and that the tasks at home as well as abroad will demand constant attention from whatever regime is in power.

In summary, then, the present Chinese leaders have not indicated that they would be responsive to changes in United States policies unless their major demands are met. However, China, like other countries, finds itself caught up in the stream of world history, and one cannot rule out changes in the future as in the past. Spectacular changes have taken place in China's position in the world and in its relations with the United States during recent decades, and no one can confidently affirm that what we see today is immutable. Present Chinese behavior and policies toward the United States give little reason for comfort, but the goals that the United States sets itself and the way in which it goes about achieving them are bound to influence the outlook and behavior of the Chinese leadership. It is not likely that the future course of events will entirely satisfy either the Chinese or the Americans. But conceivably time could alter the outlooks of both in ways that cannot now be accurately foreseen.

CHAPTER SIX

The Evolution of United States Policy toward China since 1949

The first half of the twentieth century hardly prepared the United States to deal with a hostile, unified China under Communist rule. Before World War II, we had wished the Chinese people well and had tried to bring them what we thought were the benefits of modern Western civilization. We objected to foreign encroachments on China's sovereignty and integrity but were generally not willing to do more than protest against them. Disorder, poverty, and warlordism seemed to be the natural order of things in China, but because we were reluctant to back up our declarations with power, we could only hope that they would somehow end.

This attitude changed, however, after Pearl Harbor. We then began looking upon China as an important ally in the war against Japan. It was the policy of the United States to elevate China to the rank of a great power in the hope that a friendly Nationalist government would not only establish peace in China but would subsequently prevent the revival of Japanese expansionism.

In only a few years, this dream was shattered. Chiang Kai-shek and his government were unable to defeat the Communists, and the postwar American policy of simultaneously supporting the Nationalists and favoring establishment of a coalition government to end the civil war in China failed. Neither the American people nor the United States government favored full-scale intervention aimed at complete victory for the Nationalists, and even if we

had tried such intervention, it is questionable whether it would
have succeeded.

The Attempt to End American Involvement in China's Civil War

On July 30, 1949, in anticipation of the imminent end of the
Chinese civil war, Secretary of State Dean Acheson issued a
White Paper on United States relations with China. It deplored
what was happening on the China mainland but saw nothing that
the United States could do, short of "full-scale intervention in
behalf of a government which had lost the confidence of its own
troops and its own people," to prevent Communist victory in
China. In Mr. Acheson's opinion, "nothing that this country did or
could have done within the reasonable limits of its capabilities
could have changed that result; nothing that was left undone by
this country has contributed to it." Mr. Acheson charged that
"the Communist leaders have foresworn their Chinese heritage
and have publicly announced their subservience to a foreign
power, Russia, which during the last fifty years, under czars and
Communists alike, has been most assiduous in its efforts to extend
its control in the Far East." He went on to say, however, that
tragic as the situation was, "it is abundantly clear that we must
face the situation as it exists in fact. We will not help the Chinese
or ourselves by basing our policy on wishful thinking." [1]

The views expressed in the White Paper and the documenta-
tion assembled to back them up were to become the basis of intense debate for many years over "who lost China"? Secretary
Acheson was accused by some critics of having done nothing
more than whitewash the administration's failure to give effective
help to the Chinese Nationalists.

However, he and the administration remained firm in their intention to disengage from the Chinese civil war. The United
States continued to recognize the Nationalist government even

[1] "Letter of Transmittal," in U.S. Department of State, *United States Relations with China with Special Reference to the Period 1944–1949* (Washington, D.C.: GPO, August 1949), pp. xv–xvi.

after its withdrawal to Taiwan in December 1949, and economic aid was continued. But military support was terminated, and a deliberate effort was made to minimize the importance of Taiwan to the United States in anticipation of its probable occupation by the Communists.[2]

On January 5, 1950, President Truman issued a statement intended to offset demands for increased American involvement.[3] He reaffirmed United States' support of both the Cairo Declaration of December 1, 1943, and the Potsdam Declaration of July 26, 1945, which had promised the restoration of Taiwan to China, and went on to say:

The United States has no predatory designs on Formosa or on any other Chinese territory. The United States has no desire to obtain special rights or privileges or to establish military bases on Formosa at this time. Nor does it have any intention of utilizing its armed forces to interfere in the present situation. The United States Government will not pursue a course which will lead to involvement in the civil conflict in China. Similarly, the United States Government will not provide military aid or advice to Chinese forces on Formosa.

On the same day Secretary Acheson made it clear that the President's statement was designed to counter demands that the United States intervene to prevent Taiwan from coming under Communist control. This "is not the function of the United States," he said, "nor will it or can it attempt to furnish a will to resist and a purpose for resistance to those who must provide for themselves." [4]

A few days later, on January 12, 1950, Mr. Acheson underlined the United States government's disengagement from Taiwan in a speech to the National Press Club. He defined the United States defensive perimeter in the western Pacific in a way that seemed to exclude both Korea and Taiwan; without naming Taiwan

[2] See particularly the Policy Information Paper of December 23, 1949, which was designed to "formulate information policy which will minimize damage to United States' prestige and others' morale by the possible fall of Formosa to the Chinese Communist forces," reprinted in *Military Situation in the Far East,* Hearings Before the Committee on Armed Services and the Committee on Foreign Relations, United States Senate, 82nd Cong., 1st sess (Washington: GPO, 1951), v. 3, pp. 1667–1669.
[3] *Department of State Bulletin,* v. 22, January 16, 1950, p. 79.
[4] Same, p. 81.

specifically, he also said: "We must not undertake to deflect from the Russians to ourselves the righteous anger, the wrath, and the hatred of the Chinese people which must develop. We must take the position . . . that anyone who violates the integrity of China is the enemy of China and is acting contrary to our own interest." [5] Several years afterward, during the offshore islands crisis of 1958, Mr. Acheson asserted that on four occasions between 1948 and 1950 the highest American military authorities had concluded that the retention of Taiwan in friendly hands was not essential to the vital interests of the United States. [6]

Thus, despite the demands for action made by a few influential Americans, including former President Herbert Hoover and Senators William F. Knowland and H. Alexander Smith, the administration had clearly decided against occupying Taiwan or using American military power to protect it from the Communists.

At the same time, the administration still made no moves to establish relations with the newly founded People's Republic of China. The disposition not to do so stemmed at least in part from the actions of Peking's leaders in 1949 and early 1950.

In his major policy statement of June 30, 1949, "On the People's Democratic Dictatorship," Mao Tse-tung had reaffirmed in strong terms the Marxist-Leninist character of the new government, had declared that a "people's democratic dictatorship" was necessary for China, had denounced all the "imperialist nations," and had asserted that China should not look to them for help. [7] Any illusions about the new regime's attitude toward the United States were dispelled by the Chinese Communists' treatment of American diplomatic and consular officials, which included arrests and various forms of harassment. The result was a United States decision, made on January 14, 1950, to recall all official American personnel from the China mainland.

Nevertheless, the way was apparently being left open for the eventual establishment of relations with the new Communist government. It was probably anticipated that the Communists would

[5] Same, January 23, 1950, pp. 114–115.
[6] *The New York Times*, September 7, 1958.
[7] *Selected Works*, v. 5 (New York: International Publishers, n.d.), pp. 411–423.

soon capture Taiwan and thereby end the civil war and unify China under one government with its seat in Peking and that our recognition of the regime would follow in due time.

This view was not specifically stated, but it seems to have been implied in both the declarations and actions of the 1949–50 period. In September 1949, for example, Secretary Acheson, speaking on recognition policy toward Latin American governments, stressed that recognition did not constitute a judgment on the government's origins or policies and need not be taken as "the forerunner of a policy of intimate cooperation." The primary consideration behind the act of recognition, he said, was that "we are all on the same planet and must do business with each other," and he added that there was value in keeping open "a channel of communication" with the country involved.[8] China was not specifically mentioned. But the pertinence of the argument was clear, and the Secretary's language evokes the debates of subsequent years. (Only two months later Winston Churchill, arguing for the recognition of the new Chinese government, stated that "the reason for having diplomatic relations is not to confer a compliment, but to secure a convenience."[9])

In January 1950, the Soviet Union raised the issue of Chinese representation in the United Nations for the first time and insisted that the People's Republic of China be granted the China seat on the Security Council. The United States, legalistically and cautiously, took the position that a decision as to which government was entitled to China's seat depended upon the question of recognition, but it also indicated that the issue should be viewed as a procedural one and that the United States would accept any Security Council decision made by a majority of its members (a position that was to change later). The vote on January 13, 1950, was against seating the Chinese Communists, and the Soviet Union walked out of the Security Council—a move it was soon to regret.

Although there was little reason not to expect that the new Communist government would establish control over all China, it was not beyond the realm of possibility, particularly in light of

[8] *Department of State Bulletin*, v. 21, September 26, 1949, pp. 463–464.
[9] House of Commons, *Parliamentary Debates: Weekly Hansard*, no. 141, November 11–17, 1949, p. 2232.

recent Chinese history, that forces of dissension and separation might continue to harass the Communist regime, as they had its predecessors. While waiting for the dust to settle, the United States seemed to see some basis for hope in the apparent contradiction between Peking's alleged subservience to Moscow and the underlying conflict of Chinese and Russian national interests. As was stated before, however, it is difficult to know whether the administration actually believed that the Peking regime was "completely subservient to the Moscow regime," as Secretary of State Acheson put it, or simply thought that the United States could help to arouse Chinese nationalism against a "foreign yoke." We know now, and should have known then, that the Chinese Communist movement was not effectively controlled by Moscow. At the time, nevertheless, we apparently hoped that by disengaging from the Chinese civil war we might be able to transfer from ourselves to the Russians the resentments felt by many Chinese against any form of foreign intervention, and we warned the Chinese of Soviet encroachments in China's border areas. There is little evidence, however, that Chinese attitudes were affected by what we said. It is ironical that when, ten years later, it became clear that Chinese nationalism was being directed against Moscow, what we saw was not a moderate China but a militantly hostile regime grown impatient with the Soviet Union's alleged softness toward the United States.

Thus, in 1949 and 1950 we waited for the turmoil in the Far East to settle and focused our major attention on the Soviet threat in Europe, but we continued to maintain official relations with the Nationalist government on Taiwan and initiated limited-aid programs in Southeast Asia.[10] Relations with the China mainland were severed; however, the possibility of restoring them had not been foreclosed. And there was at least some feeling among influential Americans that a permanent refusal to recognize the Chinese Communist government would simply result in the strengthening of its alliance with the Soviet Union.[11] Before

[10] For a description of the situation as seen at the time by Karl L. Rankin, the American ambassador in Taiwan, see his diplomatic memoirs, *China Assignment* (Seattle: University of Washington Press, 1964).

[11] On June 6, 1950, John Foster Dulles, who had been called in three weeks earlier to prepare a peace treaty with Japan, wrote his first memorandum in which he suggested a preliminary conference on the treaty. In the memo-

formulating a new China policy we were awaiting the answers to several questions: Would the Communist government be able to establish uncontested control over the mainland? Would the Nationalist government on Taiwan collapse or be defeated by the Communists? What would relations be between Peking and Moscow? It was expected that the answers to these questions would determine what policy we should pursue and that in the meantime we should wait and observe.

The Korean War: A New Phase

These calculations were ended by the outbreak of the Korean War in 1950. Once again the United States became actively involved in the China situation; bitter hostility toward the People's Republic of China grew; and the China issue soon became a crucial one in domestic politics. As a result of the war, a new China policy emerged.

When on June 27, 1950, President Truman ordered the Seventh Fleet to neutralize the Taiwan Strait, he left the question of Taiwan's future status open, and his executive order of that day declared that "the determination of the future status of Formosa must await the restoration of security in the Pacific, a peace settlement with Japan, or consideration by the United Nations." [12] In fact, however, this action, taken as a limited military step related to the outbreak of hostilities in Korea, soon became the pivot upon which much of our subsequent China policy was to turn.

At the time of the announcement of the emergency measure, no political or military commitment was made to Chiang Kai-shek. In August, however, the shipment of military supplies to Taiwan was resumed, and in the following spring, a Military Assistance

---

randum he proposed that both Chinese governments be represented, that each have a separate vote when they disagreed, and that the two votes be counted as one when they agreed. Three weeks later, the Korean War broke out, and no proposals of this type were put forward thereafter. See Frederick S. Dunn, *Peace-Making and the Settlement with Japan* (Princeton University Press, 1963), pp. 99–101, 127–128.

[12] *Department of State Bulletin*, v. 23, July 3, 1950, p. 5.

Advisory Group was established on the island. The administration, nevertheless, at first sought to preserve its freedom of action while it took these measures so as not to predetermine future China policy. There were some, including General MacArthur and certain political leaders at home, who argued that Chiang's interests and those of the United States were so intertwined that the Nationalist regime should be fully backed as a major anti-Communist force in Asia. But the State Department was not then willing to accept this view. Whereas General MacArthur saw Taiwan as a key to the strategy and security of the United States in the Pacific, the official American position was that political considerations argued against too close a tie with Chiang.

As was stated earlier, until the Chinese intervention in the Korean War in October 1950 the United States government apparently hoped that eventually, somehow, the Chinese Communists would realize that the Russians rather than the Western nations were China's enemy. Secretary of State Acheson, speaking on September 10, 1950, said that it would be "sheer madness" for the Chinese to intervene in Korea, and he spoke of the danger to China posed by the "great cloud from the north, Russian penetration." [13] He then went on to say:

Now I give the people in Peiping credit for being intelligent enough to see what is happening to them. Why they should want to further their own dismemberment and destruction by getting at cross purposes with all the free nations of the world who are inherently their friends and have always been friends of the Chinese as against this imperialism coming down from the Soviet Union I cannot see.

Within six weeks, the Chinese had intervened in Korea and thereby destroyed this hope on which America's China policy seems to have been based. Whatever its previous merit, it was soon swept away in the heat of battle, overwhelmed by popular feeling against the Chinese Communists, and discredited by Peking's vitriolic propaganda against the United States and strident claims to Communist ascendancy in Asia.

United States policy toward China had begun hardening to a degree even before the Chinese entered the Korean War—a fact that was reflected in the changing American position in regard to the China seat in the United Nations. In July, Secretary Acheson

[13] Same, September 18, 1950, p. 463.

opposed Prime Minister Nehru's proposal that the People's Republic of China be seated in the Security Council so as to facilitate a solution of the Korean problem and argued that the two questions should not be linked. Two months later, the United States voted against an Indian resolution to seat Peking in the General Assembly—although in November, after the Chinese had intervened in Korea, the United States was willing to support the Security Council's invitation for Peking to send delegates to appear before it. Then in January 1951, the United States House and Senate passed resolutions calling for the General Assembly to brand the People's Republic of China as an aggressor, which the Assembly did on February 1, and a Senate resolution strongly opposed the seating of Peking in the United Nations. By June 1951, Secretary Acheson was declaring "that a claimant for seating cannot shoot his way into the UN and cannot get in by defying the UN and fighting its forces." [14] The United States government moved on other fronts, too, to isolate and apply pressure on mainland China—for example, by embargoing all trade.

Now the questions overshadowing all others, of course, were how to fight the war and what American war aims should be. In a bitter and public controversy, climaxed by General MacArthur's recall in April 1951 and the debate that followed, the choice was made between fighting a limited war to achieve limited ends and widening the conflict in an effort to accomplish what America's intervention in the Chinese civil war had failed to achieve, even if this involved large risks.

General MacArthur pressed for the latter course. [15] He described China as

. . . a new and dominant power in Asia, which, for its own purposes, has allied with Soviet Russia but which in its own concepts and methods has become aggressively imperialistic, with a lust for expansion and increased power normal to this type of imperialism . . . the aggressiveness recently displayed not only in Korea, but in Indo-China, Tibet, and pointing toward the south, reflects predominantly

[14] *Military Situation in the Far East*, cited, v. 3, p. 1935.
[15] See his address before a joint meeting of the U.S. Congress on April 19, 1951, reprinted in *Vital Speeches of the Day*, v. 17, May 1, 1951, pp. 430–433, and his testimony before the Senate Armed Services and Foreign Relations Committees on May 3–4, 1951, *Military Situation in the Far East*, cited v. 1, pp. 3–320.

the same lust for power which has animated every would-be conqueror since the beginning of time.

To check Peking's "lust for power," he argued, the United States should try to "severely cripple and largely neutralize China's capability to wage aggressive war and thus save Asia from the engulfment otherwise facing it." He and other proponents of a more militant American policy pressed for blockade, naval and air bombardment, and active participation by the Chinese Nationalists in the war and an attempt to achieve "victory—not prolonged indecision."

But to the key officials in the administration who were responsible for American policy, what MacArthur and others were advocating ignored the risks of Soviet intervention in Asia, the dangers of Soviet pressure on Europe, and the general climate of international political opinion. As Secretary Acheson put it, General MacArthur was proposing "a gamble with the essential security of our nation," and General Bradley declared that such a course of action would "involve us in the wrong war, at the wrong place, at the wrong time, and with the wrong enemy." The decision was finally made, to cite General Bradley's words, not to engage "too much of our power in an area which is not the critical strategic prize." That is, we would not commit our great power, or assume the great and unknown risks involved, in an effort to try to bring about the downfall of the Chinese Communist government.[16]

Despite the decision to seek only limited war objectives, however, American policy toward Peking steadily hardened. The turmoil of debate, the pressures exerted by the leading domestic critics of the administration, and the general public mood all played a part in this process.

In an address to the China Institute in New York on May 18, 1951, Dean Rusk, then Assistant Secretary of State for Far Eastern Affairs, reflected the bitterness of public feeling and indicated the character of the official policy that was emerging out of the Korean debate.[17] The theme of Peking's subordination to Moscow continued to be important, and Mr. Rusk stressed it em-

[16] See *Military Situation in the Far East,* cited, v. 1, p. 325; v. 2, pp. 731–732; v. 3, p. 1719.
[17] See *Department of State Bulletin,* v. 24, May 28, 1951, pp. 846–848.

phatically: "The independence of China is gravely threatened. In the Communist world there is room for only one master—a jealous and implacable master whose price of friendship is complete submission." After referring to Russian ambitions in Sinkiang, Manchuria, and Mongolia, he continued:

The territorial integrity of China is now an ironic phrase. . . . China is losing its great northern areas to the European empire which has stretched out its greedy hands for them for at least a century. The peace and security of China are being sacrificed to the ambitions of the Communist conspiracy. China has been driven by foreign masters into an adventure of foreign aggression which cuts across the most fundamental national interests of the Chinese people.

Mr. Rusk went on to define United States policy as follows:

We do not recognize the authorities in Peiping for what they pretend to be. The Peiping regime may be a colonial Russian government—a Slavic Manchukuo on a larger scale. It is not the government of China. It does not pass the first test. It is not Chinese. . . . We recognize the national government of the Republic of China, even though the territory under its control is severely restricted. We believe it more authentically represents the views of the great body of the people of China, particularly their historic demand for independence from foreign control. That government will continue to receive important aid and assistance from the United States.

In sum, American policy toward China was profoundly affected by the bloody combat in Korea and the popular emotions that the war aroused. The predominant American attitude toward the People's Republic of China was no longer one of unfriendliness and annoyance combined with a vague expectation that somehow, at some time, relations might be established but one of sharp opposition and hostility. Conversely, the Nationalist government was now widely viewed not as an embarrassing remnant of a former ally but as a close and indispensable associate in the struggle against communism, one to be strongly supported by American economic, military, and political aid. The successful preservation of the Nationalist government as a rival and alternative to Peking consequently became a basic element in American policy, and the island of Taiwan, which in the months preceding the Korean War had been regarded as unessential to the vital interests of the United States, was now elevated to the rank of a crucial strong point in the United States' entire security policy in the western Pacific.

Having miscalculated the possibility of Communist China's intervention in the Korean War and underestimated China's military strength, some Americans swung violently to the extreme of depicting the Peking government as an uninhibited, almost power-mad regime with virtually unlimited aggressive appetites. More generally, there was a growing fear of direct Chinese military attack elsewhere in Asia as a result of a new assessment of the threat Peking posed to the peace and security of Asia. No longer were the Chinese Communist leaders seen as mere puppets of Moscow who might be induced to break their Russian shackles but as dangerous adversaries in their own right and perhaps bent on the open domination of all Asia. Within the next few years the United States responded to this fear with a wide network of new alliances and security arrangements.[18]

It is possible to see clearly today, even if it was not so clear in the early 1950s, that inherent in the new American approach—which was shaped partly by emotion and only partly based on sober calculation—were at least three major dilemmas. In the first place, what would happen if, over a period of years, the People's Republic of China did not collapse and was not overthrown from within or without but continued to gain international recognition and influence despite American efforts to prevent it from doing so? Second, how would security arrangements designed primarily to meet outright military threats cope with dangers arising not so much from open Chinese aggression as from the weakness of China's neighbors and more indirect forms of Chinese political influence and Communist activity? Third, what would happen if it was not possible to draw a line of clear separation between the Communist countries or countries under their direct influence on one hand and the countries of the "free world" on the other so that the former could be handled and dealt with as enemies and the latter as friends? These questions were not answered at the time and in fact were seldom even asked. Really satisfactory answers to them have yet to be found.

[18] See Chapter 8.

The Process of Consolidation

The outlines of China policy that emerged during the Korean War took even clearer and stronger shape after the inauguration of President Eisenhower in January 1953 and the appointments of John Foster Dulles as Secretary of State and Walter S. Robertson as Assistant Secretary for Far Eastern Affairs. During the political campaign of 1952 and throughout 1953, there was intense continuing debate about who was responsible for the defeat of the Nationalists on the mainland and the rise of the Communists to power. Recrimination over past policies and events greatly affected the climate in which new policies were being shaped. Sober assessment of the threat posed by China obviously was a major factor influencing Washington, but there was also a strong temptation on the part of the new administration to shape a China policy that would underline the alleged errors of the previous one.

In his first State of the Union message to Congress on February 2, 1953,[19] President Eisenhower revised President Truman's policy of using the Seventh Fleet to "neutralize" the Taiwan Strait by announcing that he was "issuing instructions that the Seventh Fleet no longer be employed to shield Communist China" from invasion by the Nationalist forces on Taiwan, a step that was hailed by some as "unleashing Chiang Kai-shek." He denied that this order implied any aggressive intent on the part of the United States but explained that "we certainly have no obligation to protect a nation fighting us in Korea."

It is doubtful that this change of policy was ever seriously intended to encourage Nationalist attacks on the mainland. There may have been some hope that it would create uncertainty in the minds of the Communists and cause them to divert troops to Fukien Province. But essentially it appeared to be a political gesture. In any case, its practical military consequences were not very important. The Korean War was already drawing to a close, and the Nationalists were not capable of making any serious military attack, either then or in later years. The political conse-

[19] *Department of State Bulletin,* v. 28, February 9, 1953, pp. 207–211.

quences were more significant, however, because the action, whether intended or not, tended to link the United States more closely to Chiang Kai-shek's ambitions.

As the years went on, however, and particularly after the 1958 crisis over the offshore islands, Washington increasingly realized that the situation in the Taiwan area involved hazards, and although the United States reaffirmed its obligation under the Defense Treaty of 1954 to defend Taiwan, it eventually imposed restraints on the Nationalists to deter them from contemplating any serious attack on the mainland.

United States objectives and expectations in supporting the Chinese Nationalists have, nevertheless, contained a number of inherent contradictions. On the one hand, the Defense Treaty concluded in December 1954, during the first offshore islands crisis, and the notes exchanged at that time by Secretary Dulles and the Chinese Foreign Minister made it clear that the United States opposed Nationalist military adventures. Moreover, it was evident that the United States intended to limit its obligations under the treaty so as not to be drawn into an attack on the mainland by actions initiated without its approval. On the other hand, the 1954 treaty not only gave the Chinese Nationalist regime indispensable political support in its competition with the Communist government on the mainland but also resulted in military assistance on a scale greater than was needed solely for the defense of Taiwan, where the protective shield of the Seventh Fleet provided the main defense. This ambiguity was heightened by the fact that the Nationalists continued their occupation and military build-up on the offshore islands, which are located only a few miles from the mainland and are geographically linked to the mainland rather than Taiwan. It was not clear in the eyes of much of the world whether the United States was in fact hoping somehow to bring about the actual overthrow of the Communist government in China—and if so by what means—or whether it simply disapproved of the Peking regime and sought to weaken its hold at home and influence abroad by more limited measures.

In January 1954, six months after the Korean armistice, United States policy was officially described as "a middle one, calculated to limit the capability of the enemy for further aggression and to build up the strength of our friends"—a policy of "pressure and diplomatic isolation" that would "at least slow the growth of the war-making potential of Communist China and retard the consolidation of its diplomatic position." [20]

A few days later, however, Mr. Robertson, the Assistant Secretary of State for Far Eastern Affairs, hinted at more ambitious aims in a statement to a congressional committee. The record of his testimony reads as follows: [21]

MR. COUDERT: Going back to your observation about China in answer to a question of Mr. Sikes, did I correctly understand you to say that the heart of the present policy toward China and Formosa is that there is to be kept alive a constant threat of military action vis-à-vis Red China in the hope that at some point there will be an internal breakdown?

MR. ROBERTSON: Yes, sir, that is my conception.

MR. COUDERT: In other words, a cold war waged under the leadership of the United States, with a constant threat of attack against Red China, led by Formosa and other Far Eastern groups and militarily supported by the United States?

MR. ROBERTSON: Yes.

MR. COUDERT: Do you believe that that posture can be maintained for an indefinite number of years?

MR. ROBERTSON: I think we must maintain it until there are some indications that the Communists have changed their objectives.

But on June 11, 1954, Secretary Dulles sharply contested the assumption "that the attitude of the United States flows from a desire for a general war with Communist China" and declared: "That is clearly false." [22]

Then in early 1955, Mr. Robertson, when asked whether his 1954 testimony still represented the position of the State Department, said that it had been a poor answer and was subject to misunderstanding:

What I tried to emphasize was that we had to maintain a position of strength throughout the area, and that the Communists must realize

[20] Walter P. McConaughy, director of the Office of Chinese Affairs, in same, v. 30, January 11, 1954, pp. 40, 42.

[21] *Departments of State, Justice, and Commerce, Appropriations for 1955,* Hearings before the Subcommittee on Appropriations, House of Representatives, 83rd Cong., 2d sess., January 26–February 3, 1954 (Washington, D.C.: GPO, 1954), p. 125.

[22] *Department of State Bulletin,* v. 30, June 28, 1954, p. 973.

that we were willing and would resist aggression with force. I
thought it was essential that we maintain a position of strength. Our
hope of solving the problem of the mainland of China was not
through attack upon the mainland but rather by actions which would
promote disintegration from within.

He denied ever having advocated the use of force but added that
he saw no possibility of easing tensions and that the State Department had no immediate plans to try since it took two parties for
such an attempt to be successful.[23]

While the principal administration spokesmen now declared
that planning for armed attack against Communist China was not
a part of United States policy, they continued to assert that the
Peking regime should be viewed as a temporary one and that
somehow the United States should attempt to contribute to its
demise or transformation. "We can confidently assume," said
Secretary Dulles on June 28, 1957, "that international communism's rule of strict conformity is, in China as elsewhere, a passing and not a perpetual phase. We owe it to ourselves, our allies,
and the Chinese people to do all that we can to contribute to that
passing." [24] A few days afterward Mr. Dulles elaborated on this
point, although still in very general terms: "American policy is
conducted on the assumption, as a working hypothesis, that free
governments in the long run are going to prevail and despotic
governments in the long run are going to go under." [25] A year
later, despite the lack of any reliable sign that the Peking government, now nine years old, was about to break up or be overthrown, a major State Department statement of August 11, 1958,
declared:

It is true that there is no reason to believe that the Chinese Communist
regime is on the verge of collapse; but there is equally no reason to
accept its present rule in mainland China as permanent. . . . The
United States holds the view that communism's rule in China is not
permanent and that it one day will pass. By withholding diplomatic
recognition from Peiping it seeks to hasten that passing." [26]

[23] *Departments of State and Justice, the Judiciary, and Related Agencies,
Appropriations for 1956*, Hearings before the Subcommittee on Appropriations, House of Representatives, 84th Cong., 1st sess., February 7–March 11,
1955 (Washington, D.C.: GPO, 1955), p. 128.
[24] See his formal address on U.S. policy toward China in *Department of
State Bulletin*, v. 37, July 15, 1957, p. 95.
[25] Same, July 22, 1957, p. 144.
[26] Same, v. 39, September 8, 1958, p. 389.

Exactly how nonrecognition or other American policies would be able to "hasten its passing" was not clearly stated, however.

The United States, nevertheless, continued to refuse to recognize the People's Republic of China, oppose its seating in the United Nations, and maintain a total trade embargo against it. Lest there be any weakening in the determination of the administration to do so, both houses of Congress, with bipartisan support, each year regularly adopted resolutions endorsing the policy of nonrecognition and reaffirming opposition to Peking's admission to the United Nations.

These annual congressional resolutions and the reiteration of a firm policy on China in both party platforms of 1956 were in harmony, though, with the administration's own views on the major outlines of China policy. Speaking in San Francisco on June 28, 1957, Secretary Dulles said:

Internationally, the Chinese Communist regime does not conform to the practices of civilized nations; does not live up to its international obligations; has not been peaceful in the past and gives no evidence of being peaceful in the future. Its foreign policies are hostile to us and our Asian allies. Under these circumstances it would be folly for us to establish relations with the Chinese Communists which would enhance their ability to hurt us and our friends.[27]

A little over a year later, on December 4, 1958, Mr. Dulles amplified his references to the responsibilities of the United States to its friends in Asia and elaborated on their vulnerability to Communist influence.[28]

Developments make it ever more clear that, if we were to grant political recognition to the Chinese Communist regime, that would be a well-nigh mortal blow to the survival of the non-Communist governments in the Far East. Such recognition and the seating of the Chinese Communists in the United Nations would so increase their prestige and influence in the Far East, and so dishearten our allies there, that the Communist subversive efforts would almost surely succeed.

During the period between these two statements, however, the development of the crisis over the offshore islands brought to the surface some of the underlying differences between United States objectives and Chinese Nationalist ambitions, and the dan-

[27] In a formal address on U.S. policy toward China, cited, pp. 94–95.
[28] For the full text of his speech, see *Department of State Bulletin*, v. 39, December 22, 1958, pp. 989–994.

gers inherent in United States involvement in the crisis aroused important segments of American public opinion.

In his news conference of September 30, 1958, Secretary of State Dulles stressed that the United States had "no commitment of any kind" to aid the Chinese Nationalists in returning to the mainland, and he now expressed the view that their return was "a highly hypothetical matter" and unlikely to be brought about "just by their own steam." He went on to say that once the crisis passed, it would be undesirable to keep the large Chinese Nationalist forces on the offshore islands.[29] This suggestion was not to be followed, though, and Chiang Kai-shek commented that he was "incredulous" at Mr. Dulles' statements, which were, he said, "completely incompatible with our stand." Nevertheless, the administration had publicly indicated that the policy of the Chinese Nationalist government with respect to the offshore islands was not entirely to its liking.

It is probable that the 1958 crisis was responsible for setting in train a growing sense of misgiving regarding aspects of America's China policy. By now the emotional atmosphere of the early 1950s was beginning to wear off, and the China question could be discussed with somewhat greater freedom than before. In the spring of 1959, when illness led to Mr. Dulles' resignation, Christian Herter replaced him as Secretary of State, and during the year, there were a few calls, both inside and outside of Congress, for a review and revision of China policy. Slowly, evidence of an increased understanding of the problems in Asia and a more realistic view of the complex problems of combating communism grew.

During the election campaign of 1960, the China question did not figure prominently, although there was some debate concerning the offshore islands. Both Presidential candidates, Mr. Kennedy and Mr. Nixon, came out against recognizing Communist China and seating it in the United Nations, but Mr. Kennedy indicated some desire to take a fresh look at secondary issues, such as defense of the offshore islands, Peking's participation in nuclear test negotiations, and the exchange of newspapermen.[30]

[29] Same, October 20, 1958, pp. 599, 602.
[30] These and other public discussions of China policy during this period are summarized in Joseph G. Whelan, "The United States and Diplomatic Recognition: The Contrasting Cases of Russia and Communist China," *China Quarterly,* no. 5, January/March 1961, pp. 62–89.

Thus, the atmosphere for public debate became freer than before, but not very much debate occurred. The policy toward China shaped during and after the Korean War and reinforced by China's inflexible policy toward the United States now appeared generally accepted, with only scattered signs of weak undercurrents of dissatisfaction. Clearly, the passions of the debate had cooled. However, the critics of prevailing policy were either still cautious about speaking out, discouraged at the possibility of having any significant influence, or genuinely puzzled as to what they might propose as an alternative to existing policy.

It should be pointed out, of course, that despite the absence of normal diplomatic relations, the United States and the People's Republic of China were not entirely without official contacts during the years subsequent to the Korean War. For example, contacts continued at Panmunjom, in Korea, even after the protracted negotiations there had produced the armistice of July 1953. In 1954, both the United States and Communist China were represented at the Geneva Conference, which resulted in a truce in the fighting in Indo-China. During the Bandung Conference in April 1955, when tensions over Taiwan were high, Chou En-lai proposed that American and Chinese meet to seek a solution of outstanding issues, and this overture led eventually to the initiation of the ambassadorial-level talks, which have already been mentioned in another context.

The first of these meetings took place in Geneva on August 1, 1955, with U. Alexis Johnson, American ambassador to Czechoslovakia, representing the United States, and Wang Ping-nan, Chinese ambassador in Warsaw, representing the People's Republic of China. On September 10, 1955, the two reached an agreement on arrangements for the release of detained nationals. Meetings then continued at less frequent intervals until their temporary suspension at the end of 1957, when Ambassador Johnson was recalled to Washington. They were resumed, however, in September 1958, and their location was transferred to Warsaw, with the Chinese and American ambassadors in that capital representing their governments.

Except for the agreement to release detained nationals, however, the negotiations produced little in the way of results, and by 1959–60, the meetings had settled into a highly formalized routine. Official statements were made, and communications were exchanged. Yet there was little actual negotiating. On key issues, unyielding positions were maintained. The American proposals that the two countries should renounce the use of force, particularly in the Taiwan area, were rejected by the Chinese, who insisted that Taiwan's status was a domestic matter to be settled by the Chinese without outside interference. The Chinese demand that the United States end its "occupation" of Taiwan became a regular feature of the talks and eventually a prior condition for agreement on other issues, but disengagement from Taiwan was now completely unacceptable to the United States. Despite the lack of accomplishment, however, neither side was disposed to suspend the meetings.

Nevertheless, it was, and still is, Washington's policy to be extremely cautious about agreeing to sit at the same conference table with representatives of the People's Republic of China. (A general policy of isolating the Peking government to the maximum extent possible and denying it international recognition, of course, provides a certain logic for this position.) For example, there was for a long period a reluctance to include the Chinese in international arms-control negotiations. In February 1959, Walter S. Robertson, the Assistant Secretary of State for Far Eastern Affairs, did state that "if it were possible to establish a sound workable system for controlling armaments or nuclear tests or surprise attacks—a system that truly protected our national security—then, of course, I believe Red China should be included." [31] The implication of Mr. Robertson's statement, however, was that after the other nations had concluded their negotiations and reached agreement, the Chinese might be invited to adhere to what had been decided. (It is worth recalling parenthetically that Peking, both before and after its rejection of the partial nuclear test-ban treaty of 1963, made it clear that it could not automatically be expected to accede to any agreements negotiated without its participation.)

Washington's policy toward unofficial contacts between Chinese and Americans was almost equally cautious and restrictive.

[31] *Disarmament and Foreign Policy*, Hearings before a Subcommittee of the Committee on Foreign Relations, U.S. Senate, 86th Cong., 1st sess. (Washington, D.C.: GPO, 1959), p. 379.

In the earlier years, this attitude was due to a considerable degree to the State Department's opposition to such contacts, but later it resulted in large part from Peking's unwillingness to ease its restrictions.

At the time of the Korean War, the State Department invalidated all United States passports for travel to the mainland, and this prohibition, instituted as part of the general wartime embargo on dealing with Communist China, remained in effect when the war ended.

In 1956, when the Chinese, presumably as part of their new "coexistence" strategy which took shape during the Bandung Conference the year before, invited fifteen American correspondents to visit the mainland, the State Department reiterated its prohibition of all travel to China by American citizens and refused to validate passports for the journalists. After considerable public criticism, this stand was modified, and on August 22, 1957, the Department validated a limited number of passports for American newsmen to travel to the China mainland. At the same time, however, it declared that the United States government would not make any agreement with the Chinese Communists to assure reciprocity for their newsmen, although it did indicate that it would examine the credentials of Chinese Communist journalists on the basis of individual applications. The Chinese rejected this proposal and retracted the invitations they had issued. No application from a Chinese Communist newsman was ever received, and Peking continued to bar the American journalists on the State Department's list, which slowly grew over the years.

Suggestions of a New Outlook

When John F. Kennedy took office in January 1961, some observers expected him to take a fresh look at China policy and to seek some improvement in American relations with Peking. Certain of his advisers were on record as favoring changes in China policy, and during his election campaign, he himself had cautiously suggested modifications, even though he had stood firm on the main elements of existing policy.

Whatever may have been President Kennedy's intentions, no significant changes in China policy occurred. Perhaps he concluded that domestic political opposition to modification of China policy was still strong, or perhaps he felt that steps to modify China policy might involve risks to other high-priority programs of the administration and that he should postpone action on China policy issues. At any rate, he took no major steps to alter policy toward Peking.

Even if he had chosen to ignore some of the existing domestic difficulties, of course, many obstacles would have stood in the way of American initiatives. China's hostility to the United States was, if anything, increasing in this period, and Peking showed every sign of actively opposing any idea of an accommodation. As the Sino-Soviet conflict intensified, moreover, the Chinese seemed to become even more militant and uncompromising than before. The years 1960–62 were also difficult ones for China at home, and some people argued that this was not the time to make things easier for them. Finally, American involvement in Vietnam was increasing, the Chinese were backing North Vietnam and the Viet Cong, and the possibility of an escalating conflict, possibly involving China, could not be ruled out.

A vague hope that somehow an improvement in relations could be achieved, however, existed in Washington even though President Kennedy was reluctant to take major initiatives. A week before his death, for example, he spoke on the question of trade with China at a press conference: [32]

We are not going to—planning to trade with Red China—in view of the policy that Red China pursues. When the Red Chinese indicate a desire to live at peace with the United States and other countries surrounding it, then quite obviously the United States would reappraise its policies.

We are not wedded to a policy of hostility to Red China. It seems to me Red China's policies are what create tension between not only the United States and Red China, but between Red China and India, between Red China and her immediate neighbors to the south, and even between Red China and other Communist countries.

Essentially, what President Kennedy was saying was that if the Chinese mended their ways, the United States would take a fresh look at China's policies but that in the meantime the present poli-

[32] *The New York Times*, November 15, 1963.

cies would continue. Only a few months earlier, at his press conference of August 1, he had warned of the "menacing situation" the Chinese could create:

I would regard that combination, if it is still in existence in the 1970s, of weak countries around it, 700,000,000 people, Stalinist Government and a nuclear power and a Government determined on war as a means of bringing about its ultimate success as potentially a more dangerous situation than any we've found since the end of the Second war." [33]

It is clear that America's overall relations with Communist China did not improve during the Kennedy years and perhaps, in view of China's increased militancy, even deteriorated. However, the United States government did try to avoid major crises. In the spring of 1962, it reportedly notified the Chinese Communists through the ambassadorial link in Warsaw that Washington would not favor a Nationalist attack on the mainland—an action that had been rumored as imminent because of Peking's domestic political and economic difficulties.[34] And later that same year, the United States joined Communist China and others to reach a temporary settlement over Laos.

Although the main lines of United States policy remained intact, there were some indications of an effort to alter the American posture and perhaps tactics as well. In early 1961, for example, the United States at the Warsaw talks again brought up proposals for an exchange of newsmen, a subject which had already been unsuccessfully revived in 1959. The Chinese brusquely rejected the proposals, however, and countered by reiterating their demand for the prior withdrawal of United States protection from Taiwan. Later in the year, the United States to a degree modified its approach to the China issue in the United Nations by agreeing that the Assembly should debate the question of China's seat, although the substance of American policy remained unchanged. When there were many reports during 1961–62 indicating a serious food shortage in Communist China and there was a good deal of subsequent public discussion concerning the desirability of selling or giving food to the Chinese, President Kennedy stated that if the Chinese submitted a request, it would re-

[33] Same, August 2, 1963.
[34] See *The New York Times*, June 27, 1962.

ceive consideration. At the same time, he made no outright offer of food.

There was also some evidence of subtle changes in Washington's outlook, assumptions, tone, and expectations. These were most apparent in an address made by Roger Hilsman, Assistant Secretary of State for Far Eastern Affairs, on December 13, 1963. The date was three weeks after President Kennedy's death, but the main outlines may well have been sketched out when he was still alive.

Mr. Hilsman's speech said nothing about an expected demise of the Peking government; rather, it expressed optimism about "evolutionary forces" that would gradually change the character of the regime. For the present, though, the Chinese leadership was seen to consist of dogmatic, inflexible men who are ignorant of the outside world, convinced of their own righteousness, and full of hatred for the United States, and all blame for the lack of more contacts between the two countries was placed on them. The United States' pursuit of different policies toward the Soviet Union on the one hand and Communist China on the other was explained by reference to the Chinese Communists' greater suspicion of the outside world, their refusal to recognize the existence of common interests, the greater vulnerability of China's neighbors, and Peking's insistence on the recovery of Taiwan. The speech suggested, however, that the principal American objective regarding Communist China was not to produce its downfall or to subject it to complete, long-term isolation but to make it impossible for Peking to "subvert or commit aggression against its free-world neighbors." In a phrase harking back to the pre-Communist period, Mr. Hilsman proclaimed a policy of the "open door," a door open to the possibility of change. However, until Communist China changed, he said, the United States would maintain its current policy positions and not "betray our interests and those of our allies to appease the ambitions of Communist China's leaders." [35]

In short, although the speech did not introduce any major new changes in American policy, it did suggest that that policy would

[35] The full text of the speech may be found in *Department of State Bulletin*, v. 50, January 6, 1964, pp. 11-17.

no longer be based on the assumption that the Peking regime would collapse but on the hope that it would be transformed, and it indicated that the United States would be responsive to changes in Communist China's policy. In this respect, some change of tone, and perhaps of posture, was implied. But no immediate policy conclusions were drawn.

It could be argued, of course, that this new approach contained within it the seeds of some kind of "two-China" policy. Otherwise, how else could one reconcile the commitment to the Nationalist government, which Mr. Hilsman restated, with the assumption that the Peking government was here to stay—albeit, it was hoped, under less militant leaders—and the assurance that the United States would respond positively to changes on Peking's part? Undoubtedly, one aim of the speech was to introduce a less passionate tone in American public debate on China and thereby to prepare the way for future changes in American policy.

If there was any serious intention of moving toward a change in policy, however, it was halted, or at least interrupted, by President Kennedy's death. The change of Presidents and Lyndon B. Johnson's takeover introduced fresh problems and new priorities. And before long the deteriorating situation in Vietnam appeared to create once again an unfavorable climate for changes in American policy aimed at improved relations with mainland China.

France's recognition of the Peking government in January 1964 put additional strains on the American position. The French action seemed to call for a reaffirmation of United States policy lest silence be interpreted as approval. This was not slow in coming. Speaking in Tokyo the day after the French announcement, Secretary Rusk declared: "We are loyal to our commitments and we will never abandon the 12 million people on Taiwan to Communist tyranny." He then went on to observe: "When mainland China has a government which is prepared to renounce force, to make peace, and to honor international responsibilities, it will find us responsive." [36] The continuation of existing policies was emphasized again on March 13, 1964, when Secretary Rusk explained to the Senate Foreign Relations Committee why the United States maintained a total embargo on trade with mainland China, North Korea, and North Vietnam but not on trade with

[36] Same, v. 50, February 17, 1964, pp. 233–234.

the Soviet Union and the European Communist nations.[37] Referring to the three Asian countries, he said:

Our decision to impose a total trade embargo is based primarily upon political considerations. Each of these Communist countries is actively engaged in aggressive activity. . . . When regimes are engaging in aggressive activities of such character and intensity, we must design our trade policies accordingly. Our complete trade embargo is a reflection of these relationships.

In 1965, when the China issue confronted the United Nations once more, the United States again took an unyielding position. By a major effort, it managed to mobilize sufficient opposition to the seating of Peking to prevent it, but barely. The vote was 47 to 47.

Later that year, however, the State Department did indicate a willingness to validate passports of doctors and medical personnel as well as journalists to travel to mainland China. Subsequently, this relaxation in policy was extended to include scholars too.

American policy thus seemed to be oscillating. Unyielding positions were maintained on matters of important substance. At the same time, there was tacit recognition that the Chinese Communist government was in power for the indefinite future, and hope was expressed that it might in time mend its ways. The primary emphasis, though, was on the position that there could be no change in basic United States policy until changes had occurred in Peking's attitudes and policies. President Johnson put it this way on April 20, 1964: [38]

As for China itself, so long as the Communist Chinese pursue conflict and preach violence, there can be and will be no easing of relationships. There are some who prophesy that these policies will change. But America must base her acts on present realities and not on future hopes. It is not we who must re-examine our view of China, it is the Chinese Communists who must re-examine their view of the world.

Nor can anyone doubt our unalterable commitment to the defense and liberty of free China. . . .

In the background of these declarations was the Sino-Soviet dispute and debate that had reached a climax in 1962 and 1963, subsided briefly after Khrushchev's downfall in October 1964,

[37] For the full text of his remarks, see same, March 30, 1964, pp. 474–484. The quote is from p. 480.
[38] Address at an Associated Press lunch, same, May 11, 1964, p. 730.

132

and then was renewed. Whereas the United States had a few years earlier emphasized the solidarity of the Communist bloc countries and asserted that the links that bound Peking to Moscow required a firm policy toward China, it was now commonly argued that Peking's militancy, which seemed to disturb Moscow about as much as Washington, justified the continuation of a very hard policy toward China while American-Soviet tensions were being reduced. Some observers emphasized that China was now more vulnerable, for it was isolating itself from its former ally and could no longer count on Soviet assistance in case of trouble. The Soviet Union and the Communist countries of Eastern Europe were hailed as examples of how a desirable evolutionary process could take place in Communist societies, and it was hoped that similar trends might eventually take place in China. For the present, however, it seemed that the Soviet Union and the United States had, in many situations, a common interest in opposing the extension of Chinese influence and limiting China's ability to upset the peace of the world. In short, the United States government appeared to be more interested in sustaining an improved relationship with the Soviet Union than in seeking fresh approaches to China.

Any argument that the Sino-Soviet dispute might provide opportunities for new American initiatives toward Peking, now that the Chinese were breaking away from the Soviet Union, was countered by references to Peking's undeniable hostility and uncompromising policy toward the United States. In fact, the Sino-Soviet dispute and the war in Vietnam appeared, if anything, to accentuate the hostility between Peking and Washington. The Chinese focused on the United States and the Soviet Union as special targets of abuse but at the same time attempted to improve their relations with other Western countries as well as with the new nations of the Afro-Asian world, and the United States concentrated on improving its relations with the Soviet Union and the Communist countries of Eastern Europe. Secretary of State Rusk reflected a widespread American feeling of bafflement about China when he said: "It is difficult to enter each other's minds across that vast ideological gulf." [39]

[39] See *The Washington Post*, August 9, 1964.

Summary

During the years since American policy toward China hardened as a result of the Korean War, there has been no disposition to alter the fundamentals of our policy—nonrecognition, support of Taiwan, opposition to seating Peking in the United Nations, and the American trade embargo. But there has been some willingness to be flexible, at least to a degree, on secondary aspects of our dealings with mainland China. The bilateral talks at Warsaw, for example, have continued, albeit for very limited purposes. (By the middle of 1965, about 130 meetings had taken place. This fact has led some American officials to claim that despite the lack of formal diplomatic relations between the United States and Communist China, the United States has in actuality had more sustained, high-level diplomatic contacts with Peking than other non-Communist governments have.) The United States and the People's Republic of China have sat at the same international conference tables on two occasions, at Geneva in 1954 and again in 1962. After first barring all nonofficial contacts, the United States has in recent years pressed actively for an exchange of newsmen and begun to relax other restrictions. And the United States has accepted—perhaps in part because it has no choice—the steady reduction of the existing restrictions on China trade by our allies, most of whom by 1957 had placed their trade with mainland China on the same basis as their trade with the Soviet Union.

It has been possible to accomplish little, however, toward arranging an exchange of newsmen or other forms of unofficial contact, despite the skirmishing with the Chinese on such issues at Warsaw. In a small number of special cases, to be sure, the State Department has granted certain Americans authorization for travel to the mainland, and in some instances—for example, relatives of Americans imprisoned in China and two or three writers—Peking for its own reasons has granted visas. Nevertheless, most American journalists have been unable to enter Communist China, and no Chinese journalist has come to the United States. Moreover, contacts between American and Chinese scholars and scientists have been almost nonexistent, although there have been limited exchanges of publications and occasional encounters at international conferences.

Despite the continuity of basic United States policy toward China, some of the original assumptions underlying that policy have now been altered. The People's Republic of China is not about to collapse, and its life expectancy seems long. The international Communist movement is no longer unified, and Peking is certainly no satellite of Moscow. Domestic passions over the China issue seem to have subsided in the United States, and public opinion no longer appears to be such an obstacle to policy change. It seems probable, in fact, that the American public would accept changes in China policy if Washington were to make new moves.

However, new problems and premises seem to have replaced the old ones as the justification for an unchanging policy. The commitments to the Nationalist government and other allies and friends in Asia obviously cannot be dealt with as if they should not have been undertaken in the first place or as if they did not now exist as realities. The weakness and vulnerability of China's small neighbors—most notably Vietnam—have been demonstrated too often for the United States to overlook them, and there are uncertainties as to how any change in American policy might affect them. The Chinese Communists' uncompromising hostility toward the United States and their increased international militancy seem to argue, in the minds of many Americans, for unyielding opposition, not conciliation. And in the eyes of many, the first Chinese nuclear explosion is a symbol of the growing dangers which China's achievements and its expanding role in international affairs pose.

The American response to these new circumstances has been essentially to continue old policies and to wait, in the hope that a change of Chinese Communist behavior will eventually open the door to reduced tensions and perhaps a new relationship.

CHAPTER SEVEN

An Appraisal of
United States Policy
toward China since 1949

It is tempting to make sweeping judgments as to the success or failure of a particular foreign policy. This temptation is perhaps especially great in the case of United States policy toward China because it has been so distinctive and has involved so much passion. However, it is not easy to make an overall appraisal.

Machiavelli wrote "that fortune is the arbiter of one-half of our actions but that she still leaves us to direct the other half, or perhaps a little less." [1] Many decisions in foreign policy are taken in the heat of crisis, and while there may be hope that they will bring satisfactory long-term results, the main purpose is to solve a specific immediate problem or to influence a particular current situation. The relationship between individual decisions and major objectives is frequently obscure and uncertain. Urgent choices have to be made among limited alternatives when the consequences can only be dimly perceived. And neither at the time the decision is taken nor later can it be definitely known what results an alternative choice would have yielded. Not even the wisdom of hindsight can tell us this.

Even a great power can seldom fully achieve all its foreign-policy objectives. Moreover, a nation's foreign policy includes many differing objectives, some of which may conflict with others. Foreign-policy making and diplomacy must attempt to rec-

[1] *The Prince*, Chapter 25.

oncile existing contradictions and establish priorities, and one can only hope that subsequent events will prove the choices to have been right.

Often decisions taken to meet an immediate situation become deeply imbedded in long-term policy and form the core around which major objectives are reformulated and commitments made. This was true of the decision in 1950 to protect Taiwan and of that in 1954 to support President Ngo Dinh Diem of Vietnam. Ideally, of course, one would like to see each major decision fit neatly into a coherent long-term perspective. But the slate is never clean, and it is necessary to deal with the present without being able to predict the future clearly. It is important, however, for the policy maker to have some vision of the future, imperfect though it may be, and for individual decisions to be related to that vision.

Even if it were possible to make a completely dispassionate and accurate appraisal of past policy and sharply define its successes and failures, we would still not have a sure guide for the future. Conditions change, interests shift, and old solutions may not be applicable to new situations.

In midstream, however, let us look at what the United States has tried to accomplish and attempt to appraise how it has succeeded. We start with the Korean War because present policy derives directly from it.

The Hope that the Chinese Communist Government Would Not Last

President Truman's decision to recall General MacArthur in April 1951 was related to the American decision during the Korean War not to take direct military action against China itself and therefore not to attempt to destroy the Peking government by force. No one can say what would have happened if General MacArthur's views had prevailed. The overwhelming force of the United States presumably could have destroyed the major centers of power in China. But it is difficult to say that this action would have brought down the Chinese Communist government, and it is impossible to know what the consequences would have been, not only in China itself but also in the rest of Asia, the Soviet Union, and the United Nations.

Despite President Truman's decision not to strike against Chinese territory, however, the China policy that emerged from the Korean War was one involving efforts not only to contain but also to exert continuing pressure on the Chinese Communist regime, and it seemed to be based on an underlying hope that American action could contribute to the weakening and ultimate demise of the Peking government. It is difficult to say whether this hope was genuine or was merely intended to provide the rationale for American efforts to limit the expansion of China's influence. In any case, it was argued that the particular United States policies which evolved could contribute to this end.

American policy, nevertheless, clearly has not hastened the hoped-for demise of the Chinese Communist regime. And while we cannot clearly foresee the future, there is no present evidence that the Peking regime is a temporary phenomenon. In fact, its power and influence have steadily grown. During the past few years, we have seen a large measure of recovery from the domestic crisis created by the failures of the communes and the Great Leap Forward in China, and in its foreign policy, Peking has defied Moscow, conducted increasingly active diplomacy in Asia, Africa, and Europe, exerted new pressures on South and Southeast Asia, and exploded its first nuclear devices. The Chinese population has many sources of dissatisfaction, but there is no evidence of effective organized opposition to the regime. In short, the hope that the People's Republic of China would not long survive has not been fulfilled. Recent statements from Washington have implicitly recognized this fact and, in effect, acknowledged that the People's Republic of China is likely to rule mainland China for the indefinite future.

The Desire to Isolate Communist China

Isolation and containment have often been identified as the two principal ingredients of the China policy of the United States.

The policy of isolation has included the refusal of the United States to recognize the People's Republic of China or move toward establishing normal relations with it, the discouragement of other nations from dealing with Peking, opposition to the seating of the Chinese Communists in the United Nations and in all other international organizations, and the maintenance of an American embargo on all American trade with mainland China.

Determined itself not to recognize the Chinese Communists or do anything that might increase their prestige, the United States has also felt a special responsibility to set an example for others and not to waiver in its policy lest other countries, weaker than the United States, succumb to China's and communism's influence and thereby erode the American position. Washington at times has argued that any country dealing with the Chinese was helping the Communist cause and exposing itself to serious dangers.

This policy has been criticized on many grounds, including the fact that one "cannot ignore 700 million Chinese." This particular criticism is not very convincing. In fact, the entire Asian policy of the United States, however subject to criticism, focuses on the China mainland. Moreover, the United States has dealt directly with the People's Republic on a *de facto* basis on a number of occasions and has negotiated with Chinese Communist representatives at Panmunjom, Geneva, and Warsaw. Moreover, it is clear that Peking is also responsible for the restriction of communication. Certainly, the Chinese population is even more ignorant about the United States than Americans are of them. If the United States is charged with ignoring 700 million Chinese, then the Chinese government must be accused of ignoring "200 million Americans, the most powerful nation on earth." Actually, while neither country has ignored the other, both have shown deep suspicion and hostility, and both have adopted toward each other a posture of minimum communication.

The United States has tried to induce other countries to follow its policy of being restrictive in dealings with the Chinese Communists, but the price has sometimes been the charge that the United States has interfered with the independence of others for the sake of an "unrealistic policy." Few other countries genuinely believe in the wisdom of attempting to isolate China, even though most are aware of the very real limitations, under the best of circumstances, on freedom of contact with the Chinese Communists and many know the risks of dealing with them.

The success of the policy of trying to isolate China has therefore been very limited. A few countries, including some that feel most threatened by China or most fear China's interference in their internal affairs, have welcomed the policy and want to see it maintained. They have tended to regard it as a symbol of the United States' determination to oppose any expansion of Chinese Communist influence, and they have been fearful of any weakening of American commitments. Other countries, including most Latin American nations, have been prepared to follow the American example mainly because they have had no strong reasons to do otherwise and have wished to avoid friction with Washington. Some of our close allies and friends, including the Federal Republic of Germany, Italy, Japan, and Canada, have accepted the American lead with respect to nonrecognition of the Peking government but have done so with varying degrees of doubt and reluctance and have developed trade and other contacts with the China mainland. Other allies, however, including the British and French, have not followed the American lead in regard to either recognition or trade. Their development of trade relations with mainland China has been especially noteworthy. As a matter of fact, despite American opposition to trade with the mainland, the share of non-Communist countries in Communist China's total trade increased, as was stated before, from roughly one-third in 1957 to roughly two-thirds in 1965.

A majority of the countries of Asia and Africa have actively tried to establish relations of various sorts with the Chinese Communists, and Peking has assiduously courted many of them in return. In fact, the Chinese Communists have by no means been totally isolated, as is indicated by their role in numerous Afro-Asian conferences, meetings, and exchanges, by the steady stream of visitors to China, and by the frequent tours of Chinese leaders to other capitals, especially in Asia and Africa. Many Asian and African countries, indeed, have been openly critical of the American position.

Some supporters of present American policy claim that it is only the Chinese who isolate themselves by their own policies and behavior and not the United States that isolates them. While there is an element of truth in this argument, it is nevertheless clear that the goal of isolating Communist China has been an explicit and major objective of the United States. It is true that the Chinese leaders themselves do try to isolate the Chinese people from the outside world in many respects and do control their foreign dealings with care. But they also press China's participation in world politics with great energy and determination, and they have obviously had some success in their efforts.

What has been the total effect of this aspect of American policy? Some would contend that it may have reinforced the tendency of Chinese Communist leaders to be rebellious members of the world community and that it has doubtless intensified their animosity toward the United States. It would be difficult to argue, however, that it has fundamentally shaped their basic attitudes, for these were already inherent in Chinese Communist doctrine. One can thus only speculate as to whether a different American approach would have induced a more favorable Chinese response. However, it does seem fairly clear that the policy of trying to isolate China has precluded alternative efforts to explore what influences might be brought to bear on the Chinese to try to induce them to be more moderate and more accommodating.

A few years ago, critics of current policy were charging that the United States was forcing Communist China closer to the Soviet Union by its policy of isolating China from the rest of the world. Supporters of American policy, on the other hand, stressed the indestructible bonds of ideological affinity and the hostility to the West that joined the two Communist countries. The Sino-Soviet split has proved both critics and supporters wrong. American policy makers, however, can take relatively little credit for this development since few foresaw or consciously encouraged it.

In any case, the split has contributed little to the American objective of isolating the Chinese Communists. As the Chinese broke away from their intimate relationship with the Soviet Union, they set about increasing their economic ties with Japan and the Western world and expanding their political relations with the countries of Asia and Africa. In many respects, the rift with the Soviet Union probably stimulated them to carry out these plans and provided an added impetus for more active and independent Chinese diplomacy.

The Chinese have more than reciprocated American suspicion and opposition to normal intercourse, and it would certainly be wrong to conclude that we bear sole, or even primary, responsibility for this state of affairs. The existing situation, however, doubtless troubles the Chinese much less than it does the Americans. The Chinese, for example, have no attachment to the ideal of a free flow of people and ideas, and they regulate their dealings with other nations with deliberate selectivity. From the United States' point of view, on the other hand, the price is a significant one. For many reasons, it is undesirable for the United States to be cut off from free access to other countries. The result is to reduce the level of contact and knowledge and the degree of understanding that are essential for sound political judgment. Moreover, if the United States is to search for ways of influencing and moderating Peking's leaders, it is difficult to see how this can be done through a policy of isolation.

The Policy of Containment

Unlike the broad aim of isolating the People's Republic of China, the policy of containment aims more specifically at limiting the extension of China's direct territorial, political, and ideological influence.

As in Europe, where containment aimed at the Soviet Union has focused on certain crucial areas, there have been in Asia a few key points of maximum tension or pressure. When the Korean War broke out, the United States stepped in to protect South Korea against attack from the north and also to defend Taiwan against possible attack by the Chinese Communists. Thus, the beginnings of a military containment policy in Asia took shape when the Chinese were still in the flush of their revolutionary victory.

142

However, in Southeast Asia, to which both Chinese interest and American attention turned after Korea [2] (at first in a small way with economic and technical assistance programs and then very emphatically with the French withdrawal from Indo-China in 1954), the containment policy ran into a set of problems quite unlike those in Europe. Military containment was more difficult to apply in an area where the local means of resisting Chinese pressures were diffuse, weak, and uncertain and where the military threat was often an indirect rather than a direct one. As a result, the United States has been less clear on exactly what containment of China should involve and what means would be the most effective.

Speaking in June 1958, Walter S. Robertson, Assistant Secretary of State for Far Eastern Affairs, praised the success of American policy and asserted: "For four years now the Communists have been deterred from outright military aggression." He then went on to declare: "The Far East today is not all that we would like to see . . . but I do believe that there has been a turning of the tide. . . ." [3]

It is doubtful, though, whether "outright military aggression" was ever the main threat, and as has already been emphasized, it is much more difficult to deal with other problems, dangers, and threats through a policy of military containment. Today, moreover, it is not easy to be so confident that there has yet been, in fact, a clear "turning of the tide." In recent years, Communist-supported insurrectionary movements, aided by China as well as the Communist regime in North Vietnam, have increased in scope and militancy in both Vietnam and Laos. In addition, China's political influence has clearly expanded in Cambodia, and probably in Burma, and for a period of time, up to late 1965, China and Indonesia appeared to have formed a close political entente.

[2] As early as July 18, 1949, Secretary Acheson had asked Philip C. Jessup to draw up possible programs of action designed to prevent "further extension of Communist domination on the continent of Asia or in the Southeast Asia area." McGeorge Bundy, ed., *The Pattern of Responsibility* (Boston: Houghton Mifflin, 1952), p. 180.
[3] Statement to the Senate Foreign Relations Committee, May 2, 1958, *Department of State Bulletin*, v. 38, May 2, 1958, pp. 914, 917, 918.

In certain areas of Asia, however, military containment has clearly been relevant and important. Korea is the most obvious example, but there are others. When the Chinese exerted military pressure against India in 1962 and 1965, it is possible that they might have been tempted to extend their gains if they had not feared American intervention. And it is virtually certain that they would have tried to attack Taiwan at a time of their own choosing if the United States had not pledged itself to the defense of the island.

American strength and commitments have undoubtedly done much too, in a general way, to offset the influence that China might have exerted on its weak neighbors simply as a result of its growing military power, and it is undeniable that American guarantees, backed up by military strength and political determination, have had an important psychological effect, especially in Southeast Asia. This was doubtless what Mr. Robertson had in mind when, in February 1957, he stated that "the course we have pursued has had a deterrent effect and has bought some of the time needed for the free nations of Asia to build the strength which they will require to retain their independence." [4]

Today, however, one would have to be less sanguine about the progress made toward a secure and stable Asia during the time bought by the American guarantees. It is true that no nation in the area has lost its independence, but the difficult search for national stability and regional solidarity still continues, and despite heavy American involvements over the past several years, it would be hard to contend that either is yet in sight. In Northeast Asia, to be sure, the partition of Korea has to a degree been stabilized at the 38th parallel with the assistance of American forces, and in Japan there has been a remarkable process of economic and political development with the help of American aid. In South and Southeast Asia, though, instability and division have been continuing and acute.

The fact is that American military strength, diplomatic action, and economic assistance can provide only part of the barrier required for containment. Part must come from the local peoples involved. American measures designed to strengthen the will to

[4] Same, v. 36, February 25, 1957, p. 297.

independence of China's neighbors have, it is true, supplied some of the armature and incentives which these small and divided countries have needed, but where unfavorable factors have been present, as in Vietnam and Laos, containment as a policy has been difficult to apply and only partially successful.

Moreover, a policy focused solely on the aim of containing Communist China militarily clearly cannot alleviate all the difficulties which beset the area. Even if American involvement were universally welcomed, military measures offer no answers to the problems created by the idiosyncrasies of local leadership; the influence of local traditions, culture, and geography; varying interpretations of national interest; and the many weaknesses of the new countries. In short, while military containment should be an element in American policy, and an important one, there are many problems which it cannot solve.

In pursuing our policy of containment, we have at times also failed to distinguish clearly enough between the threat from China and the threat from communism. To many Americans, the "Chinese threat" and the "Communist threat" in Asia have become synonymous and interchangeable. There has also been a tendency among some to dramatize the danger as an all-encompassing one. Only a few Asian nations, however, have seen the problem in these terms, and most have not been willing to join multilateral security arrangements such as SEATO.

Among China's neighbors, the degree of fear of communism and even attitudes toward local Communist parties are closely related to the existing domestic situation in the country involved, and as was indicated before, there is a wide range of views. Thailand and the Philippines, at one end of the spectrum, participate actively in the military containment effort, are hostile to Communist China, and do not tolerate domestic Communist activity. At the other extreme, Indonesia, at least until late 1965, tolerated a strong Communist party and at various periods maintained very close relations with Peking. In between are many mixed situations. Cambodia, for example, is friendly to Communist China but suppresses communism locally. Malaysia, however, is quietly unfriendly to Peking and suppresses the local Communists but avoids formal alignment against Peking.

Most of the countries of the area have been too preoccupied

with their domestic difficulties and international vulnerability to wish to identify in an unqualified way with a sweeping crusade against communism or against China. In those cases where local interests seem to dictate and local circumstances permit, China's neighbors may selectively oppose either one or the other or both, but seldom with the passion or enthusiasm that the combination has often aroused in the United States.

The Sino-Soviet dispute, accompanied by competition between Peking and Moscow for the allegiance of Asian Communist parties, has provided a further argument for caution in analyzing the complex interrelationships between national power, Communist ideology, and local politics. A policy that has to deal with such complex factors and problems cannot hope to create a uniform and impenetrable barrier.

In other words, the simple notion of military containment, in the sense of drawing a clear line, seems inadequate alone to cope with the existing situation. Nevertheless, containment itself is one essential ingredient of an effective China policy.

Support for the Nationalist Government on Taiwan

In many respects, United States recogition and support of the government of the Republic of China on Taiwan, renewed and reinforced as a result of the Korean War, gradually became a major symbol of our present China policy. By protecting the Nationalist government and supporting it as the legitimate government of all China, the United States has given a striking demonstration of its opposition to the Communists in Peking because it has thus explicitly challenged the legitimacy of the People's Republic of China.

However, while defending, supporting, and encouraging the Nationalists, the United States has not been willing to assist Chiang Kai-shek militarily to return to the mainland, and there is no other way in sight for him to return. Thus, the United States now finds itself in the position of supporting as the government of China a regime with no foreseeable prospect of extending its authority beyond Taiwan and nearby islands.

In short, the United States has succeeded in the limited purpose of helping to defend Taiwan and preserve a Chinese government independent of Peking, of assisting this government to govern Taiwan and retain an international status of its own, but this achievement has had little effect on the situation on the China mainland.

Perhaps it is arguable whether, in terms of American interests, the consequences would or would not have been serious if the Chinese Communists had successfully attacked Taiwan soon after their victory on the mainland and before the beginning of the Korean War. It was the judgment of at least some American policy makers at the time that this would have been an undesirable but unavoidable consequence of the Communist victory on the mainland and that the United States should not try to block it. All such calculations were upset, however, by actions taken during and after the Korean War and by the climate of hostility and the changes in the power equation created by the war. We are now faced, therefore, with the necessity of judging the consequences of what actually did happen and not of what might have been.

Once it was concluded that the People's Republic of China posed a major threat, there were many arguments in favor of support for the Nationalists, and as the American commitment to Taiwan took deep root, it increasingly became a prime symbol of American firmness in opposing the Communists. To some nations which disagreed with American policies, it also became a symbol of American stubbornness and rigidity. Nevertheless, it provided unquestionable evidence of the United States' determination to oppose Communist expansionism, evidence that could not be dismissed lightly by Communist China or by any of the other countries concerned with the affairs of the area.

It is more difficult, however, to claim that the regime on Taiwan has acquired an important symbolic value either as a real alternative to the People's Republic or as a repository of traditional Chinese values. As the prospects for a Nationalist return to the mainland have dwindled, the political significance of its role as a symbolic alternative has also diminished. Today in the eyes of most of the world, "China" means the Communist mainland, the principal country in Asia, and not the island of Taiwan. The domestic accomplishments of the regime on Taiwan have in many respects been impressive, but they have not been sufficient to counterbalance the fact that it does not control and has no demonstrable influence on the China mainland.

Nevertheless, out of the confusion of the past decade and a half there clearly has emerged on Taiwan a regime much more viable and durable than the defeated regime of Chiang Kai-shek in 1949 and one which in fact if not in theory is quite separate and distinct from the Communist mainland of the mid-1960s. It now appears that much of the world, while refusing to accept the Nationalists' claim to be the government of all China, sees Taiwan as a distinctive political entity which, although less important than the regime on the mainland, deserves a continued existence. American support of the Nationalists' claim to be the government of all China is criticized by many, but the American commitment to defend Taiwan receives much sympathy. Few probably expect that this American commitment will change in the near future.

United States policy toward Taiwan has, however, involved some important liabilities. It is clear, of course, that the continued existence of the Nationalist government, under United States protection, has been a serious obstacle to negotiations and agreement between Peking and Washington on other issues, although Chinese Communist attitudes toward the United States would obviously not be totally transformed even if this grievance were removed. There are other drawbacks as well. Many nations, for example, view United States policy toward Taiwan as unrealistic and provocative because it has entailed support of Chiang's claim to govern the mainland. Militarily, the situation involves some hazards, even though the United States has sought to define its commitments regarding Taiwan with care and to avoid involvement in actions over which it has no control. These hazards became clear in 1958 during the crisis over the offshore islands and in the spring of 1962 when the United States felt it necessary to inform the Communists that it did not favor a Nationalist attack on the mainland. Politically, the tie with the Nationalists has caused the United States some embarrassment in relations with a number of countries which have been antagonistic toward the Nationalist regime.

Thus, the legacy of fifteen years of American policy toward Taiwan is a complex one, no matter how one assesses the balance of assets and liabilities resulting from past actions. Not surprisingly, there are some people who think they can turn the clock back or erase the dilemmas with simple formulas: "Recognize reality" and "face the facts" or "stand by your friends" and "we are duty bound." It would be reassuring if the problem of appraising the past and determining a course for the future were that simple, but unfortunately it is not.

Attitudes in Communist China

Relations between the United States and Communist China since 1949 have been so antagonistic that the establishment of friendlier attitudes has not been high on the list of American objectives, and relatively little thought has been given to the question of whether United States policies might be so designed as to have some moderating influence, now or in the future, on the nature of the Chinese Communist regime or the outlook of its leaders and people.

As long as there was the implication that American policy was founded on the hope that the Peking government would not last, there was little basis, it is true, for serious thought about possible means to improve relations with it. Moreover, although by the late 1950s American leaders on occasion did begin expressing the hope that perhaps, over a period of time, the Chinese would have no choice but to "mend their ways" as they were contained and isolated, there was not very much evidence that they really expected that the Chinese would have a change of heart. Nor was there any immediate sign that this prospect was to be encouraged by a greater official readiness on the part of the United States to deal with the Chinese Communists or to recognize the legitimacy of any of their aspirations. It was implied that it was up to the Chinese simply to reform themselves after effective American policies of containment and isolation had convinced them that their own policies were unproductive and dangerous to China.

Up to the present, little has happened to sustain such hopes.

The Chinese Communists have continued to be as hostile and assertive as ever. They have certainly not become more conciliatory, and there has been no sign of significant changes in their goals or attitudes. Actually, the Chinese Communists today may feel that they have even more reasons than in earlier years to look upon the United States as their principal enemy.

Whatever feelings the Chinese people may have had for Americans twenty years ago, they have been subjected to an incessant barrage of propaganda against the United States for a decade and a half, and it is difficult to imagine that this propaganda has not left its mark. It may be comforting to believe that deep inside, the Chinese people "really like us." But it is difficult to find evidence to sustain such a hope, and in any case, it is hard to see what relevance it might have to the realities and problems of international politics.

The Attitudes of Other Countries

Another criterion among the many by which our China policy can be evaluated is the degree to which it has been supported by other nations. The problem of dealing with China is not a private American concern, and the measures taken by the United States involve a large number of other countries. In fact, many elements in United States policy clearly cannot be effective unless they do receive support from others.

When judged by the criterion of international support, United States policy on China has obviously had serious weaknesses, and these have increased over time. Strong and consistent support for all components of United States policy has come primarily from a few small and relatively weak governments, especially those on China's immediate periphery, that have felt most directly menaced by Communist China and that are largely dependent on the United States for the preservation of their existence and freedom. They include the regimes in the divided nations of Asia—South Korea, Taiwan, South Vietnam—plus the Philippines and Thailand. Apart from these, one sees relatively little unity of policy or purpose toward China. Instead, whether we look at the principal countries in Asia, including Japan, Indonesia, Pakistan, and India, or at the major countries in Europe, including the United Kingdom, France, and Germany—to say nothing of those countries generally hostile or unsympathetic to the United States—we see countries which differ, in varying ways, with either our aims or our methods or both. In particular, many nations that otherwise endorse our policy of containing Communist China oppose the aim of isolating it, and their insistence on establishing contacts and trading with Peking, despite current American policies, has contributed significantly to the weakening of the effectiveness of the present American position.

United States Policy in Perspective

Clearly, the China policy of the United States, while it has acted as a barrier to Chinese expansionism, has not fulfilled many of the original hopes and promises that inspired it. The People's Republic of China has not collapsed or been overthrown. Although the conquest of Taiwan has been prevented, the Nationalists are no nearer than they were in 1949 to exercising authority over all of China. The Communists are still excluded from the United Nations, but this fact has not deterred them from vigorously developing their diplomacy outside that body. Furthermore, it looks increasingly as if the United Nations will vote in favor of seating Peking in the not too distant future. While China's neighbors have been protected from direct attacks, the Chinese Communists, through both overt political action and support of subversion, have steadily expanded their influence in certain countries, and others have been responsive to friendly Chinese overtures. The Chinese, to be sure, have had their failures as well as their successes; nevertheless, their contacts and influence have obviously grown. This has been attributable only in part to the workings of Communist ideology and tactics; China's growing power and active diplomacy have been equally important.

Since the Korean War, both Communist China and the United States have attempted to avoid direct military conflict; however, both have also opposed direct accommodation. The United States has seen Communist China develop as a regional power but has been reluctant to admit that some of the assumptions on which American policy toward China was originally based may no longer be valid. It is this fact that led Senator Fulbright in March 1964 to speak of the increasing divergence between "myth and reality" in United States policy and to say: "Particularly with respect to China, an elaborate vocabulary of make-believe has become compulsory in both official and public discussion." Mr. Fulbright declared that "we are committed, with respect to China and other areas in Asia, to inflexible policies of long standing from which we hesitate to depart because of the attribution to these policies of an aura of mystical sanctity." [5]

The dilemma is due partly to the problems we face, but it is also partly of our own making, even though emotional attitudes and partisan feelings have recently diminished. Some commitments have been undertaken without adequate appreciation of their consequences. We have been reluctant to recognize that some of Communist China's aspirations may be legitimate while others are not. We have denied ourselves flexibility by refusing to consider a variety of policy alternatives. And we have not been able to gain or hold the support of many other nations for the essential features of our present policy.

The problem is undeniably complicated. Peking, on its part, has shown no sign of moderation or conciliation. At present, its hostility is intense, and this hostility is cultivated and served by an efficient and tightly controlled Communist apparatus that is calculating and unyielding. With such an adversary, accommodation is certainly difficult and may even be dangerous. If, as both the Chinese Communists and the most extreme anti-Communists contend, the hostility between the two worlds is absolute, there is obviously no possibility of compromise. But the United States has not really tried to test whether or not this is in fact the case; and even if it is the case now, we must in developing our policies at least keep in mind the possibility of a different future.

[5] Address of March 25, 1964, of which excerpts may be found in *The New York Times*, March 26, 1964. This address was incorporated and expanded in Senator Fulbright's book, *Old Myths and New Realities* (New York: Random House, 1964), pp. 37-38.

CHAPTER EIGHT

United States Strategic Policy and Commitments in Asia

Even though the People's Republic of China today is not militarily able to threaten the United States directly, it clearly poses a serious challenge to the international order on which the freedom, peace, and security of the United States and its allies rest. This challenge creates a major strategic problem for the United States—most specifically in Asia, for it is in Asia that Communist China's influence is greatest and its force can be most effectively applied.

The character of the Chinese challenge creates a significant element of uncertainty about the nature of the strategic problem in Asia. While this challenge contains an important military component, it is not primarily military—despite China's possession of substantial conventional strength and the beginnings of a nuclear capacity.

Nevertheless, the possibility of the People's Republic of China using military force cannot be ignored. The Chinese Communists have demonstrated on several occasions, notably in Korea and in Tibet, against India, and twice (1954 and 1958) against the offshore islands, that they have an ability to use, or threaten to use, military force to achieve some of their goals. The takeover of Taiwan—which Peking regards as necessary to complete the Chinese civil war—would almost certainly have been attempted by force had it not been for American support for the defense of the island. No one can say with certainty what other areas might have felt the direct impact of Chinese military power had the leaders in Peking felt that force could be applied with impunity, although they have probably calculated, with at least some reason, that in the troubled areas of Asia on China's periphery, indirect methods of exerting Chinese influence have generally been preferable to direct military actions which involve greater risks.

All Asian countries today are militarily much weaker than China. Only Japan and possibly India have the potential to counterbalance or to challenge Communist China's existing military superiority. But Japan has not felt militarily threatened in any direct sense and has not been disposed to build up large armed forces, while India has been preoccupied with problems in the subcontinent of South Asia.

Therefore, the United States, which has made far-ranging commitments throughout the area, has provided the essential military strength to balance the power centered in Peking. Not only has the United States committed powerful forces of its own in Asia; it has also worked with and through those Asian governments which have objectives similar to our own in the effort to establish and maintain an effective defense system. The defense agreements which the United States has made with these countries, the arrangements for military bases, the training of Asian military personnel, and the provision of large quantities of military supplies and equipment have been designed not only to build up local military strength that would otherwise have been lacking but also to serve as tangible evidence of the United States' commitments to the security of the area and its determination to help in the defense of the area. We have hoped that these military measures would contribute to the increased political stability and security necessary for peaceful development.

In assessing the strategic balance and the military problems in Asia, the United States has had to consider the Soviet Union as well as China. In fact, postwar Soviet behavior in Chinese areas such as Manchuria and nearby areas such as North Korea, the Soviet Union's acquisition of nuclear weapons in 1949, and Soviet actions leading to the outbreak of the Korean War in June 1950 appeared far more threatening in the years from 1945 to 1950 than any developments in China.

Then, however, following the establishment of the new Peking regime in 1949, the formation of the Sino-Soviet alliance in early

1950, and the Chinese Communist intervention in Korea later that year, the strategic problems posed by the Russians and the Chinese appeared to merge into a single picture. Before long, the situation changed further, and it was the Chinese rather than the Russians who were seen as the main immediate threat to stability in Asia, even though our strategic power continued to be designed primarily to counterbalance Soviet strength.

The conflict between Moscow and Peking that has developed since the late 1950s has vastly altered the military relationship between the two, however, and today we are dealing with two countries which, while both presenting challenges to our interests, are themselves competitors for influence in Asia and elsewhere. In Asia, therefore, we now seek both to contain China, politically and militarily, and to maintain positions that contribute to the strategic deterrence of the Soviet Union, which, unlike China, is militarily capable of menacing us massively and directly.

Evolution of United States Policy

Although, as the Chinese civil war drew to a close in 1949, the United States proceeded cautiously to adjust its security policies and commitments to the changing situation in Asia, we were cool at the start to suggestions for collective defense arrangements in the Pacific such as those as put forward at different times by President Elpidio Quirino of the Philippines, President Syngman Rhee of Korea, and Generalissimo Chiang Kai-shek on Taiwan. When the Chinese Communists' victory was imminent, the NATO agreement for the Atlantic area and Western Europe had just been concluded, and Secretary of State Acheson asserted, on May 18, 1949, that the United States was "not currently considering participation in any further special collective defense arrangements." [1] The main focus of United States security policies was on Europe, and the European countries were in no mood to make commitments in the distant Far East. In the United States as well as Europe, moreover, there were doubts that much would be

[1] *Department of State Bulletin*, v. 20, May 29, 1949, p. 696.

gained by collective arrangements with new governments whose future was very uncertain.

While the White Paper on China, issued in August 1949, recognized the possibility of new security problems arising from the Chinese Communists' victory, it did not attempt to outline any dramatic new American strategy to meet them. Instead, the Department of State simply stated that:

. . . should the Communist regime lend itself to the aims of Soviet Russian imperialism and attempt to engage in aggression against China's neighbors, we and the other members of the United Nations would be confronted by a situation violative of the principles of the United Nations Charter and threatening international peace and security.[2]

In short, the United States moved toward ending its direct involvement in China's troubles and, instead of attempting to prescribe future policy toward China, merely expressed its hope that a favorable evolution of the situation would gradually take place. As was indicated before, Taiwan's loss to the new Communist government in Peking was anticipated by President Truman in his statement of January 5, 1950.[3]

Elsewhere, we did take some preliminary steps to strengthen our position on the periphery of China, particularly in Japan, Korea, and the Philippines. At the time, though, these measures were directed more against what was perceived to be the Soviet threat than against any clearly conceived sense of challenge from China. The implications of China's emergence as a Communist power were not yet fully grasped. Nor were the scope and consequences of decolonization in Asia fully anticipated.

On January 12, 1950, however, Secretary of State Acheson did outline a defensive position that was apparently designed to help stabilize the new situation on the basis of a redefined configuration of political power in Asia that accepted the loss of China, presumably including Taiwan, to communism.[4] In doing so, he stated that the "defensive perimeter" of the United States now ran along a line stretching from the Aleutian Islands to Japan, the

[2] Secretary Acheson's Letter of Transmittal, *United States Relations with China* (Washington, D.C.: GPO, August 1949), p. xvii.
[3] See above, p. 108.
[4] See above, pp. 108-109.

Ryukyus, and the Philippines. "So far as the military security of other areas in the Pacific is concerned," he said, "it must be clear that no person can guarantee these areas against military attack. But it must also be clear that such a guarantee is hardly sensible or necessary within the realm of practical relationship." This statement was widely interpreted as excluding from American protection not only Taiwan but also South Korea, where we were already reducing our commitments, and other areas on the mainland. If hostile attacks were to occur outside the defensive perimeter as defined, "the initial reliance must be on the people attacked to resist it" plus the commitments of the United Nations' members acting under the Charter.

Secretary Acheson also warned that we should not "become obsessed with military considerations" and stressed the political dangers of subversion. With the experience of China obviously fresh in his mind, he said that American aid cannot be the sole defense anywhere, although it can be helpful if the local will to resist is strong. He reaffirmed the United States' special obligations to the Philippines but declared that "elsewhere in Southeast Asia, the limits of what we can do are to help where we are wanted."

Any hope that the United States could draw a neat line that would both deter aggression and define the limits of its commitments was violently shaken, however, by the North Korean invasion of South Korea, which took place in mid-1950 with the encouragement and backing of the Soviet Union. Even though the United States government had failed to include Korea specifically in its "defensive perimeter"—a fact which may inadvertently have encouraged the Russians and North Koreans to believe there would be no American response—this clear act of military aggression was viewed as a major challenge to basic concepts of collective security and therefore as a threat of serious proportions. The American reaction was prompt. Consequently, within six months of Secretary Acheson's policy statement of January 1950, the United States was already militarily engaged, together with other members of the United Nations, beyond the defensive perimeter which he had defined.

Initially, the Chinese were not directly involved in the Korean

War and therefore were not the primary consideration in our calculations. We were preoccupied most of all by the need to block the extension of Soviet influence, protect the security of Japan, uphold the reputation of the United States, and support the principles of collective security.

However, even if Chinese troops had not intervened, as they ultimately did in October 1950, the Korean War would inevitably have had a large impact on United States strategic and military policies toward all of Asia and specifically toward China. Taiwan, which we had written off earlier in the year, was placed under American protection, partly because of logistical considerations related to the war in Korea but also because a new overall strategic situation was taking shape and it was no longer possible to look upon a possible Chinese Communist attack on Taiwan simply as the final and logical consequence of the Chinese civil war.

The outbreak of the Korean War and the United States' involvement in the defense of Taiwan were thus the decisive events that helped to shape a new American strategic policy for the area as a whole.

In addition, both the conduct of the war and the dismissal of General MacArthur underlined several important facts. In the war, the United States demonstrated that it was able and willing to sustain a strong Far Eastern policy and that despite its disengagement from the China mainland, it was prepared to be involved even on the Asian continent itself when such an involvement was considered essential for the protection of American interests. The protracted and indecisive fighting in Korea also demonstrated the risks and costs of heavy direct military involvement on the continent, and as later American behavior in areas such as Laos indicated, the Korean experience did not predispose the United States to intervene indiscriminately with its own forces in all Asian conflicts.

The Chinese intervention in Korea also proved to the United States that the Peking government was willing to make major sacrifices when it felt its vital security and political interests to be threatened. At the same time, the so-called "human sea" tactics of the Chinese created an exaggerated image in the minds of many Americans of a Chinese Communist regime ready to threaten much of Asia with hordes of troops. As a result, there was not only a heightened sense of a Chinese threat but also a widespread feeling that the United States should not again become committed to a direct massive encounter with Chinese troops.

Finally, the Korean War, which was waged throughout as a limited conflict, made clear the reluctance of the United States to take military action directly against Communist China. The American decision not to extend the war into China itself was influenced by many considerations, including uncertainty regarding Soviet intentions in Asia and Europe, restraints exercised by other governments that supported us in the United Nations, and our basic desire to avoid using nuclear weapons. All these factors have continued to influence our military policies in Asia.

The Korean War, as was stated above, left its mark not only on American attitudes and policies toward China but also on United States security strategy throughout all of Asia and the Pacific. The Chinese Communists were now widely viewed not merely as unfriendly but as violently hostile and aggressive. This new image of China gave impetus to the conclusion of a series of new security arrangements with countries on China's periphery. In the latter half of 1951, a security treaty between the United States and the Philippines was signed, the Anzus agreement with Australia and New Zealand was concluded, and a peace treaty with Japan was signed. In 1953, the United States concluded a defense treaty with the Republic of Korea, and in December 1954, it signed a mutual defense treaty with the Republic of China. In short, the attempt at partial disengagement, which had been briefly attempted in late 1949 and early 1950, was abandoned, and the United States now confronted the People's Republic of China with a clear policy of positive containment involving commitments on almost the entire East Asian periphery of China.

There remained Southeast Asia. The victory of the Chinese Communists on the mainland and the Korean War both stimulated increased American interest in Southeast Asia, but it was not until the French defeat at Dien Bien Phu in April 1954, only a few months after the conclusion of the Korean armistice, that the United States' major new role in Southeast Asia fully emerged. Some people tended to see the deteriorating situation in that area in oversimplified terms as being the result almost solely of a Chinese Communist drive for hegemony in Asia, but even those with a more sophisticated view, who recognized the indigenous revolutionary forces at work, were alarmed by the dangers arising from the instability of the region. As early as April 16, 1953, President Eisenhower had said that what was needed was not only peace in Korea and an armistice there but "no less importantly, an end to the direct and indirect attacks upon the security of Indo-China and Malaya. For any armistice in Korea that merely released aggressive armies to attack elsewhere would be a fraud." [5]

American fears of Chinese expansionism in Southeast Asia led to the conclusion of still another security agreement, therefore, and on September 8, 1954, the Manila pact creating SEATO was signed by Great Britain, France, the United States, Australia, New Zealand, Thailand, the Philippines, and Pakistan. This treaty represented an effort to organize the defenses of Southeast Asia on a much more systematic basis. Now that the Geneva agreements, which earlier in the year had brought a halt to fighting in Vietnam, had divided Vietnam into a northern half controlled by the Communist Viet Minh and a southern half under non-Communist Vietnamese control, SEATO was designed to stabilize the situation and prevent further Communist expansion—to draw a line which, together with those drawn in South Korea and in the Taiwan Strait, would establish three firm positions on China's periphery that could halt the outward spread of Chinese Communist influence.

In fact, SEATO never developed a fully integrated military policy or command, and in some situations the allies went pretty much their own way. During the later crises in Laos and Vietnam, for example, the primary responsibility for action was actually borne by the United States, not by SEATO.

SEATO never became a very effective alliance because the assumptions on which it was based did not fully take into account the facts of the existing situation. Its purpose was to thwart China's ambitions, even though the People's Republic of China was not specifically named in the SEATO agreement. However, in the years since 1954 China has not actually been openly involved in Southeast Asia in "aggression by means of armed attack," as

[5] *Department of State Bulletin*, v. 28, April 27, 1953, p. 601.

envisioned in the treaty, and despite Peking's encouragement and support of revolutionary forces, it has been difficult in the conflicts in Laos and Vietnam to identify China specifically as the main "threat to sovereignty or political independence by means other than armed attack," which the treaty also tried to provide for.

Since the 1951–54 period, when the United States pursued policies which some critics characterize as suffering from "pactomania," the formal security arrangements of the United States in the Asian area have undergone only minor changes. The security agreement with Japan was amended by mutual consent in a new agreement signed in 1961. Special American assurances were given to Thailand in 1962 as a result of SEATO's collective weakness in dealing with the situation in Laos, which was then causing Thailand so much concern. The same year, in response to China's attack on India, a program of military assistance and technical advice to the Indians was initiated despite protests from Pakistan, which itself had been a beneficiary of United States military assistance since 1954 but feared the build-up of Indian military power and responded by increasing its ties with Peking while it still formally remained a member of the anti-Communist CENTO and SEATO alliances.

The two crises in the Taiwan Strait, in 1954–55 and 1958 respectively, revealed still other strains in the alliance system but did not significantly alter the strategic picture. These two crises underscored both the United States' determination to defend Taiwan and its desire not to be drawn into a war against Communist China. It became apparent during these crises, as during others, that while the United States shared certain important interests with its Asian allies, the creation of military alliances did not in and of itself create a complete identity of interests.

The quickened pace of Communist-led activities in Laos and Vietnam beginning in 1959 involved the United States even more deeply in Asia, however, as American forces were gradually drawn into more direct participation in the task of combating political subversion and revolutionary warfare. Our network of military pacts, and even our assistance programs, obviously did not fully solve the problems of guaranteeing stability and security in these areas. In fact, except for a brief period during China's limited attack on India at the end of 1962, it seemed clear that the main danger now was not, as had been believed in the early 1950s, that masses of Chinese military forces would cross into their neighbors' territory; rather, it was that indigenous revolutionary forces backed by indirect Chinese support might seize power in internal struggles.

While a direct American-Chinese military confrontation was not impossible, the clear superiority of American strategic power, deployed with the assistance of the allies of the United States, made this kind of military confrontation unlikely. American strategic power could not be automatically effective, however, in making strong governments out of weak ones, in countering local subversion, or in building the social and economic as well as political foundations of regional order and stability. These tasks required new military and political instruments and new tactics focused on the problems of combating revolutionary war.

Beginning in 1964, the United States vastly increased its military assistance to South Vietnam and participated more directly in the fight against the Viet Cong in the south. Then in early 1965, it started attacking bases and supply routes in North Vietnam. For the first time, the United States was now striking militarily against not only the centers of Communist insurgency in a local conflict but also against some of its external sources of support, in North Vietnam. At the same time, it was limiting its actions to avoid conflict with China, which appeared equally desirous of avoiding any direct confrontation with the United States. The United States was also attempting to adapt and use its superiority in modern weaponry, including air power, to counter the advantages of its adversaries in the villages and rice fields.

The Dangers and the Response

During the years immediately ahead, there is little likelihood that the Chinese will choose to make a direct military challenge to United States forces unless, as apparently was the case in Korea, Chinese leaders feel that the basic security or survival of their regime requires it or unless an unavoidable confrontation develops as a result of serious miscalculation by both sides. It is difficult to visualize situations in which either country would believe that a direct, massive military clash would involve more gains than risks or losses. China's conventional power, while large and reasonably effective in conventional, pre-nuclear terms, is circumscribed in important ways by the weak industrial base of the country, which limits the modernization, mobility, and technological capacity of the armed forces. Strained relations with the Soviet Union have deprived Peking of Soviet military aid, have placed in doubt the meaning of the security treaty between the two countries and the degree to which the Chinese might rely on the Soviet nuclear shield, and have even created a potential threat to China along the extensive Sino-Soviet border. Finally, the strategic deployment and mobility of United States forces, to the east and south of China, and the immense American nuclear capability, against which the Chinese have no effective defense, must certainly give the Chinese leaders pause. Because China's nuclear strength will not really be significant for some time, Peking's leaders probably realize that attempts to use it against weak adversaries would be an invitation to devastating retaliation from the United States.

Few of the restraints on Communist China originate from its Asian neighbors, however. For the most part, these countries remain weak and divided. China has little to fear from any of them, unless Japan should rebuild its military strength, embark on aggression, and once again turn its attention to the mainland. However, American bases on the territory of China's Asian neighbors do play a role in the American-supported security system which surrounds China, and consequently, it is a major Chinese Communist aim to eliminate them as a step toward eliminating the American presence from all of Asia and the Pacific.

One can only speculate as to whether the Chinese Communists would be likely to use their military power more than they have to date as a direct instrument for extending their influence in Asia if the restraints were fewer and the opportunities greater. But it seems unlikely that they would embark on general military expansionism under any foreseeable circumstances short of general war, although they might well use their military forces for limited purposes along China's borders, as in the case of the attack on India. The simple fact of growing Chinese power does enhance the spread of Chinese influence, however. China's neighbors do not need the presence on their soil of Chinese military forces to remind them of their respective power positions. The image of millions of Chinese soldiers swarming into other parts of Asia, therefore, does not reveal the basic problem. That problem is the rise of China as a power in Asia and the spread of Chinese Communist influence by a wide variety of means other than military.

The geopolitical situation, China's strengths and weaknesses, and Communist doctrine combine to favor nonmilitary means as the principal instruments of Chinese policy. The Chinese Communist leaders have made clear that they hope to extend China's influence not only to its neighbors but around the world through the promotion of "people's war," the encouragement of subversion, the development of diplomacy, trade, and aid, and various forms of political warfare. These are not only the weapons that China has most readily available but also those that China's opponents often have the most difficulty in combating. The Chinese leaders in Peking, by pressing ahead with communism's revolutionary message and techniques, are attempting to take advantage of the strong sentiments of anti-colonialism, anti-imperialism, and in some cases racialism that exist in many new countries, and they are trying to exploit not only instability but also collectivist trends that they see in many places. They do not confine their attention to Communist movements alone. Where possible, they also try to align with and manipulate local nationalist movements and to exploit any climate of sympathy or sense of identification which may exist in forms favorable to Chinese Communist strivings and accomplishments. The Chinese have thus been able in some situations to extend their influence and advance their purposes with relative economy of effort, limited involvement, and minimum risks to China's security. They cannot be sure, however, that the forces which they may help set in motion or support through such policies will remain under their control.

If American forces were to be removed from Asia, the Taiwan Strait would be the area where there would be the most clear-cut danger of overt Chinese Communist military action. Elsewhere, Chinese involvement is less direct, and the danger of open military conflict less real. However, the Asian situation is still generally so unstable that one cannot rule out the possibility of military struggles developing which might involve Communist China in conflicts with other Asian countries. The American military presence in Asia is intended to prevent such conflicts from occurring, to help create situations of stability which will minimize the danger of them developing, and to counterbalance Chinese force if they do occur.

Politically, the United States system of alliances and bases in Asia serves as tangible evidence of a continuing American commitment. However, it involves political costs as well as advantages. These vary a good deal from country to country. In Korea, American forces are still involved in the aftermath of the 1950–53 war, and there is little doubt that in the situation there any sign of American withdrawal at present might be accompanied by serious trouble in South Korea. The present generation of South Korean leaders, having tasted Communist rule, have had their fill and do not want to repeat the experience. While not having abandoned all hope for ultimate reunification of the country, they are today preoccupied with the problems of nation-building in the south, while United States troops protect their independence and deter the possibility of attack from the north. Although it may be questionable whether the United States should look forward to maintaining this military presence on the Asian continent permanently, disengagement from Korea is difficult to contemplate at present and probably will not be possible unless and until there is a marked improvement in the Asian situation as a whole or in the relations between the two halves of Korea under conditions that are not now foreseeable.

Security problems relating to Japan involve many political uncertainties that will come into clearer focus before 1970, when the existing security treaty will be up for reconsideration. At present, the security treaty symbolizes important political ties between the United States and Japan and provides the latter with protection and the former with bases of some value. However, in looking to the future, various Japanese groups favor widely differing policies, ranging from closer ties with the United States to neutralism and accommodation with Communist China. If opposition to a continued American military presence in Japan and to American control of Okinawa determined future Japanese policy, the result might be movement toward neutralism and the ending of the security treaty, which would have serious implications for United States policy. There is strong sentiment among important Japanese groups, hitherto restrained by official policy and somewhat counterbalanced by opposing groups in Japan, favoring closer relations between Japan and the China mainland. Any major move in that direction would also have important effects on the American position. On the other hand, some Japanese, encouraged by China's acquisition of nuclear weapons, may in time begin to press for Japan's own rearmament. This development, too, would call for important adjustments in American policy. The political stakes involved in American-Japanese cooperation are obviously high. Militarily, Japan is in a position to provide support and facilities unmatched elsewhere in Asia. If close cooperation on the basis of real mutual interests can be continued in the future, it will contribute greatly to the security of Asia. In the context of close cooperation, it might well be desirable for Japan to play a role of increasing importance in Asia, economically, politically, and even militarily. However, Japanese neutralism and accommodation with Communist China would create new problems and dangers, as would any re-emergence of trends toward right-wing militarism or expansionism.

As a result of United States decisions at the time of the outbreak of the Korean War and subsequently, Taiwan is also a key element in our current Far Eastern policy. In the eyes of some, in fact, it has become, in a sense, the touchstone of our China policy. The specific American military commitments to Taiwan, however, are limited and defensive. Under the Mutual Defense Treaty of December 2, 1954,[6] the United States recognized that "an armed attack" directed against Taiwan or the Pescadores "would be dangerous to its own peace and safety" and "that it would act to meet the common danger in accordance with its constitutional processes." The offshore islands were consciously excluded from this guarantee, but by the congressional resolution signed by the President on January 29, 1955, "the securing and

---

[6] The treaty is reprinted in Peter V. Curl, ed., *Documents on American Foreign Relations, 1954* (New York: Harper and Brothers for the Council on Foreign Relations, 1955), pp. 360–362.

protection" of "related position and territories . . . now in friendly hands" were authorized if the President judged such measures "to be required or appropriate in assuring the defense of Formosa [Taiwan] and the Pescadores." [7]

Once the decision was reached to keep Taiwan out of Communist hands and to continue recognizing the government of the Republic of China as the only legal government of China, the American involvement in Taiwan, both political and military, steadily grew, and today, with the growing complexity of the United States' military position and commitments throughout Asia, Taiwan has come to play a significant role in our overall Far Eastern strategy, since it has been integrated into the area-wide system of supply lines, maintenance facilities, and deployment plans. The United States presence on Taiwan, which is situated midway between Japan, the Philippines, and the Indo-Chinese peninsula, is now related not only to the protection of Taiwan itself but also to the broad American-supported security system. However, United States military needs throughout the area are also served by extensive facilities in Japan, Okinawa, and the Philippines and by more limited ones elsewhere, and while there are clearly strong arguments for denying the Communists the use of Taiwan as a military base, the military value of the island should not be the only, or even the most important, factor determining our political objectives there. These, as will be discussed in a subsequent chapter, need to be carefully re-examined and redefined.

In Southeast Asia, the Chinese Communists have not to date directly intervened with military force as they have in Korea and in the Taiwan area. They have provided matériel, supplies, and advice to fellow revolutionaries and other friends in Vietnam and Laos and on occasion have exerted military pressures and made threats. But so far, at least, their overt military acts have been prudent, and the problems and challenges in the area can be attributed only in part to China. This fact is one among many reasons why it has been difficult to formulate and apply an appropriate American response to the dangers posed by the bitter strug-

[7] The resolution is reprinted in Paul E. Zinner, ed., *Documents on American Foreign Relations, 1955* (New York: Harper and Brothers for the Council on Foreign Relations, 1956), pp. 298–299.

gle in Vietnam. SEATO, which was intended to be the major instrument for coping with situations of this sort, was based on a presumed but by-no-means-complete identity of security interests among its members; moreover, it was really designed, as was stated before, to cope mainly with unambiguous aggression and military problems rather than with the complex problems of revolutionary war. SEATO has been largely ineffective in this situation, therefore, and the major responsibility for supporting the South Vietnamese regime has fallen on the United States.

Within the context of American strategic objectives generally and of American policy toward China, it is important that the Vietnam area not be allowed to fall under Chinese domination. This would probably be the case even if a non-Communist government ruled China, although it is even more so now because of the character and aims of the Peking regime. If the Chinese came to dominate the area, the consequences would be widely felt, and not in Southeast Asia alone. Such a development would certainly be a blow to American influence in other areas, and it would encourage rather than deter those who promote revolutionary violence in many unstable areas throughout the underdeveloped world. Whatever the degree of direct Chinese involvement, therefore, the United States and its friends could not but suffer from Communist victory by violence in Vietnam, and the effects would be not only political and psychological but strategic and military as well because the political losses would inevitably weaken many American military positions.

It is unrealistic to expect, however, that American policy can aim at the complete elimination of Chinese influence from the Vietnam area or from Southeast Asia as a whole. A look at the map and a cursory glance at history should make it clear that this would be not only difficult but probably impossible to achieve. In the long run, though, there are strong arguments in favor of limiting great power competition in Southeast Asia and perhaps even immunizing it from excessive outside interference—whether by China, the United States, or others—so that the countries there can develop without being viewed simply as strategic or political pawns of any other country.

It would be utopian to believe that this can be achieved in the near future. Nevertheless, while trying to deal with the immediate frustrations created by a complex and intractable situation and while accepting the necessity of American military intervention to insure the survival now of a non-Communist South Vietnam, the United States, in looking to the future, should not lose sight of the fact that a neutralized Vietnam and Southeast Asia would be preferable to an area of intense, continuing great power confrontation and conflict. There are, of course, many developments in the area over which we have no control and often little influence, so we of necessity have to adjust our course of action to events without losing sight of our basic interests and purposes.

Until recently, the United States saw no major Chinese military threat to the subcontinent of South Asia, but the Chinese attack on India in the fall of 1962 and renewed pressure on the border during the India–Pakistan crisis in 1965 have created uncertainty about the future. In 1962, the Chinese successfully demonstrated that, faced only with the relatively weak Indian defenses of the time, they were able to penetrate Indian territory almost at will. However, they carefully limited their actions and showed little desire to become heavily involved militarily in India itself. Having demonstrated their power, they soon withdrew and retained only limited territorial advantages. This episode served to stimulate the Indians to take more effective military measures, and it helped to induce the British, Americans, and Russians to assist the Indians in strengthening their defenses. It also induced the United States to explore possible means of strengthening its military posture in the Indian Ocean area, although the American government was cautious about becoming further involved in military commitments to Pakistan or India, with all the complications such commitments might entail. These complications became amply clear during the 1965 Indian–Pakistani conflict over Kashmir when Peking strongly supported the Pakistanis while Washington and Moscow both maintained neutral positions and pressed for a cease fire.

Both the Sino-Indian border episode of 1962 and the crisis of 1965 demonstrated once again that the United States' strategic striking power alone has only limited relevance in many Asian conflicts. And Pakistan's behavior in the two instances illustrated that formal alliances are often of limited significance and that even an ally of the United States may, if it believes it to be in its immediate interests, pursue policies of partial accommodation with the Chinese Communists.

Military Instruments and Political Purposes

It is easier to look back over the experience of recent years than to anticipate what lies ahead. Security problems relating to China have some continuing features, but there is a vast area of unpredictability due to shifting local situations and the impossibility of foretelling accurately the actual influence and effectiveness of various alternative American policies. It would be wrong to assume that there is always a "sure" or "right" approach which will insure the achievement of all our purposes. Many actions and many influences are at work, and in each situation that we confront, there are many interests, ambitions, and emotions besides our own. However, certain basic problems and needs can be defined with some confidence.

As an overall deterrent, we have and need strategic forces adequate to deter Communist China from major military adventures, to prevent Peking from engaging in nuclear blackmail, and to dissuade the Soviet Union from backing the Chinese. The credibility of such a deterrent and retaliatory force is already high in areas such as Taiwan and Korea, where there has already been a direct confrontation between Chinese and American military forces and a military line has been drawn. Elsewhere, as in Laos and Vietnam, any Chinese temptation to provide large-scale, overt support for "people's wars" may be checked by the fear that in any future direct clash the United States might not again, as during the Korean War, refrain from bombing targets in China. The vulnerability of China's new nuclear plants, which would be especially tempting targets in such a situation, doubtless gives Peking's leaders pause at present.

In addition to these strategic capabilities, the United States will also continue to need other naval, air, and land forces readily available for rapid deployment in the area. The availability of such forces has made it possible for us to inject our power and influence into critical situations such as those in Korea from 1950 on, in Thailand in 1962, and more recently in Vietnam. Our ability to take rapid, limited, and discriminating action, and to do it efficiently, is an important political as well as military asset.

In most cases, however, it must be recognized that American power must be used with self-restraint since indiscriminate use of our military strength can involve great political costs as well as military risks. In Vietnam, the United States has applied pressure on North Vietnam by direct attacks on sources of supplies for the Communist-led guerrillas in the south, but it would be a mistake to view this action as a precedent to be followed in all comparable situations or to escalate these attacks without restraint and extend them to sources of supply in China itself. To assume that military action against China would automatically bring an end to Communist-inspired revolutionary activities outside of China's borders not only would be a gross misunderstanding of the nature of China's influence and of the forces at work in Vietnam but would ignore the large risks of provoking major conflict without the prospect of commensurate gains. Military responses must be relevant to existing problems and situations, and there is little reason to believe that the use of our superior military power directly against China would be a useful way of attempting to solve either the refractory political problems in other countries or the long-term problem of dealing with the multifaceted Chinese challenge.

China's possession of the beginnings of a nuclear capability complicates but does not yet alter the basic strategic picture or call for dramatic new security measures. At present, there appear to be no strong reasons for deploying American nuclear weapons in Asian countries bordering on China. It is doubtful, in fact, whether any of these countries would want such weapons anyway. Attempts to involve non-Communist Asian nations in this way would probably require a higher degree of military cooperation than now exists, and they would introduce many complex problems of command and control such as those that have caused so much difficulty in NATO. Moreover, they would probably not strengthen the existing security arrangements or significantly bolster American nuclear capacities in Asia.

It is possible, however, that in time countries such as India and Japan, which possess the capability of manufacturing nuclear weapons, may be tempted to decide to join the nuclear club themselves, either for political reasons—to gain prestige—or because of a lack of confidence in American support. Such nuclear proliferation, in Asia or elsewhere, would be undesirable from the United States' point of view, and it might increase instability in the region rather than create a more stable balance. However, if the United States wishes to forestall such a development, it may have to make a special effort to convince countries such as India and Japan that both their security needs and desire for political status can be satisfied without possession of nuclear weapons. Unless such an effort is made, simple American disapproval might not affect their policies any more than it did in the case of France. Formal American guarantees of protection against Chinese nuclear attack might be one alternative, but it is not certain that they would be welcomed. The Indians, in particular, might not want to alienate the Russians by moving closer to the Americans in this fashion. However, should the nuclear danger from China increase, we may encounter certain situations in which the Russians and the Americans may make common cause, if only tacitly, in the Asian area.

As was indicated before, the Chinese have argued, during a period when they have had no nuclear capability or a minor one, for the creation of a nuclear-free zone in the Asian and Pacific area. Their motives in making these proposals have been clear: to reduce the striking power of their adversaries without weakening their own position, to diminish the confidence that America's friends have in United States guarantees, and to score points in the propaganda war by speaking out against nuclear weapons. These purposes are not compatible with American interests, so it is difficult at present to see what interest the United States would have in agreeing to the Chinese proposals. In all probability, moreover, the Chinese would not be satisfied with a nuclear-free zone restricted to Asia. The range and flexibility of modern missiles are such that missiles based in the United States and the Polaris submarines can reach China, and Peking might well insist that they too be included in any agreement for the Pacific and Asian area. Chou En-lai's proposals of August 1, 1960, did, in fact, include the United States. Acceptance of such proposals would, of course, affect the entire American strategic defense system.

Nevertheless, if tacit or explicit agreements to limit China's nuclear development could be reached or Chinese pledges not to pursue policies of nuclear proliferation in Asia could be achieved, it might conceivably be to the United States' interest to consider accepting limitations on the use of nuclear weapons in Asia, especially since even existing restraints make it unlikely that they would actually be used in most situations.

There are strong political and psychological as well as military reasons, however, for maintaining a significant American military presence in Asia—including, at present, a nuclear striking force. Just as in Europe, United States installations and forces in Asia provide a tangible symbol of our commitments to the countries in the area, a warning to our adversaries, and a reassurance to our friends. There are obvious political drawbacks involved, but the simple pursuit of some formula for major military withdrawal would not solve them and might, in fact, create new and even more serious difficulties.

The Chinese Communists, it should be noted, have repeatedly insisted that they will not be bound by any arms-control agreements negotiated without their participation, while the United States has asserted its willingness to include the Chinese in such negotiations at an appropriate time.[8] It is not clear at what point Washington would consider Chinese Communist participation to be useful and desirable. The question is a complicated one, involving many political as well as technical problems. It is difficult to argue that the painful negotiations that have gone on between the United States, the Soviet Union, and other countries during recent years would necessarily have been advanced by the participation of the Chinese. Nor can one argue convincingly that to date China's absence has hampered progress of the negotiations. The Chinese demonstrated by their refusal to sign the limited nuclear test-ban treaty of 1963 that they were presently unwilling to be bound by any arms-control agreements which might impair China's drive to achieve status as a great power and to develop nuclear strength. However, there will come a time when, if certain types of arms-control measures are to be seri-

[8] See above, pp. 86–88, and p. 125.

ously considered, an effort will have to be made to include Communist China, for some measures would obviously be impractical without Chinese participation. It remains to be seen whether Peking's leaders will in time show a greater willingness to consider such measures.

However, a direct confrontation of American and Chinese armed strength is not at the heart of the difficulties between the two countries. As was stated above, Chinese armed forces do not now directly threaten the United States at all, and the danger of their large-scale use against China's neighbors is limited as long as the United States' commitments to resist Chinese aggression remain firm.

If one thinks only of the present arms balance and the short-run hopes and prospects of arms-control negotiations themselves, therefore, one might argue that because of all the above factors there is no urgent need to include the People's Republic of China in the negotiations. There remain, however, the broader and longer-run political questions concerning the pro's and con's of including the People's Republic of China in various international councils such as the United Nations [9] and arms-control forums— whether it is wiser to exclude or to try gradually to include the Chinese Communists in the most important institutions that have been established by the international community.

Although the United States' alliances and bases have indeed been important means of extending American power into the Asian area, there is also another side to the picture. The present security system has evolved in response to changing circumstances over a period of years and reflects a variety of motives— the fight against communism, defense against Communist China, the desire for a strategic advantage over the Soviet Union, the bolstering of old friends, and the making of new ones. As a result, these arrangements have sometimes grown or endured without adequate re-examination of the threats to be met, the motives of those seeking our support, or the best means to achieve desired ends. Moreover, their existence on occasion seems to have shaped policy rather than been determined by it. Some Asians have tended to view them as undesirable intrusions that may actually, at times, have accentuated rather than reduced their perils. In

[9] See Chapter 11.

some cases, our military presence has tended to intensify domestic strains in Asian countries and to exacerbate relations between neighbors by altering the local balance of power. Overemphasis on military matters in situations where the principal difficulties have been political and economic has sometimes meant that we and our friends have been misguided in our efforts and have misspent our energies. Especially in the 1950s, the sharp line that we tended to draw between those nations prepared to "line up" with us and other nations which insisted on being nonaligned, even if they shared many of our values and goals, sometimes ignored local political realities and relationships in the Asian area and overlooked the fact that our own basic interests might be involved regardless of the formal political alignments which existed. These factors, as well as other considerations, suggest the need for a re-examination of what we want to accomplish in Asia and the instruments we require.

On February 18, 1965, when American military involvement in Vietnam was rapidly growing, Secretary of Defense McNamara told the House Armed Services Committee that the choice for the United States was "not simply whether to continue our efforts to keep South Vietnam free and independent but, rather, whether to continue our struggle to halt Communist expansion in Asia." [10] This statement raises a question as to how such a struggle is to be waged and to what extent it can or should involve direct American military participation. Too sweeping military commitments or involvements may prove to be politically unsound or militarily unfeasible if we consider the variety of conditions in the several Asian countries. Even though military security and domestic peace and order are certainly essential for the Asian countries, communism cannot best be fought at all times and places primarily by military means. Moreover, as has already been emphasized, China's influence in the area does not derive mainly from military threats, and the use of Chinese armed forces outside its borders is not now the major instrument of Peking's policy.

The value of the major American bases and alliances in Asia, thus, needs to be reassessed in relation to our strategic objectives and our expectations during the coming years. For example, even

[10] *The New York Times*, February 19, 1965.

though SEATO has a record of some useful accomplishments, it has obviously not fulfilled all its missions and does not function as it was originally intended to do. Indeed, the basic security interests and policies of its members have been too disparate for all its major purposes to be fulfilled. Changes in this or other security arrangements, however, should be made only with great prudence and over a period of time so that the inevitable tremors which will accompany the changes will be limited and so that whatever new arrangements emerge will be well suited to a clear conception of political purposes.

Past experience does not support the view that new multilateral arrangements drawing together diverse Asian and Western nations are likely to provide the most satisfactory way of dealing with present difficulties. There is an insufficient sense of unity among the Asian countries, the interests of the European countries in contributing to Asian security remain to be clarified, and the disparity between the position of the United States and that of the other interested countries is too great.

In working out our future security policies and arrangements, this country needs to take full account of the requirements and attitudes of others. Perhaps this can best be done by making varied arrangements tailored to fit individual situations rather than through comprehensive schemes that may look attractive on paper but do not correspond to the realities of the situations. The practical experience acquired in coping with the main military crises of recent years—in Korea, the Taiwan Strait, Vietnam, Laos, and India—indicates that each of these situations had to be met in a different way even though in each case the United States bore the major burden of outside support. No general formula was applicable, and much had to be improvised. Even where the United Nations played a useful role, it was generally a supporting rather than a primary one.

Not all these American operations have been outstanding successes; nevertheless, it is by no means certain that reliance on other United Nations measures or multilateral regional procedures would have been more effective. International collaboration should certainly be encouraged as part of the whole United Nations peace-keeping effort. But under existing circumstances, the United Nations cannot be relied on to cope effectively with every contingency, and in some situations, international procedures may be too cumbersome and may hamper both the United States and its allies in the pursuit of their best interests. These interests, it is true, include the objective of a broader sharing of international responsibility, but this can only be achieved where there is a community of outlook with regard both to goals and to the best methods of attaining them. Such a consensus does not now exist with regard either to Communist China or to the whole complex area of political warfare. Appraisals of the threat from China differ, and even where they are similar, there is not always agreement on what should be done.

In a broad political sense, on the other hand, our effort should be a multilateral one, aimed at establishing an international political consensus compatible with our policies. If such a consensus can be achieved, it may then be possible for international measures for peace-keeping to play a larger and more useful role in Asia.

American security guarantees should also be selectively attuned to the problems that we face. They must take into full account the danger that ill-conceived security agreements may undermine the achievement of some political objectives, either within individual countries or in relations between countries. For example, some types of alliance arrangements which the United States might support may risk the impairment of the important political objective of encouraging greater regional cooperation among the Asian countries. The establishment of bases and the dispatch of armed forces should not be seized upon as the easiest way of meeting virtually any difficult political situation. We should have learned by now that there is no easy substitute for political wisdom, skill, and sensitivity in the execution of policy.

From time to time, the suggestion is made that there should be a more active use of Asian military forces to help insure the security of the area. However, the weaknesses in the area are too great, the divisive tendencies and rivalries too strong, and the neighboring power of China too persuasive for regional cooperation in military matters to be very significant at the present time. Moreover, many proposals that national Asian military forces in excess of needs at home be made available for use elsewhere often seem to be divorced from political reality (although Korean troops now in Vietnam do appear to be serving a useful purpose).

The suggestion is periodically advanced, for example, that the Chinese Nationalist troops on Taiwan be employed elsewhere, and it is not for lack of desire on the part of the Nationalist government that these forces were not used in Korea and have not been invited to play a role in Vietnam. However, clearly the political complications would be too great, and the political risks and costs would far outweigh the conceivable military gains. If the United States wishes to enhance the influence of the Nationalist government in Asia, the use of Nationalist troops abroad is surely not the way to do it. Nor is it an effective way of challenging Chinese Communist power. Neither American interests nor the security of the area would be enhanced by introducing additional complications into what are already extremely difficult situations.

The case of the Chinese Nationalists, to be sure, poses special difficulties, but even if one views the problem more generally, it is hard to see an effective system of regional military cooperation developing in the near future. In all probability, the United States will continue to bear the major overall responsibility, and it should not seek unwise short cuts to reduce its own burdens.

Nor can we expect much direct support from our European allies, who have played a diminishing role in Asia ever since we entered actively on the scene at a time when their power and influence were declining. When the SEATO agreement was concluded, after the French defeat in Indo-China, both the British and the French joined in it, but it was not long before the French began going their own way in Asia, even though they continued to retain nominal membership in the organization. The British have maintained a special interest in the Commonwealth countries in Asia, as they have demonstrated by their actions during crises in South Asia and by their support of Malaysia in its confrontation with Indonesia, and they have retained, perhaps precariously but with clear American approval, their positions in Singapore and Hong Kong. There have also been other situations, in Korea and more recently in Vietnam, where the United States, for a variety of reasons, has sought the participation of its European allies, if only in a token capacity. Above all, we have wanted to demonstrate to the Asian countries that the United States has not stood alone.

Clearly, however, both the interests and the strength of our European allies are now more limited than our own in Asia, and we have been reluctant to bind our own policies and actions to meet their wishes. In addition, there have been some sharp differences between us. For example, differences with the French have been great, not only over Laos and Vietnam but also over China policy—a fact that was dramatized by French recognition of the Peking government early in 1964. Consequently, NATO, which has had difficulty enough maintaining cohesion when dealing with European problems, has not provided a very useful forum within which there could be systematic coordination of strategic policies in Asia. To the extent possible, we should certainly seek to reconcile our differences with our European allies, but we are not going to achieve this end by summoning them to share our responsibilities in Asia.

Even if the obstacles already mentioned did not exist, there would be obvious drawbacks to approaching our main tasks in Asia through the vehicle of a Western military alliance. In the eyes of many if not most Asians, it would arouse deep fears of revived Western imperialism.

The situation might change, it is true, if China develops major strategic power capable of directly threatening both the United States and Europe—a development that might affect the resources which the United States could make available to meet its European commitments—or if China challenges the Soviet Union to such an extent that the balance of forces between the Soviet Union and the NATO powers is significantly affected. In the immediate future, however, it is not easy to see any real possibility that NATO will play a significant part in handling the strategic problems of the Far East.

In the long run, the European nations will certainly be concerned if Chinese power and policy aggressively challenge the peace, destroy security, and upset the balance of power in the Asian area. For the present, most of them do not see this possibility as imminent. If European nations felt that the Soviet danger was increasing, some might even welcome a strong China on the Soviet Union's Asian frontier. Conversely, at least some European nations may tend to look increasingly to the Soviet Union to do its share in offsetting growing Chinese power.[11] At any rate, all tend to see limited roles for themselves in Asia at the moment.

In summary, there are certain things that American military strength can accomplish effectively in Asia and others that it cannot accomplish at all. It can deter military aggression if the United States has sufficient political will to do so, and it can stop such overt aggression should it occur. It can help immensely to provide external protection for countries that require a period of peace in order to build up their national strength and unity. On the other hand, military power cannot make strong nations out of weak ones or create political resolve in countries that have none, and it must be combined with political measures to cope with guerrilla warfare. It cannot prevent one nation from extending its influence over others through political, diplomatic, cultural, and other nonmilitary means.

If the task of containing Communist China could be accomplished by military means alone, it would not be too difficult. However, the task is not simply military. China's strength and influence make themselves felt in a variety of different ways, and military instruments are simply not capable of coping with many of them.

In short, the United States can establish a balance between itself and China, but doing so will require not only the protection provided by military power but the exercise of effective leadership and wise policies in a wide variety of fields. We certainly are

---

[11] At his second press conference on November 10, 1959, General de Gaulle stated:

"Doubtless, Soviet Russia, although having helped Communism become established in China, realizes that nothing can happen to prevent it, Russia, a white European nation which has conquered part of Asia and, in short, is quite well endowed with land, mines, factories, and wealth—nothing can happen to prevent it from having to reckon with the yellow multitude which is China—numberless and wretchedly poor, indestructible and ambitious, building by dint of violent efforts a power which cannot be kept within limits and looking around at the expanses over which it must one day spread. . . ."

See *Major Addresses, Statements and Press Conferences of General Charles de Gaulle, May 19, 1958–January 31, 1964* (New York: French Embassy, Press and Information Division, n.d.), p. 58.

not going to see Chinese Communist influence completely eliminated from all areas in which we have an interest. We will have to deal with many varieties of neutralism and nonalignment and with alignment with one side or the other, and we will have to adapt and alter many aspects of our policies as the balance shifts, as local forces contend, and as the Chinese and we ourselves gain and lose advantages. The situation will continue to be fluid rather than static, and we may eventually discover that in Asia, as in Europe, Communist governments themselves are subject to change.

Military strength provides evidence for friend and foe alike of our political commitments. However, it cannot be a substitute for wise and timely political action by ourselves and those with whom we are associated. Military weakness can lead to disarray and loss of confidence. However, if military strength is used indiscriminately and unwisely or without regard to our political purposes, the result can be failure, despite our immense power and good intentions.

CHAPTER NINE

The Framework for a China Policy

It has already been emphasized that the United States has not achieved many of the objectives or hopes that originally underlay its China policy. American policy, it is true, has checked the extension of Chinese Communist influence in Korea, Southeast Asia, the Taiwan Strait area, and elsewhere. But the Chinese Communists have proved to be more durable than some American leaders expected, and few other countries have been prepared to join the United States in a policy aimed at indefinite isolation of the Peking regime.

Any critical judgment of the accomplishments of United States policy should not, however, obscure the fact that the Chinese too have failed to achieve many of their goals. As was stated earlier, they have not established control over Taiwan; their ambitions for hegemony in Asia continue to be challenged and blocked, not only by the United States but also by other countries in Asia; and they have made relatively little progress toward their objective of world-wide revolution. Despite some successes, therefore, the Chinese Communists have in their accomplishments fallen far short of their aspirations, and the difficulties which still confront them are enormous.

Some critics of American policy would like to see it speedily and totally reformed, and in their attempt to change what they believe to be an "unrealistic" policy, they themselves often ignore significant realities. Past decisions and commitments and the expectations these have created throughout Asia, on the part of friend and foe alike, must be part of our present calculations.

China policy, it should now be clear, involves much more than simply deciding whether to recognize the government of the Republic of China in Taipei or the People's Republic of China in Peking or supporting one or the other as the legitimate claimant to China's seat in the United Nations. Even if by some magic these two questions could be solved, the major problems of China policy would still be with us—the problems involved in appraising China's strength, ambitions, and position in the world, in taking into account the evolving attitudes of other countries whose interests may or may not be the same as either ours or those of the Chinese, and in determining what posture and policies we should adopt in order to achieve our long-term goals vis-à-vis the Chinese in Asia.

It would be romantic and wrong to think that we need only make a few friendly acts and wise decisions and that these will then be applauded by our friends and welcomed by the Chinese Communists and will lead us out of the dark. Equally romantic and just as wrong is the notion that we can achieve our purposes simply by demonstrating toughness and unyielding determination in the face of enemy challenges to our policy.

Our problem is to determine not just specific actions to meet specific short-term problems but the overall relationship that may be possible and desirable between ourselves and China in the long run. We need to have a sense of both our strengths and our shortcomings, and while firmly opposing certain Chinese actions and goals, we also need to be sensitive to their legitimate aspirations. History gives us little reason to believe that, unless there is a catastrophic war, decisive victory or complete defeat for either side will be the result of the confrontation and struggle that are now unfolding. However, history does suggest that those who have a clear idea of what they are trying to achieve and who adjust their hopes and expectations to the facts of the real world have the best chance of achieving their goals.

The Broad Goals of Our China Policy

We have already noted that those who expected the government of the China mainland to collapse or be overthrown have been disappointed, and there is even less reason today than there was in earlier years to believe that such hopes will soon be fulfilled. The government in Peking faces enormous domestic problems, but to date it has been remarkably successful in maintaining its political control.

One cannot, of course, rule out the possibility that we may in time see another period of disruption, civil war, and fragmentation in China. However, this is not a development that we can now foresee; there is no reason to believe that it is imminent, and overt steps on our part to try to bring it about would probably boomerang. Should a major disruption of Communist China's unity and stability occur, the consequences for the United States would be unpredictable and not necessarily favorable. There would be no guarantee that out of the turmoil a government well disposed to the United States, able to restore peace and order, and less ambitious internationally would emerge. Soviet intervention would be very possible, and even the Japanese might be tempted to step in once again. One can envision, in fact, a situation in which the United States might be confronted with even worse dilemmas than it faces at present.

On the other hand, while internal breakdown in China appears unlikely in the foreseeable future, it is difficult to predict what success the Chinese Communist leaders are likely to have during the years immediately ahead in overcoming the formidable obstacles that they face in trying to remake their country into a truly world power. Population pressure, agricultural difficulties, technological weaknesses of many kinds, and the competing demands for limited resources will not soon be solved. There are many reasons to expect a long-term growth in China's strength, but China's development will doubtless encounter great difficulties and numerous setbacks.

Communist doctrine and organization now provide the driving force for China's development, but it is the strength and vitality of Chinese society and the abilities of the Chinese people which provide the foundation. The ambitions of Peking's leaders derive not just from ideology; they spring also from aspirations for national independence and power and impulses toward social and economic development that are shaking much of the world. To imagine that the disappearance of the present Chinese Communist leaders and their doctrine would change all this picture overnight and would suddenly make China both friendly and docile is to ignore the facts of twentieth-century nationalism in the Chinese context. The virtual identity of views of the Communists and Nationalists regarding the unity of China and its territorial claims illustrates an important continuity and identity with which Chinese of varying ideological outlooks view their national interest. China's geographical position and history and its striving for modernization and for great power status are bound to stir the world, whoever rules China. Communist doctrine, with its apocalyptic vision of world-wide revolution, has added enormously to the problem by infusing China's present leaders with intense, revolutionary militancy, but it is not the only source of the problem.

Ideally, the United States would like to see a China that is democratic, unified, and prosperous, that is always observant of the rights and interests of its weaker neighbors, and that is playing a constructive and peaceful role in its participation in world affairs. But there is no realistic basis for believing that a China of this sort will emerge in the foreseeable future, and we must deal with China as it is, not as we would like to see it. China today is not a unique case. Great nations undergoing revolutionary change, attempting to cope with the major challenges of internal reform, and pursuing broad national goals are rarely either democratic or restrained in their ambitions.

The history of recent years suggests, also, that short of massive physical intervention, the outcome of which would be unpredictable, there is relatively little the United States can do to determine the political system within China—or, for that matter, other major countries. What we can do is help to shape the relations between China and ourselves and in the world community as a whole and determine ways in which undesirable Chinese policies and actions abroad can be prevented or offset. We should constantly remind ourselves, however, that relationships of hostility or friendliness between nations are not immutable—the changes involving ourselves, the Germans, the Japanese, and the Russians in the last thirty years should make this clear—and we should be alert to the potentiality of change inherent in all situations and be ready to adapt our policies, not merely remain bound to the past.

Faced by the Chinese Communists' current uncompromising

hostility, what objectives should the United States now pursue? Should we seek a mutually acceptable basis for living at peace with the Chinese and, while opposing attempts on their part to impose their will on others, recognize their legitimate ambitions and interests? Or is such a quest bound to be unsuccessful because of antagonistic doctrines and interests, and is there the danger that in making the attempt we may risk undermining our own resolution and weakening the position of our friends?

Today, a kind of armed truce exists, with the United States and the People's Republic of China confronting each other directly in some situations and competing everywhere on the Asian periphery, each seeking to undermine the other's positions not only in Asia but throughout the world. China has been checked in some ways, but fundamental questions still remain: How do we counter China's revolutionary zeal? How do we define China's rightful position in Asia? How do we establish a more normal relationship between China and the United States? If our point of departure is to oppose everything that China favors and to seek no grounds for accommodation and compromise, where will this lead?

Conceivably, we might attempt to establish a clear-cut position of American hegemony in Asia designed to contain China at every turn and keep it weak and isolated in the hope that eventually Peking will reform its behavior. On the basis of our experience during the past years, however, such a policy would not be likely to succeed. It would lack the indispensable support of even the non-Communist nations in the area and therefore would not be effective in preventing the extension of China's influence through political and subversive means.

What is required is that we work, with vigilance and perseverance, to find some kind of balance between the legitimate interests of the United States, China, and the other countries in the region. This will take a long time at best. It will be a slow, step-by-step process and will depend on the ability of the nations of Asia to put their own houses in order and work out cooperative relations with their neighbors. To say that it will require a combination of firmness and flexibility may seem trite. Yet there are still some Americans who think that only toughness and intimidation will pay off, while others, equally naïve, believe that if only the United States made a few friendly gestures, the Chinese dragon would be appeased.

If the United States seeks some kind of acceptable accommodation with China, one designed to reduce the chances of conflict but at the same time to allow other nations as well as China to develop peacefully, it will have to do so in a way that does not vindicate China's assertions that it is the wave of the future. Peking's claims at present are so extravagant and its pretensions to universal wisdom so sweeping that this task will not be easy. The current Communist leaders in Peking have demonstrated their dogmatic militancy time and again and have shown that they are little affected by the sentimental euphoria that envelops much talk about peace, friendship, and good will. Because they are tough, tenacious, and suspicious of the United States, they can be expected to continue their attempts to turn any opening to their advantage. Certainly, therefore, the job of bringing about an improvement in our relationship with China without at the same time eroding our present position will require continued firmness as well as flexibility.

The startling transformations that have taken place in the world in the wake of World Wars I and II and the Communist revolutions in Russia and China are evidence enough that one cannot speak of straightforward solutions to problems. Problems and solutions evolve and change, with new ones emerging from the old, and there are risks inherent in every important decision. It is not easy to make a simple list of national objectives with ordered priorities. Any nation, in seeking its goals, may have to work toward them in seemingly contradictory ways. One goal may have to be emphasized more than others, and the pursuit of any one of them has to take into account the pursuit by other nations of their goals. Success may elude us if we grasp for it too avidly. Toward China, for example, our objectives are necessarily contradictory, and there is no certain answer as to what our priorities should be at any given time. We want a peaceful and friendly relationship, but we do not intend to be dupes. We want other nations to support our policy, but not if the price compromises our own interests. We want to insure our own security and that of our friends, but we have no clear way of measuring present and future threats. We want to avoid provocative actions, but weakness would endanger both our interests and those of others.

Consequently, the best we can hope for is to set forth our major goals and work slowly but steadily toward achieving them while we constantly reappraise our situation, our resources, and the alternative courses of action most likely to yield results. Senator Fulbright's advice to discard old myths in favor of new realities is a worthy call which we should heed. The difficulty, however, is that one man's myths are another man's realities. In no situation is this truer than that regarding the China policy of the United States.

Containing the Danger

More than half a century ago, Eyre Crowe, Senior Clerk and later Permanent Under-Secretary of the British Foreign Office, described the system of the balance of power in the following terms:

History shows that the danger threatening the independence of this or that nation has generally arisen, at least in part, out of the momentary predominance of a neighbouring State at once militarily powerful, economically efficient, and ambitious to extend its frontiers or spread its influence, the danger being directly proportionate to the degree of its power and efficiency, and the spontaneity or "inevitableness" of its ambitions. The only check on the abuse of political predominance derived from such a position has always consisted in the opposition of an equally formidable rival, or of a combination of several countries forming leagues of defence.[1]

Today, one would add ideological militancy and revolutionary subversion to the threatening side of the equation.

In effect, the United States has sought in Asia—first in its policies toward Japan and now in its policies toward China—to maintain a balance, in the words that Eyre Crowe used for Britain, "by throwing her weight now in this scale and now in that, but

[1] "Memorandum on the Present State of British Relations with France and Germany," January 1, 1907, in G. P. Gooch and H. V. Temperley, *British Documents on the Origins of the War, 1898–1914* (London: HMSO, 1928), v. 3, p. 403.

ever on the side opposed to the political dictatorship of the strongest single State or group at a given time." [2]

Even if one recognizes that the Chinese are in some respects reacting to past injustices, that historical circumstances have doubtless contributed to a fear of American encirclement, and that at times the United States may have tended to exaggerate China's aggressiveness, the fact remains that China today over-shadows most of its neighbors with its mass and power, has pro-claimed its intentions to promote world revolution, and has ex-erted growing pressure on much of its periphery. For the United States to turn its back on this situation would be to abandon many commitments and responsibilities already assumed, and such an action would probably compel most of China's eastern and southern neighbors to make their peace with the China mainland as best they could. This does not imply that China would then neces-sarily subjugate the area physically or that all the Asian nations would soon become Communist. It does suggest, however, that those who tried to resist China's hegemony might well find them-selves isolated and constrained and that most of Asia would prob-ably become a zone of great Chinese influence from which the influence of other major nations would be largely excluded. Only United States power and influence can provide the requisite sup-port for Asian nations to prevent this from happening. Alone, the Asian nations themselves are too divided and too weak.

The United States would be making a great error, though, if it attempted, from across the Pacific, to establish an American hegemony or to eliminate Chinese influence in Asia. China's role there is bound to be great, no matter who rules China. It is a legit-imate American aim, however, to help China's Asian neighbors feel strong and independent enough to resist and avoid Chinese domination, whether through military occupation, political con-trol, or subversion. At the same time, the United States must rec-ognize that China can be expected to oppose any power balance which looks to it like encirclement by a ring of hostile countries under American tutelage. Few nations are willing to accept situa-tions which they believe to pose threats to their security or cause obvious diminution of their influence.

The United States must also oppose the challenges posed by in-

[2] Same.

digenous Communist parties throughout Asia, but without over-simplifying the problem. We should try to be clear, in other words, about the conditions that we face. In numerous Asian situations, communism is an aggravating factor and often the most dangerous one, but it is not the root cause of Asia's present difficulties. Secondly, a populous, modernizing, and unified China would pose major problems for the balance of power in Asia whether it was Communist or not. Third, anti-imperialism, the idea of planned economic development, and impulses toward socialism and political discipline are, as has already been emphasized, characteristic of many of the countries and peoples of Africa and Asia and would be so even if they lacked indigenous Communist parties—as some do—and were unaffected by the Chinese example. Finally, one should not assume that all Communist-motivated or Communist-oriented groups in Asia are subject to the direct discipline and control of Peking or Moscow. The recent history of Sino-Soviet competition and the evolution of local Communist parties throughout Asia and elsewhere clearly demonstrate that this is not the case.

While these observations do not automatically point to a specific line of action for the United States, several consequences do flow from them.

We should seek to identify China's basic interests and the specific means adopted in their pursuit and then distinguish these from other Communist or indigenous forces which the Chinese may attempt to manipulate or use. In practice, Chinese policies have usually been more temperate than their slogans of doctrinal battle, which if accepted at face value would appear to offer almost no hope for the future.

We should recognize the diversity of Asia and realize that there is no single political or ideological mold, even in the Communist movements of Asia. National forces are strong, and the interplay of international currents, including those from both Peking and Washington, in practice presents various options to nations that are caught up in confused situations and are struggling for survival. The United States will speak to many deaf ears if we regard as friends only those whose interests and values are identical to our own. Many non-Communist Asian nations practice various forms of political dictatorship, even if they profess democracy as their ultimate goal. They have strong feelings about their own national interests, but many are very sensitive to the special problems of having China as a close neighbor. Some are also conscious of pressure from the United States, which in many cases is not to their liking either. Countries that feel threatened by China or communism may seek American support to counteract their influences, or they may assume that American help will be forthcoming in the event of a crisis. Nevertheless, they are not all prepared to join in a general anti-Communist crusade, which, as they see it, might create new dangers and risks.

Despite Peking's desire for major-power status, obvious geographical and historical factors make Asia the area of principal interest to China and the one most accessible as a target of Chinese ambitions. In shaping policy toward China, however, we cannot think entirely in terms of the situation in Asia. China's goals are revolutionary and world-wide. Africa, the Middle East, and even Latin America are now areas of important and growing Chinese diplomatic influence and revolutionary activity. Peking, as well as Moscow, now cultivates Communist parties throughout the world. And even the United States' allies in Europe and the Commonwealth are now targets of Chinese diplomacy. China's world-wide presence or influence is increasingly felt—through trade negotiations and cultural exchanges as well as diplomatic contacts, in debates at the United Nations, in international Communist gatherings, and in numerous Afro-Asian conferences and meetings of unaligned nations. Clearly, there is an increasing need to deal with the China question as a world-wide problem and not merely as an aspect of our Asian policy.

The United States cannot be indifferent to the extension of Chinese power and influence, and it should try to prevent any growth of Communist parties and governments even when these parties and governments are not under direct Chinese control. International communism may have lost its unity, but the Chinese Communists have been indefatigable in their efforts to obtain support from Communist parties and groups throughout the world and to infuse them with Peking's own ideological fervor. Numerous links with other Communist parties unquestionably give Peking additional leverage and means of influence for its international diplomacy.

Americans would be on surer ground, however, if they gave more emphasis to the practical explanations of these relationships rather than attribute them solely or even primarily to doctrinal considerations. It seems probable, for example, that whatever the government in Peking in recent years, it would have attempted to establish regimes friendly to China in neighboring Korea and Vietnam. In Asia as in Europe, therefore, certain traditional and basic political forces continue to operate, even though they are now complicated by fresh dangers and new appeals and methods.

Communism has certainly not become a universal solvent of basic social and economic problems, in Asia or elsewhere. Indeed, we may be seeing what Richard Lowenthal has called "the disintegration of a secular faith." [3] Even so, the strength of its appeals has not completely disappeared, and the Chinese have known how to use them to good advantage. However, a policy that is overly preoccupied with Communist ideology risks underestimating the thrust of Chinese power and the skill of Chinese diplomacy, just as, conversely, a policy focused too narrowly on the objective of containing China militarily risks underestimating the significance of revolutionary faith and the challenge of Communist techniques for subversion and the seizure of power. Communism is not, in fact, a tidal wave threatening to engulf the world; to think so is to exaggerate its power and influence. At the same time, we cannot afford to ignore the use to which Communist doctrine and methods are put by our adversaries.

Military measures, as was stated before, must play an important role in any containment policy. They can deter or repel direct physical aggression, provide the means of retaliation when aggression occurs, and give some sense of security to those who are threatened. But they can be effective only within the framework of a policy that clearly prescribes their political purposes and strictly controls their use so that they serve, in fact as well as theory, the political ends. Military measures afford a limited guarantee and insurance, but the history of recent years, particularly in Asia, shows that except for well-defined tasks they are no substitute for diplomacy, political action, and national will.

[3] Richard Lowenthal, *World Communism: The Disintegration of a Secular Faith* (New York: Oxford University Press, 1964).

In some places, where the threats are direct, American military measures are clearly essential, and in others, American military power is required to support broad strategic policy. Moreover, American military commitments, bases, and weapons can in some cases be important in providing local support if they are not looked upon as a substitute for political and economic action. That is, they can sometimes provide the protection and security which are necessary prerequisites for the solution of political and economic problems. The display of superior force must not, however, be allowed to obscure the more difficult underlying problems, without whose gradual solution nothing will have been accomplished, and there is a danger of neglecting these problems if we focus too narrowly on military objectives. The fact that the political and economic problems are really more difficult than military tasks to deal with, require greater patience, and are often discouragingly refractory should not provide excuses for policies that lean toward "easy military solutions." Also, while military measures may be a precondition for some political solutions, they can also create new complications that add to the political dilemmas. Korea, SEATO, Laos, and Vietnam have all created, as well as solved, some of the political problems that we have faced —and still face today. A political price may have to be paid, but the payment should not be made blindly in the expectation that if, in military terms, the adversary can be deterred or defeated, all other problems will disappear.

Some observers have argued that because the Chinese have so many problems at home and their strength is still so limited, they really do not have the ability to establish their predominance over foreign areas and that even if they continue to attempt to expand their influence through diplomacy, subversion, and other means, the nationalist urge in other Asian nations is so strong and the fear of the Chinese so great that the other nations will be able effectively to resist Chinese domination. Others have argued that international communism has become so fragmented that neither Peking nor Moscow can really establish its authority over Communist regimes elsewhere and that, therefore, even if other Communist governments were to be created, following the examples in North Korea and North Vietnam, they would have their own policies and, like the countries of Eastern Europe, would resist centralized Communist domination from any outside capital, whether Peking or Moscow. It has also been argued that the United States does not really have the capacity to control events all over the world and that consequently it should not allow itself to be drawn into commitments all around China's borders in Asia since these commitments may simply dissipate American energies, incur resentments, and result in frustration. Finally, it is sometimes argued that by continuing its commitments and involvements on the present scale, the United States constantly risks being drawn into escalating conflicts that could involve even the Soviet Union.

Such arguments are used by a variety of people who believe that the United States should seek to reduce its commitments and, if necessary, even accept some losses to the Communists so long as we do not sacrifice our overall strategic superiority. Disengagement, it is maintained, should be carried out selectively but with determination in order to limit the United States' commitments and make them conform more closely to its limited capabilities. These arguments have been applied with special vigor to such seemingly intractable situations as Laos and Vietnam, and they also appear to influence many of those disillusioned with foreign aid.

Such arguments frequently reflect a discouraged awareness that the problems of the new nations are far more complicated than we once thought and a realization that America's great strength is not the whole answer to them. They also reflect a realization, of sorts, that neither communism nor China provides the full explanation for our difficulties and that the complex pattern of problems we face is going to take a long time to resolve. They underline the dangers of regarding each crisis as cataclysmic and of failing to weigh sufficiently the bearing that immediate responses may have on long-term objectives, and they point up the peril of describing in black and white terms the complicated and fluid patterns of international behavior.

Nevertheless, they should not be allowed to become an enticing path to defeatism and withdrawal. There are dangers and tasks that must be faced. Many other countries do rely on American protection, and it is in the American interest to support them. Communist China is dedicated, as its leaders are the first to

194

insist, to expanding Communist and Chinese influence, and the United States has entered into numerous commitments that have given rise to legitimate expectations which can be ignored only at great risk to ourselves. In the kind of world we now live in, the future of Asia is too closely linked with our own for us to be indifferent to what happens there.

It is not by accepting any sweeping abstraction such as "disengagement," any more than "roll back" of communism, that an effective foreign policy can be formulated and applied either in the short run or the long run. We need to appraise in a discriminating way our own interests and differentiate between China's legitimate interests and China's ambitions to expand its influence at the expense of others. We must learn how to distinguish in many other countries between an understandable and probably inevitable acceptance of a degree of Chinese influence on the one hand and a subservience to Chinese ambitions on the other. Finally, these considerations have to be weighed against the ability of the United States to influence specific events without becoming more deeply committed than its interests warrant.

The application of all these tests to the shaping of United States policy toward China, of course, has to be put in the context of our relations with other countries.

The Role of the Soviet Union

The crucial problems in relations between the United States and China have not been solved by the Sino-Soviet rift. Despite the depth of their dispute, both nations remain opposed to the United States. Today they compete for primacy in the Communist world, but both challenge the United States and its allies for a preponderant influence in the world.

It is in the American interest that the Soviet Union and Communist China should remain divided and that each should offset the power and oppose the influence of the other. Even if this situation leads on occasion to increased militancy, with anti-American postures important in their competition with each other, the risks are less than those involved in facing two such opponents united in both doctrine and policy.

The weakening of Communist unity in Eastern Europe can be attributed in considerable part to the divisive effect that the Sino-Soviet dispute has had on the solidarity of the Communist world. So far, there has been nothing comparable at the eastern end of the Communist land mass, in North Korea or North Vietnam. These two small Communist countries are far more isolated than the East European nations and, for historical and cultural reasons, are likely to find it hard to avoid heavy Chinese influence, but it is conceivable that over time they may be able to play Moscow off against Peking in ways that enhance their own freedom of action. And it is in the American interest that such a situation should develop. As long as the Soviet Union sees its interest to lie in a less militant and aggressive policy and in limiting the growth of Chinese influence, as now seems to be the case, there may be some advantage, from the American point of view, in encouraging a limited degree of Soviet involvement in situations where Soviet and Chinese interests are competitive.

Although Peking can no longer assume, despite the continued existence of the Sino-Soviet alliance, that the Soviet Union will come to the help of China if it gets into trouble unless, in Moscow's opinion, Soviet interests justify the effort and risk, it would be reckless to take for granted a general harmony of Russian and American interests in opposing Communist China. There has already been and may continue to be a limited convergence of interests in individual situations and for particular purposes, but beyond this, it is difficult to make predictions. There may well be cases where Chinese and Russian interests coincide because both gain at the expense of the United States. Moreover, one cannot rule out the possibility of renewed collaboration, especially if the United States gravely threatened the major interests of either one. Despite the major differences between the two countries over policies within the Communist world and despite the serious conflicts of national interest that have developed between them, the Russians can hardly be expected to look with favor at any significant encroachments of American power on the Asian mainland or on the humiliation, serious weakening, or destruction of a Communist government in China by the United States.

It is paradoxical that at present there do, in fact, appear to be some opportunities, however limited, for American cooperation with the stronger antagonist, the Soviet Union, against the weaker one, the People's Republic of China. The explanation lies in the greater frustration, militancy, and hostility of China and the seemingly increased willingness of the Soviet Union to avoid inflammatory pronouncements, to meet at the conference table, and to attempt to work out acceptable arrangements aimed at reducing tensions. With Communist China, neither the United States nor the Soviet Union is currently able to engage in an effective conversation, except for a *dialogue des sourds,* in which each side hears mainly the abuse poured on it by the other. In contrast, the United States and the Soviet Union have in recent years been able to maintain constant contact despite continuing suspicion and serious crises. The Berlin crisis, the competition for nuclear superiority, the U-2 incident, the Cuban crisis, and other landmarks in the cold war have not interrupted, except momentarily, the continuing dialogue between the Americans and the Russians carried on in Moscow, Washington, Berlin, and Geneva and at the United Nations.

It would clearly be in the American interest to have improved contacts and communications with Peking as well as with Moscow. The ability to establish ties depends as much, or more, on the Chinese as it does on the Americans, but increased American efforts in this direction would be desirable. The evolution of relations between the Soviet Union and the United States during the past few years indicates that under certain circumstances, at least limited progress in resolving conflicts may be possible even when deep-seated suspicion and antagonism persist. The dogmatism of the Chinese Communists and their fierce anti-American propaganda do not augur well for such an evolution, it is true, and we have no assurance that the Chinese regime will become less dogmatic or that its foreign policy will mellow with age. Regardless of the dimness of these prospects, however, the United States should not be content to remain in a state of total impasse with such inadequate contacts with one of its principal adversaries.

The Soviet Union will not be an idle spectator to the competition between the United States and the People's Republic of China, and the United States cannot afford to overlook likely Soviet reactions to the evolution of Sino-American relations. These can probably be expected to range widely—from major support of China, if the destruction or complete humiliation of the Chinese Communist government were to be threatened, to actions compatible with or paralleling American policy, in situations where Soviet and Chinese interests clash and where the Soviet Union wishes to counteract Chinese influence or dampen a conflict in which it does not wish to become involved. One can conceive of many shadings between these positions, including situations in which Moscow may adopt an attitude of neutrality when the United States and China appear to be counterbalancing each other without detriment to major Soviet interests.

The fear of displeasing the Soviet Union should not, however, be a persuasive argument against the United States' seeking a reduction of tensions or even an accommodation with Peking if such were possible. In all situations, Moscow will obviously regard Soviet national interests as its primary consideration.

Any appearance that Moscow strongly backs Washington's policies might jeopardize Moscow's authority throughout the Communist world, and the Soviet Union, while deploring the ideological extravagances of Peking, will doubtless be reluctant to abandon the leadership over all militant Communist parties to Communist China. Therefore, Chinese successes in Southeast Asia or elsewhere might stimulate the Soviet Union to enter into fresh competition with Communist China not in support of American policies but against them. Developments in Vietnam have demonstrated, for example, that the Russians cannot be totally passive spectators in conflict situations of this sort and that even if they act cautiously, they may feel compelled to play an independent role aimed at offsetting both American and Chinese influences. Moreover, the Vietnam experience also suggests that similar conflict situations are likely to impel the Russians to draw back from any policy of accommodation with the United States, either because of genuine hostility toward American action or because of a feeling that they cannot afford to seem too tolerant of American policies.

There are many imponderables in the triangular relationship involving the United States, the Soviet Union, and China, and the

United States should have maximum flexibility, which it does not now have, if it is to maneuver its way successfully through future crises and emerge from them with its broad objectives closer to realization.

Relations with Other Non-Communist Countries

China policy cannot be dealt with in isolation from United States relations with many other non-Communist countries, for they are closely intertwined. American policy toward China affects other countries, and they influence what the United States is able to accomplish. This interaction has important effects on the American position and American interests throughout the world.

It is no mere sentimental desire to please others that makes the link between our China policy and our relations with others important. The record shows that many aspects of our current China policy have been weakened or vitiated by the actions of other non-Communist countries, including our friends and allies, who have felt differently about the nature of the China problem and how to deal with it than we have. Through trade with the China mainland, recognition of the People's Republic of China as the legal government of China, and support for the seating of Peking in the United Nations, for example, many countries have worked at cross-purposes with American policy and have reduced its effectiveness.

These considerations will continue to be important in the future. The United States itself can, of course, continue to oppose recognition of Communist China and the seating of Peking in the United Nations and continue to maintain the American trade embargo, but experience shows that these policies are likely to receive declining support from other nations and that they cannot effectively isolate Communist China without support from others. It is predictable, also, that other nations will resist pressures to follow the American example even more in the future than in the past as the shift of world opinion on these issues continues.

Whereas the United States government has defined the objective of isolating the Chinese Communist regime as an integral part of the policy of containing China, most other non-Communist countries have not. In fact, many now feel that any attempt to ostracize Peking simply exacerbates the problem by antagonizing the Chinese and minimizing their participation in normal international discourse. Therefore, while there is fairly strong and broad support for the American strategic objective of restraining China's expansionism, there is sharp disagreement as to how best to accomplish this.

In the Afro-Asian world, as has already been suggested, there is considerable sympathy for Communist China, despite Peking's recent setbacks, and in not a few places, admiration for its accomplishments. Echoes of approval greet many of the anti-imperialist and anti-colonial slogans Peking trumpets. Although the harshness of the Peking regime and its arrogance are often deplored, its success in establishing its authority over such a vast country and its "socialist" goals and achievements are frequently applauded. Undoubtedly, there are racialist undertones in some of these attitudes.

Because of these views, as well as for other reasons, many African and Asian countries criticize American attitudes toward China, even though others that are most exposed and vulnerable to China's influence look to the United States for protection. Some of this criticism can be ascribed to sentimentalism, but the importance of the trend should not be underestimated.

China stands to gain and the principle of international cooperation to lose if the picture of a divided world—white versus colored, rich versus poor, capitalist versus socialist, exploiter versus exploited—gains increased currency. The danger is multiplied if in combating communism we assume postures which make it easier for the Chinese Communists to succeed in posing as the champions of one-half of a divided world.

We should do our best, therefore, to avoid two opposite dangers, both of which seem tempting to some Americans. On the one hand, we should avoid any simple and naïve conclusion, based on sympathy with the newly independent nations, that somehow any use of American power in Asia or Africa is immoral and that the most strident expressions of anti-Americanism are no more than the righteous voices of the downtrodden. On the other hand, we should avoid the temptation to listen only to opinions that are in harmony with ours and to dismiss all others as representing dupes, if not allies, of the Communists. Sentimental internationalism that in effect leaves it up to others to pursue their interests at our expense and a narrow interpretation of the national interest that accepts no challenges or dissent are both dangerous.

Because of the divergences among our friends and allies on how best to deal with the extension of Chinese influence to other countries, each nation has in effect pursued its own policies, and despite consultation, there has been little serious attempt to arrive at agreed-upon positions. The argument that diversified approaches to China are in the general interest because they permit greater flexibility is largely specious. It would have merit only if it were the result of calculation—which has not been the case.[4] In fact, the Chinese have seen in the divergence of policies among the Western nations an opportunity to try to exploit the "contradictions" among the "imperialist" nations to their own advantage.

We obviously cannot expect complete unity in approaching the China problem, for the interests of the different countries are not the same. The United States in particular now has many responsibilities and concerns not shared by the other non-Communist nations. Our European allies, as was stated before, have shown little disposition to increase their responsibilities in Asia, and perhaps even if they did so, we might find ourselves working at cross-purposes. However, a greater measure of consultation would clearly be desirable, at least to increase mutual understanding of differing points of view. Little more is likely, though, until the policies themselves are more compatible.

Experience has shown that major aspects of the China policy of the United States cannot really be effective unless its policy and that of its friends are much more compatible than they have been in recent years. The responsibility for proposing more active

4 Edgar Faure, former Prime Minister of France, who prepared the way for France's recognition of the Peking government, said rather grandly in a radio interview in January 1964 on the eve of the French action: ". . . France has an Asiatic culture and calling. She no longer has colonial interests in Asia, but she knows Asia. . . . Because of this historical mission, because of this Asiatic calling, France can open the Chinese window for the West." *Le Monde* (Sélection hebdomadaire), January 12–22, 1964.

consultation lies primarily with the United States, which bears the greatest responsibilities in the area and suffers the most if each nation goes its way. Even if significant differences remain on certain issues, it should at least be possible to evolve much more imaginative and active joint programs to promote economic and social development in the Asian countries on China's periphery, and in the long run, these may be as important, or even more important, in meeting the problem posed by China as the necessary but essentially negative policies required for military containment.

In sum, the policy of the United States toward China is not a bilateral matter. Any policy is likely to be inadequate and sterile unless it fits into some overall conception of Asia in which both China and its neighbors, as well as the United States, have a place. It cannot, moreover, be effective if pursued alone. The aim of containing China is necessary but is not enough, and the resources of many nations, including eventually those of China itself, will have to be drawn on to create an Asian community that satisfies the aspirations for both survival and development of the Asian peoples. A long and difficult period of transition will probably be required before the present emphasis can shift to more constructive and in the long run more fully acceptable forms of American participation in Asian affairs. But a determined effort to move in that direction should be made, and present difficulties should not be allowed to obscure the ultimate goal.

CHAPTER TEN

On Dealing with the Chinese Communists

Relations between the United States and Communist China present an incongruous picture that future historians will try to explain but may not be able to understand fully. These two nations, one the most powerful in the world and the other the most populous, with no common boundary except the wide expanse of the Pacific Ocean, have come to look upon each other as the bitterest of enemies. Their hostility is expressed less through direct military conflict than in fear and distrust and actions to thwart each other's influence throughout the world.

As was indicated before, no persons from the mainland of China, except for refugees and a Communist delegation to the United Nations in 1950, have come to the United States since 1949, and Americans have gone to Communist China in only a few scattered and exceptional cases. It is true that delegations of the two governments have met at the truce talks in Korea and at the two international conferences held in Geneva in 1954 and 1962, that their ambassadors have met, and still meet, periodically in Warsaw for limited purposes, and that there have occasionally been incidental encounters in the course of unofficial international gatherings at which nationals of both countries have been present. But that is all. At a time when most other channels of international contact are clogged with conferences and travelers and in an era which some have heralded as the prelude to One World, this picture is indeed a barren one.

On the American side, this extraordinary situation has resulted in part from the depth of feeling that has infused American attitudes toward China and in part from the fact that recognition of the Nationalist government on Taiwan as the government of China has seemed to make necessary an attempt to deny the People's Republic of China on the mainland all normal international contacts. For the Chinese Communists, anti-Americanism has been a calculated instrument of national policy, at home and abroad, and the isolation of Chinese from Americans has been deliberate and purposeful.

The United States should not willingly accept such a state of affairs with the explanation that the principal responsibility for a change rests with the Chinese, nor should it rely on the vague hope that somehow time will automatically bring about an improvement. The hard fact of Chinese hostility and Communist China's challenge to a stable international order should not prevent us from doing what we can to explore the possibilities of establishing the minimum conditions for normal international intercourse with mainland China. As in the case of United States relations with the Soviet Union, the establishment of channels of contact and communication is not a substitute for vigilance in the defense of national interests and the pursuit of national objectives, and the attempt to deal with the Chinese Communists should not reduce anyone's alertness to the seriousness of the confrontation. Nevertheless, increased contact is essential.

Attitudes and Approaches

Today, just as a century ago, the authorities in Peking try to isolate the Chinese people from undesirable contacts with the outside world. Most sweeping analogies with the past are not valid, however. The Communists are now modernizing Chinese society and not trying to keep it untouched by outside influence. Moreover, they do not remain confined behind their wall of secrecy, restraint, and superiority as did their predecessors. Instead, from behind their protective shield they launch the words and deeds designed to promote the world-wide Communist cause and advance China's interests generally. Finally, for other powers, the priority problem is not that of forcing a breach in the wall through which commerce might flow, as it was believed to be in the nineteenth century, but rather of coming to know, understand, and possibly over time influence a society that has become a vigorous actor in the world even while it remains partly aloof from it.

This task has special significance for the United States because Chinese and Americans now have almost no contact, because the two governments are suspicious of each other, and because the two societies are misinformed about each other. In magnitude and character, of course, the problem is not the same in the two countries. In the United States, information can flow freely, debate flourishes, and there is an eagerness to learn. Unfortunately, though, these circumstances have not prevented prejudices from being nourished both by a lack of information and by misinformation. In China, the manipulation of "truth" is an instrument of policy, which is in turn guided by an ideology that permits no challenge or dissent, and the system is one under which all means of information and communication are controlled.

What is called China's "isolation" has several aspects. Not only is the Communist government excluded from the United Nations and other international gatherings but the Chinese leaders themselves, for political reasons, have assiduously restricted contact with Americans. Perhaps most important of all, the Chinese Communists live in a rigidly controlled world characterized by an exceptionally self-centered view of human affairs and a devotion to a sectarian interpretation of history. The immensity of the country and its own strong national heritage tend to reinforce an isolationist and uncompromising arrogance that makes it difficult to find a "rightful" and "proper" place for Communist China in the international community.

This state of affairs is a perilous one that creates many problems for the world. Embittered by Peking's hostility, however, the United States has done little to alleviate the situation. The Chinese Communists have done even less.

Such an impasse is both psychologically undesirable and politically dangerous. In the United States, for example, the result is that many Americans look at China largely in terms of oversimplified stereotypes. In short, not only are official relationships almost totally lacking, but there tends to be an atmosphere of impenetrable mystery and a sense of remoteness which obscure and blur modern China in the American consciousness. This situation, in turn, tends to reinforce preconceptions, freeze attitudes, and make the climate for political debate difficult.

During recent years, as has previously been mentioned, Chinese Communist rigidity and militancy, more than American obstinacy, have prevented any improvement in relationships. The disciplined paroxysms of anti-American propaganda among the Chinese people and the militant assaults on the United States interests everywhere have not been hopeful auguries of fruitful contacts or a useful dialogue. Even the most prudent official American suggestions that ways should be sought for better understanding have been rejected outright by the Chinese Communists as camouflage for attempts to advance "imperialistic" interests. At home and abroad, the Chinese Communists have apparently felt a compelling need to nourish their anti-American policies with fervor and without compromise.

It can be argued that this attitude is, in part at least, the result not only of conflicts of interest but also of deep Chinese resentment over the policies pursued by the United States. However, it is doubtful that spontaneous indignation and righteous anger are key determinants of Chinese Communist policy. The Chinese leaders have demonstrated a notable capacity to manipulate political activity and propaganda campaigns in a disciplined and unsentimental manner. They do not make neat distinctions between basic conflicts of interest and fostered antagonisms prescribed by ideological dictates. Still, these facts do not provide grounds for Americans to be smug or spiteful, and China's current hostility is not a good reason for not trying to improve the situation.

We cannot, of course, expect that conciliatory actions on our part—short of satisfying Peking's major demands—or even the establishment of increased contacts between Americans and Chinese will basically change the character of the Chinese leadership or lead to any dramatic and rapid change in China's international behavior. In the future as in the past, the men in Peking can be expected to take a hard and probably skeptical look at any proposals made by the United States. They are unlikely to be quickly responsive to conciliatory moves, any more than they are to threats. Moreover, they are skillful practitioners of a dialectical approach which combines conciliation and pressure, thrusts and withdrawal, harshness and moderation in progression toward their goals. Proposals from the United States will be viewed in this framework. Under the best possible circumstances, therefore, it will probably take a long time before useful dialogue can be established.

What the situation calls for, however, is not a refusal to deal with the adversary but a patient, sustained, and hardheaded approach that combines firmness with understanding and, in the absence of agreement, at least seeks to establish improved contacts and better communications. This is essential, moreover, if we are to hold or gain the support of our friends on issues relating to China—support which is necessary for any long-term success in the search for means to settle issues on their merits.

We must not expect unrealistically to be able to reach the Chinese people over the heads of their leaders—except insofar as we may be able to have a limited influence upon the long-term evolution of the Chinese Communist system, which might induce changes in the society. Nor should we assume that we can easily convince the Chinese leadership of our good faith simply by bold gestures. If, in time, the Chinese leaders modify their attitudes, they will do so in response to many influences, including the problems that they face at home and the world environment as it evolves and as they perceive it as well as changes in United States policy. Nevertheless, the policies that we pursue are bound to play a part in shaping the future.

For the present, the usefulness of traditional diplomacy seems to be limited, but this situation need not prevail indefinitely. Regularized diplomatic contacts might be important in the future. Informal contacts, if they could be established, might also be of help, as they have been in the case of the Soviet Union. If conducted in good faith, they might eventually lead to somewhat improved mutual knowledge and perhaps even appreciation. Only if the will to bring about a better climate is strong, though, will there be any chance of achieving it. To date, the will seems to have been almost totally lacking in Peking, and it has been only mildly and somewhat ambiguously present in Washington.

To argue that it would be better to let the Chinese "stew in their own juice" may be emotionally satisfying to some but is neither realistic nor constructive. The United States' refusal to deal with the Chinese Communists, as has already been emphasized, has not been very effective in limiting the growth of their power or the spread of their influence. Nor is there convincing evidence that it has caused them internal strains. In fact, it has probably helped to throw them back on themselves and may have reinforced their sense of defiant solidarity. To the extent that other nations have become wary of the Chinese Communists, it is because of the behavior of the Chinese and not because of the American attempt to quarantine them. On balance, then, the American policy of isolating Communist China has not been successful. For the United States, moreover, it has involved a significant price in frictions and strains in relations with many friendly nations, and it has required the expenditure of considerable political capital to persuade some of our friends to follow our lead.

There are also risks, however, in any major change of policy, and these must be carefully weighed and taken into account in determining the timing and method of any new steps that are taken. There is clearly the possibility that the Chinese may rebuff or ignore American initiatives and simply pour additional scorn on the United States for attempting them. Some people have pointed to the danger of humiliation for this country, but this danger would be serious only if the United States unwisely gave the impression that it was, from a position of weakness, currying favor with the Chinese Communists and ignoring both its own interests and those of its friends. If the United States proceeds with caution and dignity and makes clear that it is not abandoning its essential interests or weakening in its opposition to Chinese Communist encroachments on others, there can be no serious risk of humiliation.

In sum, what is now needed is a reshaping of the American outlook that would involve a greater readiness to deal with the People's Republic of China as a durable and important power whose presence is inescapable even though its behavior and policies conflict with our interests. There is little prospect that a speedy improvement in relations can be achieved, and in the short run, there is some risk that new initiatives may unsettle friends. But these facts should not prevent us from doing whatever seems necessary to work, with vision and resolution, toward the long-term improvement of what is now an unsatisfactory situation, and no progress can be made, even in the long run, unless we have more active dealings with Communist China than we now have.

Trade, Contacts, and Exchanges

It must be emphasized that it is not easy to see how more active dealings with the Chinese Communists can be brought about in the immediate future or to anticipate exactly what future prospects for active and useful negotiations are likely to be. Nevertheless, these obstacles and uncertainties should not deter the United States from probing for possible openings.

One step which we could take without prior negotiations with the Chinese would be to modify our present controls on commercial and financial transactions with Communist China. For trade actually to develop, of course, the Chinese would have to be willing to allow it.

The American embargo on all trade with mainland China has been in force since the Korean War. In recent years, some voices in the United States have been raised in favor of placing China trade on the same basis as American trade with most other Communist countries, and the other major trading nations now trade with China in nonstrategic goods. The American government's policy on this issue, however, has remained essentially unchanged.

In a speech of June 28, 1957,[1] Secretary of State Dulles said that "normal peacetime trade with China, from which the American and Chinese people would benefit, could be in the common interest," and he expressed the view that such trade "could exist, to a limited degree, without recognition." But he then went on to assert that trade with Communist China is not normal trade because it is wholly controlled by the Chinese for their military and political purposes.

In recent years, however, the available evidence suggests that with a few exceptions, the Chinese have conducted most of their trade primarily on the basis of economic rather than political

[1] *Department of State Bulletin*, v. 37, July 15, 1957, pp. 91–95.

considerations. It is difficult to believe, moreover, that the Chinese could manipulate future trade with the United States so as to obtain special political and military advantages beyond those which accrue to all trading nations. American companies would certainly not be in a weaker position than their counterparts in other non-Communist countries that are now trading with mainland China, and, presumably, legislative and administrative regulations would be available to prevent abuses. The fact that China's foreign trade is managed by the government should not itself be a deterrent, for the United States already engages in trade with a number of countries, including other Communist nations, that have state control of trading.

During 1962 and 1963, when the Chinese were suffering from a serious food shortage, there was some discussion in the United States of the possibility of selling or offering them wheat. Former President Truman and some other prominent Americans reportedly favored an unconditional offer of a gift. But the administration, as was noted before, and was more cautious—perhaps because it feared a snub from the Chinese as well as domestic political criticism. It intimated that we would not rule out the possibility of shipping grain and other surplus food if the Chinese submitted a request. Nothing came of this suggestion, however, and when the Chinese emerged successfully from their crisis, partly as a result of large-scale purchases of grain from Canada, Australia, and other non-Communist countries, the issue fell into the background.

After this brief episode, President Kennedy, in a press conference on November 14, 1963, reaffirmed that the United States was not "planning to trade with Red China—in view of the policy that Red China pursues. When the Red Chinese indicate a desire to live at peace with the United States and other countries surrounding it, then quite obviously the United States would reappraise its policies." [2]

This policy was restated a few months later by Secretary of State Rusk,[3] who explained that "since the Communist countries no longer form a completely monolithic bloc in political terms, it

[2] *The New York Times*, November 15, 1963.
[3] Testimony on East-West trade before the Senate Foreign Relations Committee, March 13, 1964, *Department of State Bulletin*, v. 50, March 30, 1964, pp. 474–484.

follows that we should not treat them as a monolith in trade terms." He went on to acknowledge that none of the areas subject to the American trade embargo (Communist China, North Korea, and North Vietnam) is really very vulnerable to it since all of them can trade in nonstrategic goods with other Communist and non-Communist countries, but he justified United States policy in the following terms: "Our decision to impose a total trade embargo is based primarily upon political considerations. Each of these Communist countries is actively engaged in aggressive activity. . . . When regimes are engaging in aggressive activities of such character and intensity we must design our trade policies accordingly. Our complete trade embargo is a reflection of these relationships." Just what political purposes are now served by the trade embargo was not clear, though. Nor was it clear why the embargo is applied to certain nations accused of aggressive activity and not to others.

Present evidence, in fact, suggests that the embargo serves no important political or economic purpose. Since the latter 1950s, at least, it has neither weakened the Chinese significantly nor retarded their economic development in any major way. It has not made the Peking government more amenable to United States policy, nor has it prevented the Chinese from expanding trade with other non-Communist countries, including the principal allies of the United States. It is simply a residual expression of our dislike for the Chinese Communists, and there is very little to be said in favor of maintaining it. Perhaps the principal reason why the United States has done so is that since the embargo was adopted in a highly charged political atmosphere, the government has been wary of the political consequences of taking steps to abandon it.

It is paradoxical that the United States, which normally supports the principle of separating economics from politics and criticizes the Communists for not doing so, should in this case cling to an outdated economic policy solely for reasons of political symbolism. In some respects, of course, the removal of the trade embargo and the authorization of trade with Communist China on the same basis that it is permitted with the Soviet Union might themselves be largely symbolic acts at the start, for they might not immediately lead to trade on any significant level. We should not, in other words, entertain illusions that the Chinese would leap at the prospect of trading with the United States or that even if they welcomed the opportunity, the results would be substantial in the absence of American credits. However, the longer the United States adheres to its present policy for noneconomic reasons, the more difficult it will be to disengage from it.

In short, the important thing at the moment is to take the first steps, which the United States can do alone, and then to follow them up with quiet inquiries and negotiations. These might or might not produce immediate practical results or tangible political or economic benefits, but they would at least open the door to the possibility not only of trade but of increased contacts in the future. If trade relations between the United States and Communist China were established even on a limited basis, for example, some increase in contacts between Americans and Chinese would almost certainly occur. These would naturally be restricted and would not by themselves go far toward normalizing relations or changing attitudes in the absence of more fundamental changes in outlook and policies. Nevertheless, they might help reduce ignorance and misrepresentation as factors contributing to poisoned relations.

The United States can by no means insure increased contracts between Chinese and Americans by introducing elements of flexibility into its policy. The controversy over the exchange of newsmen, discussed before, amply illustrates the additional problems involved. With regard to this specific issue, however, it is important for the government not only to continue to press the Chinese Communists but to make its position as clear and unambiguous as possible both to the American public and to opinion abroad—even if the Chinese remain adamant and there are no expectations of early progress toward an exchange. Indeed, the United States should take a very strong stand in light of its traditional faith in the freedom of international communications and the free flow of news.

At present, much of the American news coverage on China originates in Hong Kong or is based on United States government sources. If American newsmen were admitted to Communist China, they could add some but not an enormous amount to the information already available. Several Western correspondents are already stationed permanently in Peking, but serious restrictions impair their ability to observe and report. Even though there is no formal censorship of outgoing dispatches, strict controls over the sources of news plus the likelihood that a wayward reporter may find his stay in China curtailed effectively limit the news that can be gathered and sent out.

It should not be imagined, moreover, that there is a vast American public thirsting for news about China and that the coverage of China in the American press would necessarily change in a dramatic fashion if only American newsmen could get to the mainland. Unfortunately, even today there is inadequate use made of the sources available, and, with perhaps some exceptions, American publications have not tried as hard as they should have to do better or to do more.

Despite all the problems, however, the fact that American newsmen would be reporting from the mainland would probably help in some degree to dissipate the prevailing sense of impenetrable barriers between Americans and Chinese, a feeling which reinforces an atmosphere that is psychologically unsound and politically stale.

If arrangements can be worked out in the news fields, they will doubtless involve reciprocity. And as long as the present hostility exists, Chinese Communist newsmen stationed in the United States could doubtless be expected to feed the Chinese propaganda machine firsthand reports of the seamiest side of American society, carefully selected for maximum effect. Independent reporting would hardly be likely, and Peking would probably quickly suppress any signs of it. It is possible, however, that some of the Chinese newsmen would come to recognize that not everything which is believed in Peking is true and that their understanding of the United States might increase. Conceivably, such a development might have some influence on leaders at home, whatever the character of the regular reporting of the newsmen.

Nevertheless, we should not expect quick returns from an exchange of newsmen if one can be brought about, and those who look for early visible results in the form of improved relations are likely to be disappointed. The overriding consideration is that within the limits of our power to influence the situation we should do so.

The same considerations apply to cultural and scholarly exchanges, which are almost totally absent today. It seems incredible that except for a flow of some publications, limited exchanges between a few libraries, and very occasional meetings of individuals at international gatherings, Communist China and the United States now have virtually no direct contact with each other's worlds of culture and scholarship. Not only American specialists on Chinese affairs are affected by the present barriers; American artists, scientists, economists, and students generally are deprived of contact with and knowledge of one of the most important countries in the world where developments of universal significance are taking place. This state of affairs cannot but affect our whole outlook in many fields.

As in the case of journalists, the main responsibility for such a situation rests with the Chinese, for it is they who have deliberately isolated themselves. They strictly control all cultural and scholarly contacts with other countries, most notably the United States, and while they welcome organized delegations from other countries on short-term tours, they have not freely opened their doors to individual foreign scholars or encouraged their own students to go abroad except, in earlier years, to some other Communist countries.

During one brief period, it is true, the Chinese did seem to want to work out some cultural exchanges with the United States. In his speech of June 28, 1957, however, Secretary of State Dulles said that we "doubt the value of cultural exchanges, which the Chinese Communists are eager [at that time] to develop," and he attributed the eagerness of the Chinese to promote such exchanges primarily to their desire to induce their Asian neighbors to open themselves to Chinese subversion.[4] (Perhaps it is worth noting parenthetically that even today, when no one could accuse the Chinese of being eager to develop cultural relations with the United States, many Americans have an unwarranted suspicion that cultural contacts cannot be separated from subversion.) As a consequence, the matter was dropped. By the time it was revived, the Chinese attitude had changed.

Although the main responsibility for the present situation lies with the Chinese and although we alone cannot remedy it, it is

[4] *Department of State Bulletin,* cited, vol. 37, p. 93.

214

not enough simply to blame the Chinese for the impasse. We should make our purposes quite clear and do what we can to encourage the desired contacts. As guide lines, we might ask ourselves: Have we sufficiently encouraged the unrestricted flow of publications? Are we ready to receive cultural groups from mainland China? Will we welcome international conferences to the United States that include delegates from Communist China? Are American scholars, scientists, artists, and their professional associations encouraged sufficiently to do what they can on a private and unofficial basis to develop relations with their counterparts in China? The answer to all of these questions should be a clear and unambiguous "yes."

For scholars, scientists, artists, and others, the first contacts with China, when they come, may be disappointing. Access to information is likely to be limited, travel controlled, inquiries unanswered, and the well-marked path reserved for foreign visitors frustrating. Nevertheless, we will have created an opportunity to produce, in time, a better understanding of developments in China and a greater sense of awareness of what is taking place there. In addition, we might slowly be able to raise the understanding of at least some Chinese about the United States, for there should be reciprocity in such exchanges, even though the two political systems are so different that precise reciprocity in each situation would be neither possible nor desirable.

We are still far from negotiations on these matters, but when they do become possible, the handling of exchanges and contacts with the Soviet Union, which have been arranged both officially and privately, may provide a useful model. Until that time comes, and in order to hasten its coming, we need to be firm in our conviction that the present situation is unsatisfactory and show persistence and determination in taking whatever steps we can to bring about an improvement.

Diplomatic Relations

During the past seventeen years, nonrecognition has become such a mark of United States policy toward Communist China that the question of recognition has often been taken to be the essence of policy itself. Many of those both for and against recognition have seemed to presume that we could expect to settle the fate of China for decades to come by our decision on this issue alone.

There is little evidence, however, that our nonrecognition policy has weighed significantly in the calculations of the Chinese Communists regarding their policy toward us. They have probably viewed it as simply one of many marks of American unfriendliness and not as the heart of the matter, which is the incompatibility of the two systems and the opposition of the United States to what China considers its rightful place in the world.

Moreover, the arguments for and against recognition have been reiterated with such ritualistic passion that their relevance to existing political reality has not always been adequately assessed. Indeed, debate on the subject sometimes seems to have focused not on questions related to political action at the moment but on the rightness or wrongness of actions long since past. Some, that is, have argued as if recognition of the Peking government would right a wrong committed against the Chinese people, while others have argued as if continued nonrecognition were a striking demonstration of the moral virtues of the American people.

Today, neither China nor the world is the same as it was when the present American policy was first shaped. Among the great changes which have taken place are the rift between China and the Soviet Union, the growth of Peking's prominence in the world Communist movement, China's increased activity among the new states of the non-Western world, the nuclear stalemate between the Soviet Union and the United States, China's increased stature in Asia, and China's development of nuclear weapons.

As a consequence, a number of the arguments which have been advanced over the years in favor of the policy of nonrecognition certainly appear to have lost whatever relevance they may once have had. For example, in a speech on May 18, 1951, Dean Rusk, then Assistant Secretary of State for Far Eastern Affairs, asserted that "the Peiping regime is not the government of China," for "it is not Chinese." [5] He apparently meant that the People's Republic of China was essentially an alien regime because it was Commu-

[5] Same, v. 24, May 28, 1951, p. 847.

nist and had close ties with the international Communist movement, then dominated by the Soviet Union. Six years later Secretary of State Dulles described the unquestionable hostility of the Chinese Communists toward the United States and its allies and then concluded that under the existing circumstances "it would be folly for us to establish relations with the Chinese Communists which would enhance their ability to hurt us and our friends." [6] A statement issued by the Department of State on August 11, 1958, declared: "The United States holds the view that communism's rule in China is not permanent and that it one day will pass. By withholding diplomatic recognition from Peiping it seeks to hasten that passing." [7] But how nonrecognition was to "hasten that passing" was left unclear.

Many arguments which have been made against nonrecognition are also difficult to reconcile with reality. Whatever the original wisdom or folly of the policy of nonrecognition, today it has to be judged in light of a decade and a half of troubled international relations, and one cannot ignore the accretions of controversy, antagonism, and sensitivity relating to the issue.

Refusal to recognize another government despite its obvious viability is not so extraordinary as some of the critics of American policy would have us believe. The United States is not alone in refusing "to face the facts." Spain and the Soviet Union, the Arab states and Israel, most of the African nations and South Africa, Indonesia and Malaysia have all used recognition as an instrument of political policy and an expression of national sentiment rather than simply as a recognition of the "facts." In addition, the existence of divided countries with competing governments—China, Germany, Korea, Vietnam—has forced all other countries to use recognition as a discretionary instrument of national policy. Some persons reasonably argue that it might be preferable for all nations to follow similar recognition policies and to avoid trying to use nonrecognition as an instrument of political pressure. But as of today, they do not do so, and American nonrecognition of the Peking regime is by no means a unique phenomenon.

There remains, however, the question of whether or not this

[6] See his speech of June 28, 1957, cited, p. 95.
[7] *Department of State Bulletin*, v. 39, September 8, 1958, p. 389.

policy is a wise one. Much of what was said during the debate over recognition of the Soviet Union can be said today regarding our China policy. In fact, the arguments used then sound so familiar that there really seems to be little originality in today's debate over the recognition of Communist China. Here is the way the issue was summarized in 1933: "On the one hand, the arguments against recognition are frequently prompted by assumptions and bigotry; and . . . on the other hand, the arguments for recognition are often prompted by a pale liberalism, a sentimental policy of universal tolerance, or by the exigencies of trade." The specific arguments against recognition included the following:

We should not, in the words of Mr. Coolidge, be willing to "barter our principles" for the sake of trade or other advantages. . . . The Soviet government is really the creature and agent of the Communist Third International. It does not fulfill the American requirement that a government shall exist by the consent of the governed. . . . Recognition would open up the United States to the promotion of the Communist doctrine of world revolution. . . . Our opportunity to aid the great masses of the Russian people (who are non-Communists) lies in nonrecognition, since nonrecognition is our only hope of discouraging communism.

Those advanced in favor of recognition were summarized as follows:

The Soviet government has been in control of Russia for sixteen years. It has demonstrated beyond a shadow of a doubt its ability to rule and maintain order. To refuse to recognize a *de-facto* government that has established order is to contradict the traditional policy of this country since the time of Jefferson. . . . The withholding of recognition has become an ostrich-like gesture. . . . Russia . . . will obviously continue to exist and develop whether the United States recognizes her or not. An attempt to "ignore" officially the existence of 165 million people, occupying over $\frac{1}{6}$th of the earth's surface, is impracticable. It would be quite as logical to refuse to recognize the Rocky Mountains. . . . Recognition—the establishment of diplomatic relations as the necessary mechanism of intercourse—does not imply sanction of *anything*. It is not our business to pass upon other people's form of government; and to maintain the attitude of so doing is a form of interference. Recognition does not imply approval of the recognized country, does not endorse its "legitimacy," its method of coming into being, its conception of government, its principles or morals. Nonrecognition, on the other hand, as the United States has applied and practiced it in the case of Russia, does imply that we feel a right to act as moral censor of the rest of the universe. . . . If the arguments that it is impossible to recognize a country that does not rule by the consent of the government was ever sound, it is certainly no longer tenable. The United States is at this moment in formal diplomatic intercourse with countries that are the declared enemies of democracy. . . . To recognize the Soviet Union is the best means of lessening or weakening communism. . . . If our refusal to recognize has been based upon a hope of discouraging the Soviet regime by failing to countenance it, our ambition is plainly doomed to failure. . . . If the desire, so often expressed by our presidents and departments of state to "help the Russian people" is genuine, we shall have to get near enough to hear them, and we shall have to establish the ordinary machinery by which nations talk with and deal with each other. Recognition is the only method by which the channel of discussion can be kept open.[8]

Although the arguments are familiar, there are some significant differences between the situation in 1966, seventeen years after the Chinese Communists came to power, and that in 1933, sixteen years after the Bolsheviks took over the Russian government. Perhaps the two most important differences are the existence of the divisive issue of Taiwan and our continuing recognition of the Nationalist government as the government of all China, both of which are currently enormous obstacles to the establishment of diplomatic relations between the United States and the Peking government. No common threat draws mainland China and the United States closer, whereas Germany and Japan tended to have this effect on Russia and the United States in the 1930s. In 1933, the political philosophy of the New Deal and the apparent liberalization of the Soviet system made the United States more receptive to establishing relations with the Soviet Union than it had been in the 1920s. Furthermore, the Soviet Union was then in the relatively moderate "Litvinov phase" of its foreign policy, whereas the Chinese Communists today are militant and defiant, particularly toward the United States. During the 1920s, moreover, there had been contacts between the United States and the Soviet Union in the form of famine relief, limited trade, and the

---

[8] *The United States and the Soviet Union, A Report on the Controlling Factors in the Relations Between the United States and the Soviet Union* (New York: Committee on Russian-American Relations, The American Foundation, November 1, 1933), pp. 2–8.

employment of some American technicians in Russia.[9] There has been nothing comparable in our relations with Communist China. American involvement in the Chinese civil war, the subsequent fighting in Korea, and clashing interests in Southeast Asia and elsewhere have infused both China's policy and ours with intense passion, which may now be subsiding somewhat on our side but is not yet doing so on the Chinese side. For all these reasons, and despite the dangers of conflict, the United States and Communist China continue to view each other with a high level of hostility, and great obstacles to the establishment of diplomatic relations remain.

Consequently, no comparison with the Soviet precedent and no neat tabulation of arguments—some relevant and others not, some emotional and some dispassionate, and some simply inherited stereotypes—can prescribe a ready answer to the dilemma of America's recognition policy toward the People's Republic of China. Nonrecognition was originally part of a broader policy that included support for the Nationalist government on Taiwan as the government of all China and looked forward to the "passing" of the Communist regime. Now we are faced by a new situation that calls for a general redefinition of United States policy toward China, and along with this there should be a re-examination of the issue of recognition.

The People's Republic of China, while not close to being a superpower at present, is nevertheless a power in the world, and it is likely to remain one and become even stronger regardless of whether the United States recognizes it as the government of China. At the same time, although it is not now flagrantly aggressive in a purely military sense, it does openly and relentlessly espouse policies and support actions which aim at the expansion of China's influence and which jeopardize the existing international order. It directs the full fury of its hostility against the United States and those allied with this country and currently gives no indication that it desires accommodation except on its own terms, which include not only the immediate withdrawal of

[9] For an interesting comparison of the recognition policies of the United States toward the Soviet Union and Communist China respectively, see Joseph G. Whelan, "The United States and Diplomatic Recognition: The Contrasting Cases of Russia and Communist China," *China Quarterly*, no. 5, January/March 1961, pp. 62–89.

American forces from the Taiwan area but in the long run the removal of American influence from all Asia.

It is by no means clear that the policies of the Peking government would have been substantially different even if the United States and most other countries had recognized it at the outset. The behavior of the Chinese Communists suggests that diplomatic recognition is in their eyes not primarily a matter of formal international law, essential to the conduct of diplomacy and the development of political relations, but an action incidental to a policy purpose.

With basic issues such as Taiwan unresolved, moreover, the Chinese Communists might well not reciprocate any American extension of formal diplomatic recognition to their government but prefer to embarrass the United States by rejecting the move. Conceivably, the Communist leaders might repeat to the United States, in less ceremonious language, what the court in Peking told American Consul Forbes in Canton in October 1843, when it was informed that Caleb Cushing was on his way to negotiate the first treaty with China:

The August Emperor, compassionating people from afar, certainly cannot bear that the American Minister by a circuitous route should go to Peking, wading through overflowing difficulties. The Consul ought, therefore, to intercept the American Plenipotentiary from repairing, in every respect unnecessary, to the Imperial Court.[10]

If recognition were not reciprocated and if unilateral action by the United States were interpreted as a concession made from weakness, the results might be damaging to American prestige. Moreover, even if recognition were reciprocated and diplomatic relations established, the treatment of the foreign diplomatic missions in Peking and the ways of Chinese Communist diplomacy are such that we could not be certain that a very effective channel of communication would automatically be created, although it would probably be better than what exists at present. Certainly, it is true that recognition has not always had the results hoped for. The British, who were among the first to recognize the new Chinese government, have not yet been allowed to sta-

[10] Tyler Denett, *Americans in Eastern Asia* (New York: Macmillan, 1922), p. 147.

tion an ambassador in Peking but have had to be satisfied with representation of lower rank.

Fortunately, recognition is not an absolute prerequisite to the development of certain types of relations. The Chinese have shown a good deal of flexibility in dealing with other countries irrespective of their policies on recognition. For example, they have conducted active dealings with Japan and more recently trade with countries such as Canada and Australia despite their displeasure at not having been recognized by the governments of these countries. In addition, they have obviously felt it important to keep open the diplomatic channel of the ambassadorial talks in Warsaw as a means of communication with us.

Under existing conditions, therefore, formal diplomatic recognition of the Peking government does not appear desirable. The Chinese do not seem sufficiently interested in American recognition even to reciprocate. In the near future, moreover, recognition or continued nonrecognition alone will probably not be a major influence on the general international behavior of the Chinese Communists or on their attitudes toward the United States.

Although there are no strong arguments for the United States to take steps now toward formal diplomatic recognition of the People's Republic of China, we should make clear that we do accept the fact that the government in Peking is the *de facto* government of mainland China and that we will be prepared to enter into diplomatic relations as soon as there is evidence that the Chinese Communists would reciprocate and that such a move might open the way for fruitful attempts to reduce the present conflict between the two countries. In the meantime, despite the lack of formal relations, the United States should show its readiness to deal with the Chinese Communists on all issues where useful discussions or negotiations might be possible—including, as has previously been mentioned, matters such as trade, cultural contacts, and the exchange of newsmen. We might explore more actively the possibilities of discussing many issues in the talks between the American and Chinese ambassadors in Warsaw, and we should be willing to have more frequent and direct diplomatic contacts even without formal recognition. There should be no reluctance to sit at the same table with the Chinese Communists at international meetings.

What Cardinal Richelieu said concerning negotiations in his *Political Testament* is pertinent. Although Richelieu never had to cope with any nation quite like Communist China, he did deal with formidable opponents, and no one has ever accused him of naïveté or lack of political skill. Here is what he wrote on "The Need for Continuous Negotiation in Diplomacy":

. . . It is absolutely necessary to the well-being of the state to negotiate ceaselessly, either openly or secretly, and in all places, even in those from which no present fruits are reaped and still more in those for which no future prospects as yet seem likely. . . .

Some among these plantings produce their fruits more quickly than others. Indeed, there are those which are no sooner in the ground than they germinate and sprout forth, while others remain long dormant before producing any effect. He who negotiates, continuously will finally find the right instant to attain his ends, and even if this does not come about, at least it can be said he has lost nothing while keeping abreast of events in the world, which is not of little consequence in the lives of states. . . .

Important negotiations should never be interrupted for a moment. It is necessary to pursue what one has undertaken with an endless program of action so ordered that one never ceases to act intelligently and resourcefully, becoming neither indifferent, vacillating, nor irresolute. It is also necessary not to be discouraged by a bad turn of events, since it sometimes happens that the wisest undertakings produce unhappy results. It is difficult to fight often and always win. . . .[11]

No spectacular results can be expected from the course of action proposed here. No one can say with confidence that even with increased contact and negotiation between the United States and Communist China, major differences could soon be settled. The negotiations with the Soviet Union since 1945 have not succeeded in resolving the many deep controversies over Berlin, NATO, Germany, and Eastern Europe. There have, however, been some important agreements with the Soviet Union, including the Austrian settlement and the nuclear test-ban treaty. Moreover, a continuing dialogue goes on between Russian and American representatives inside and outside the United Nations, and there are few who would deny its value. Increased contacts do provide a means for reducing some misunderstandings, avoid-

[11] *The Political Testament of Cardinal Richelieu: The Significant Chapters and Supporting Selections*, trans. by Henry Bertraum Hill (Madison: University of Wisconsin Press, 1961), Chapter 6.

ing some conflicts, and coming to a better appreciation of competing positions. It is this that we should seek with the Chinese Communists. We should stand firm on essentials but make clear our willingness to meet with them and negotiate on selected issues whenever and wherever there is evidence of a desire to do so on their side.

CHAPTER ELEVEN

China and
the United Nations

Differences of opinion in the international community on "which China" should be seated in the United Nations have existed ever since 1949. This question transcends the competition between the governments in Peking and Taipei and involves broad issues relating both to Communist China's place in the international community and to the character of the United Nations.

On November 18, 1949, only seven weeks after the Chinese Communists formally assumed power, Chou En-lai, then Peking's Foreign Minister, sent to the United Nations Secretary-General a telegram in which he claimed that the new government was "the sole legal government representing all the people of the People's Republic of China." It should, he said, replace in the United Nations as it had in China "the Kuomintang reactionary government," which "has lost all *de jure* and *de facto* ground for representing the Chinese people." [1]

The Position of the United States

During the first few weeks after the issue was raised, as was indicated before, the position of the United States government was less categorical and more flexible than it later became. Even so, it was difficult to keep open avenues of accommodation between Washington and Peking in view of the Chinese Communists' abuse of United States personnel and arbitrary confiscation of

[1] U.N. General Assembly, Document A/1123, November 21, 1949, p. 3.

224

property on the mainland and in view of the signing of the Sino-Soviet alliance on February 14, 1950. Then the Korean War reinforced the views of those Americans who favored total opposition to the new Chinese government. As a result, American policy hardened and crystallized. Opposition to the seating of Peking's representatives in the United Nations became, together with continued recognition of the Nationalist government and the refusal to recognize the Communist regime, a basic pillar of America's China policy. It has been reaffirmed by successive congressional resolutions, upheld in the platforms of the major political parties, and supported by both Democratic and Republican Presidents.

Actually, there is no necessary connection between the question of recognition and the question of membership or seating in the United Nations. It can be argued, in principle, that recognition should be based on the prevailing *de facto* situation and involve no moral judgment on the government in power, while the United Nations Charter stipulates in Articles 2 and 4—provisions largely disregarded in practice—that membership in the organization is to be based on certain standards of international behavior. At the same time, it can also be argued that while the United States has no obligation except to itself in deciding its China policy and many believe that there is no immediate advantage in recognizing a government which is provocatively hostile, these special considerations may not be relevant to other United Nations members for whom universality of membership is accepted as a desirable general goal and the representation of mainland China is considered to be a rational objective.

The problem facing the United States, therefore, is not simply to choose among abstract principles but to determine what it is trying to achieve both in its China policy and in the United Nations and to take the steps most likely to bring about the desired results.

Frequently, Americans have failed to distinguish sufficiently between the goals of China policy and the bearing of that policy on American objectives in the United Nations. Once the United States government had decided that we would not recognize the People's Republic of China and would try to restrict its influence, some concluded that we should place equal stress on the effort to prevent its delegates from occupying the China seat in the United Nations. Indeed, it was argued that the seating of Peking "would vitiate, if not destroy, the United Nations as an instrument for the maintenance of international peace." [2] There was a tendency to project to the United Nations our views regarding China without giving very much thought to the implications for the future.

The degree of success with which the United States linked the idea of nonrepresentation in the United Nations with American nonrecognition can be attributed to the leading position the United States occupied in the organization and the fact that the United Nations declared Communist China to be an aggressor in the Korean War and mobilized its forces to combat the Chinese in that war. Other countries which might, over the years, have been equally disposed to see nations hostile to them excluded from the United Nations have not enjoyed the special influence of the American position. In fact, if every member of the United Nations had been able to make its will felt to the same extent as the United States and had been able to keep out of the organization those governments of which it disapproved, the United Nations might now be a much smaller body.

In some respects, however, the China situation is unique. China, represented by the Nationalist government, was an original member of the United Nations and, along with the other big powers, an original permanent member of the Security Council. As President Kennedy stated in October 1961:

The United States has always considered the government of the Republic of China the only rightful government representing China and has always given full support to the position and to all the rights of that government in the United Nations. Therefore, the United States firmly opposes the entry of the Chinese Communists into the United Nations or into any of the components of the United Nations.[3]

Technically, therefore, the United States does not deny the principle of universality for the United Nations but claims that

[2] Statement issued by the Department of State, August 11, 1958, *Department of State Bulletin*, v. 39, September 8, 1958, pp. 385–390. This document is reprinted in Paul E. Zinner, ed., *Documents on American Foreign Relations, 1958* (New York: Harper and Brothers for the Council on Foreign Relations, 1959), pp. 423–432.

[3] *The New York Times*, October 20, 1961.

China, a member, is already represented by the Nationalist government and should not be represented by the Communist government on the mainland.

However, John Foster Dulles, writing in 1950 before he became Secretary of State and before the Korean War broke out, questioned whether Communist China should be kept out of the United Nations indefinitely and stated that in the long run the United States could not expect to maintain a "fictitious" preponderance of influence in the world organization.

If the Communist government of China in fact proves its ability to govern China without serious domestic resistance, then it, too, should be admitted to the United Nations. However, the regime that claims to have become the government of a country through civil war should not be recognized until it has been tested over a reasonable period of time.

If the United Nations membership were made substantially universal, that might end a preponderant voting superiority of the United States and its friends which, while pleasant, is somewhat fictitious.

Communist governments today dominate more than 30 per cent of the population of the world. We may not like the fact; indeed, we do not like it at all. But if we want to have a *world* organization, then it should be representative of the world as it is.[4]

In anticipating a trend toward universality of membership and a change in the degree of United States influence, Mr. Dulles foresaw some of the developments that were in fact to occur. He also seemed to imply that in practice the qualitative tests for membership in the United Nations set forth in the Charter should receive less emphasis. As events have developed, however, the United States has not altered its opposition to the seating of Peking in the United Nations even though it has modified the tactics it pursues to keep the Chinese Communists out of the world organization.

The available evidence appears to indicate that this stand has been supported by American public opinion, although it is prob-

[4] John Foster Dulles, *War or Peace* (2d ed.; New York: Macmillan, 1957), pp. 190–191. In the 1957 edition of this volume, which was first published in 1950, these paragraphs were left unchanged, but Mr. Dulles wrote in the Preface that in light of Communist China's behavior in Korea, Tibet, and Indo-China, she should not be admitted to membership so long as she persisted in this behavior and so long as the Charter applies a qualitative test to membership. Same, p. ix.

able that government policy has influenced such opinion as much as or more than it has been influenced by it. The public-opinion polls conducted on the question since 1950 tend to show fairly consistent results, though some minor variations. American sentiment against the seating of the Chinese Communists continued to be strong in August 1953, immediately after the Korean truce, when the percentages were 50 against and 37 in favor. A year later, opposition had actually increased, and 8 out of 10 Americans opposed the seating of the Chinese Communists, while only 1 out of 10 favored it. More recently, opposition has been less strong, but it continues at about a 2-to-1 ratio.

At the same time, the American public has apparently held the view, with equal consistency and even greater strength, that the United States should not withdraw from the United Nations, even if Peking is seated. This opinion was held by a 3-to-1 majority in 1953. The majority dropped to 2 to 1 in 1954, when opposition to the seating of Communist China was at its highest point, but then rose to 10 to 1 in two separate polls conducted in 1964.[5] These results, together with the figures from other polls on related questions, seem to indicate that although the American public has continued to oppose the seating of Communist China in the United Nations, the issue no longer arouses deep passions or irrevocable commitments except among a minority.

The United States has been the target of a good deal of criticism in the world community, however, as a result of its stand on this issue. Even among countries that have voted to uphold the American position, there has been considerable uneasiness and doubt as to its soundness. Many have gone along only reluctantly. Some countries whose basic opposition to the spread of Communist China's influence matches that of the United States have felt

[5] For a tabulation of the polling results on these questions for the period 1950 to 1961, see Sheldon Appleton, *The Eternal Triangle?: Communist China, the United States and the United Nations* (East Lansing: Michigan State University Press, 1961), pp. 208 and 210. More recent polls include a comprehensive study by the Survey Research Center, University of Michigan, conducted in May and June 1964 under the sponsorship of the Council on Foreign Relations and published by the Council as a pamphlet, *The American Public's View of U.S. Policy toward China*. A poll was also conducted in November 1964 by Louis Harris Associates for *Newsweek* magazine.

that the effectiveness of the United Nations and the long-run cause of world peace would be better served if Peking were represented. They see American policy and the American commitment to the Nationalist government—which, however one assesses its merits, cannot, as they see it, "represent" the 700 million Chinese on the mainland—as dictated primarily by domestic political considerations.

Among some countries, opposition to the American position on the China issue in the United Nations has been clear from the beginning. Many of the new member states from Asia and Africa, for example, have consistently refused to support the United States. Moreover, there has been a steady decline in support for the American position throughout the membership generally. Even though the formal votes still back the American position, it is likely that today a substantial majority of members favors seating the representatives of Peking in place of those of Taipei unless, somehow, arrangements could be worked out for both governments to be members of the United Nations.

Chinese Attitudes

Neither the Chinese Communist government nor the Chinese Nationalist regime has shown any disposition to compromise by accepting the idea of simultaneous representation for the other. The Peking regime has reiterated dozens of times its determination to stay out of the United Nations "if the so-called 'Taiwan clique' is to appear in the United Nations, under whatever form and in whatever name." [6] The government on Taiwan has made equally clear its opposition to the idea. Faced by the whittling away of their support, the Nationalists have shown no inclination to yield ground but have continued to claim to be the government of all China, to point to the continuity of Chinese Nationalist representation in the United Nations ever since delegates of

[6] See Chou En-lai's statement to Edgar Snow as reported by the latter in *The Other Side of the River* (New York: Random House, 1961), p. 760.

the Republic of China signed the Charter in San Francisco in 1945, four years before the Communist victory on the mainland, and to try to play a useful, if unobtrusive, part in the organization.

The United States has not encouraged the Nationalist government to seek or accept any alternative to the present arrangement, and the tortuous legal and procedural complications involved in most of the conceivable changes other than a simple replacement of one regime by the other have further contributed to the stalemate and the general sense of frustration.

For example, it is possible, even though unlikely, that if separate delegations from Peking and Taipei were to present their credentials and claim to represent the member state of "China," the Security Council and General Assembly might take conflicting actions, with one body recognizing one delegation and the other recognizing the other. There are uncertainties, however, as to what sorts of actions taken in the Security Council are subject to the veto and what sorts are not, and it is not wholly clear which actions taken by the General Assembly would require a two-thirds vote and which ones a simple majority since the General Assembly can itself partially determine this. Moreover, the delegation occupying the permanent seat in the Security Council could attempt to veto the election of any new member to the United Nations. Legalistic debates over these and other issues have tended to divert thought from the basic political issues involved in the situation.

Obviously, there is no way in which either the Nationalists or the Communists can be compelled to accept a "two-China" or a "one-China-and-one-Taiwan" solution against their wills. There are some who argue, though, that the international community could take its own stand on the issue despite the opposition of the two Chinese regimes and that if an international consensus developed, it might in the long run have some effect on attitudes in both Peking and Taipei. That is, while the short-run result might be a boycotting of the United Nations by both regimes, the pressures operating on them over the long term might lead both to reconsider their opposition.

In the welter of proposals and ideas which have been advanced to deal with the situation, there have been various formulas for attempting to bring about a solution which would give both governments representation. For example, if the membership of the United Nations decided to regard the Republic of China on Taiwan and the People's Republic of China on the mainland as "two Chinas," it might designate them "successor states" to the former single state of China, in which case both could be considered members of the organization. If the membership adopted a "one-China-and-one-Taiwan" viewpoint, however, it might grant the Peking regime the one existing China seat and then consider the regime on Taiwan for admission as the new state of Taiwan. In the latter case, of course, the Nationalists might withdraw completely and seek no form of representation. Should they later change their minds and seek re-entry as a new member, they might have extreme difficulty getting in. The admission of new states is subject to the veto in the Security Council, and the Chinese Communists, if members, might well be able to block them.

There has always been a question as to whether the Chinese Communists wanted to be in the United Nations on any terms.[7] Some maintain that Peking's leaders may not have wanted to subject themselves to the discipline of the world organization because they may feel that they enjoy greater freedom of action as a nonmember—specifically, because they may believe that they can use their absence from the United Nations as a means of mobilizing support for themselves and their policies in other bodies, especially those consisting solely of Communist or Afro-Asian members, and that their absence permits them to avoid votes in the United Nations which might cause them embarrassment in their relations with one nation or another. In support of this interpretation, it is pointed out that Communist China has not pressed as vigorously as it might have for representation in the United Nations, has frequently attacked the organization as a "tool of the Americans," and has recently not only supported Indonesia's withdrawal from the organization but laid down several conditions for its own entrance (including abrogation of the United Nations' 1951 resolution branding Communist China an aggressor). The Chinese statements backing the Indonesian withdrawal also reiterated the charge of "U.S. imperialist control over

[7] This and certain other aspects of the attitude of the Chinese Communists toward the United Nations have already been touched upon in Chapter 4.

the UN," called for the overhauling of the organization, and suggested that perhaps the time had come to establish "another United Nations, a revolutionary one."

To date, however, Peking has not made progress toward setting up any organization that would be genuinely competitive with the United Nations, if that is indeed its hope. The Afro-Asian members of the United Nations have shown no inclination to follow the Indonesian example or to support the Chinese Communist attacks on the organization. Peking is unlikely at present, therefore, to press an attack that has yielded such a poor result, although it can be expected to continue its efforts to assert its leadership of the Afro-Asian world.

The recent behavior of the Chinese Communists may have hurt their chances of being seated immediately in the United Nations, but as was indicated before, they do not appear to be in a hurry. From outside the United Nations, they can continue to work for increased support from the Asian and African nations, denounce the "imperialist" behavior of the United States, deride the Nationalists' claim to represent China in the organization, and continue to profess their support for some sort of world organization genuinely devoted to "peace." They are unlikely to close the door to membership in the United Nations, but they do not at the present time seem prepared to pay any significant price for it.

The Effect of Communist China's Absence

It is difficult to assess the effect on Communist China of its absence from the United Nations. If one looks at the behavior of the states that have been members, it seems clear that while the requirements of membership and the operation of the institution have established certain obligations and procedures which may have influenced their behavior, membership does not seem to have altered the basic features of their foreign policies dramatically. Each country's policy and behavior within the organization have reflected its overall objectives, and one finds a wide range of performance, with substantial support and commitment by some and halfhearted participation by others.

There is little reason to believe, therefore, that if the People's Republic of China had been a United Nations member its international policies and behavior would have been radically different from what they have been in recent years. Like all other members, it would have approached the United Nations in terms of its own interests, and like many of them, it probably would have opposed the building up of the organization in ways that might have inhibited its own behavior. It is questionable to what extent Chinese behavior during the Korean War, the Taiwan Strait crises of 1954–55 and 1958, the occupation of Tibet, and the Indian border conflicts would have been basically different had the Chinese Communists been in the organization. One can point to many instances in which member states, both Communist and non-Communist, have tended to pay relatively little attention to the organization when they felt their vital interests were involved.

Nevertheless, if they had been members, the Chinese Communists, like other members, would have been exposed far more than they have been to the normal give and take of international relations. They would have been involved in the intricate system of specialized agencies, commissions, and committees and in the political, technical, and cultural activities of the United Nations. They would have had to take more frequent stands on a wide range of issues, and in the international politicking that goes on in the United Nations, they would have had to pay more attention to the views of others. They might well have been an obstructive and disruptive influence in many situations, but it is doubtful, as some claim, that they would have simply set about disrupting the whole machinery, for they would soon have learned the political costs of such a strategy. It is even more improbable that they would have been docile, compliant participants. In fact, they would certainly have worked vigorously to get support for their views.

It is also difficult to determine how the effectiveness of the peace-keeping mission of the United Nations might have been influenced by Communist China's involvement. Possibly the Security Council might never have been able to endorse the action taken by the United States in Korea if Peking had then been in the United Nations—in which case the United States might have had to proceed on its own, with perhaps some support from its allies. Conceivably, however, if China had been a member, the United Nations might have become involved in some situations, such as the Sino-Indian border conflict of 1962, which it has to date stayed clear of. Some supporters of Peking's participation argue, in fact, that if Communist China had been in the United Nations, it might have been called to account for the attacks in both Tibet and India. It is not certain, however, that the United Nations' role in crisis situations involving China would have been any greater.

It is a striking fact that except for a period of limited involvement in Laos, the United Nations has not played a significant role in most of the major crises in Southeast Asia. From 1946 to 1954 the French did not want international bodies to have anything to do with what they considered to be their private affair in Indo-China. Nor has the United States relied heavily on the United Nations to support its actions in Laos or Vietnam during recent years. (Perhaps it should be noted parenthetically that if the People's Republic of China had been in the United Nations, it might have tried to involve the organization by initiating a complaint against the United States over American intervention in Laos and Vietnam.)

Furthermore, Communist China's representation in the United Nations might make other countries, and particularly the United States, even more cautious than they have been in the past about involving the organization in some of the most complicated political issues. As Afro-Asian representation in the United Nations has grown over the last decade, all the major powers have found it necessary to take into account an increasingly complex variety of forces there. Inevitably, the United States has found it more difficult to mobilize support for all its views and has encountered increased criticism in many situations. If Communist China were represented in the organization, it would undoubtedly lobby actively among the delegations from Asia and Africa, where it would hope to have special influence, and this situation might well increase the difficulties the United States would experience in trying to deal with various problems through the United Nations.

On the other hand, as was stated earlier, Communist China

would find itself in more direct confrontation with the complicated forces operating on the international scene. Therefore, it might be subject to greater pressures and restraints.

Although it is impossible to say with certainty how particular circumstances might have differed if Communist China had been in the United Nations, it is easier to say with confidence that its absence has had a definite impact on the organization. Many members believe that the lack of real representation for a nation of 700 million people whose role in international affairs is of increasing importance is bound to be felt by a body whose tasks, as stated in Article 1 of its Charter, are "to maintain international peace and security . . . to develop friendly relations among nations . . . to achieve international cooperation . . . to be a center for harmonizing the actions of nations. . . ." That is, they feel that Communist China's absence reduces the prospect that the United Nations can fulfill its purposes.

The Charter, it is true, requires that the membership be limited to "peace-loving states . . . able and willing" to carry out the obligations of membership, but if these requirements were strictly and impartially enforced, there would be far fewer countries in the organization than there are. Indeed, it might be a very select group. In practice, therefore, the principle of universality has become generally accepted. Universality cannot be achieved, however, with mainland China absent.

The legalistic argument that China is represented by the delegates of the government of the Republic of China on Taiwan cannot, moreover, satisfy the majority of nations for whom the mainland of China—whether Communist or not, friendly or not—is a major presence and force in the world.

The Argument for Seating Communist China

International law and the rules governing the behavior of states are still so fluid that it is difficult to contend that Communist China, and Communist China alone, is guilty of behavior that makes it an outlaw nation ineligible for membership in the United Nations. If the organization is to consist only of members who meet the theoretical requirements of the Charter, it should be much more exclusive than it now is. However, if it is to reflect fully the major currents of international political life and the competition and discord that the United Nations was set up to alleviate, Communist China should certainly be inside and subject to the same rules and discipline as the others.

Washington and Peking obviously look at the same problem from two entirely different points of view. The United States has not wanted to see the Chinese Communists come in if their entry would result in the disruption of the organization. The Chinese Communists, on the other hand, have resented their exclusion but see no reason why they should forswear their policies and ambitions in order to join an organization in which the United States has had the predominant influence.

As was stated before, however, the fact is that the voice of the United States is not as strong in the United Nations as it once was. The large number of new members from Asia and Africa has blurred the focus of leadership, and there is now a widespread desire not to get involved in rivalries between the great powers. The crisis during the 1964–65 General Assembly over enforcement of the provisions of Article 19 concerning financial payments highlighted this fact. The majority of the members was not prepared to accept the American point of view because to do so meant choosing sides between the United States on one hand and the Soviet Union and France on the other. Instead, the majority preferred some sort of solution that would accommodate divergent interests and encourage maximum participation.

Increasingly, moreover, the membership of the United Nations has shifted toward support for representation of Communist China. American arguments pointing up Communist China's misbehavior and emphasizing the requirements of the Charter have seemed less and less convincing to many—including most of the principal allies of the United States.

Indeed, it seems probable that a majority of the organization will not accept the existing situation much longer. Most members entertain few illusions that Chinese Communist representation in the United Nations would suddenly convert Peking into a force for peace or that it would, in particular, facilitate any quick or easy solution to the current troubles in Southeast Asia. In their view, Communist China's presence is a necessary recognition of China's special importance as a world power, whether one looks upon the government in Peking as peace-loving or not. How can the issues of world peace and cooperation be dealt with, they ask, if the principal parties are not present?

Perhaps it is more comfortable not to have to face one's adversaries, but the United States is clearly losing support for its present position. In the United Nations, it must eventually face the choice between defeat or giving evidence of a willingness to adjust to the views of the other members. Fighting stubbornly to the end and then yielding to the general will would be one way of meeting the situation, but this would have serious drawbacks. It would probably jeopardize the American position of leadership on issues other than the specific problem of China.

Although Communist China would almost certainly be a troublemaker and a source of special harassment for the United States in the United Nations, the sort of disruptive influences that it could exert exists even in its absence. Abuse of the veto, regular denunciations of the "imperialists" and "colonialists," and opposition to many efforts at conciliation and peacemaking would not be new if it were seated.

To continue basing the American position on the propositions that the Chinese Communists are not peace-loving, that they would have a disruptive effect on the United Nations, and that there is no possibility of satisfactory negotiations with them, therefore, may satisfy our moral righteousness, but it does little to advance the solution of major problems either inside or outside the United Nations, it is not responsive to the general climate of world opinion, and it jeopardizes support for the United States on other issues without producing sufficient compensating advantages.

Time will be needed, of course, to work out with care and foresight the best means for bringing the People's Republic of China into the United Nations. Still, during the years since 1949, we have not adequately laid the groundwork for change, and unless we use the period immediately ahead to good advantage, we will find the situation getting worse rather than better. The divisive tendencies already evident in the world, exacerbated by conflict over whether Communist China should be seated in the

United Nations, may be intensified. The prospects for acceptable, let alone satisfactory and forward-looking, settlements in Asia may become even dimmer. And the position of leadership of the United States in the United Nations may be weakened if other member states lose patience and decide to try to bring Peking into the General Assembly despite American objections.

Both the situation in the United Nations and the need to seek a fresh approach to United States relations with China and to the settlement of Asian problems argue for an American initiative on this issue in the United Nations. The United States should indicate its readiness to see Peking represented and should initiate exploratory talks to this end. If the situation seems favorable for doing so, these negotiations might be related to the search for settlements in critical Asian areas and to plans for encouraging more constructive programs of regional development.

In short, we must work out a fresh strategy, the details of which cannot be prescribed but which would provide for membership for Peking in the United Nations. We must combine a sincere will to bring about a change, however, with a firm demonstration that we are without illusions regarding Communist China's ambitions and recognize the continuing need to check them.

Clearly, this task will require time. But we may have the time only if we show promptly that we will do our best to use it to good advantage. Otherwise, we shall simply be outvoted.

What about the Nationalist government on Taiwan, which now represents China in the United Nations? It will not be possible for the United States to continue supporting the claim of the Nationalist delegation to occupy the one existing China seat in the United Nations. The United States should insist, however, on trying to work out some formula that would at least keep open the possibility of representation for Taiwan as well as mainland China. The most desirable situation would be one in which the government of Taiwan, whatever its status and composition, were a member of the United Nations in its own right. As long as it continued to receive American protection, Taiwan could doubtless survive with its own government even outside the United Nations—just as other halves of divided nations and a few other countries not in the organization manage to do. Nevertheless, it would probably become more and more isolated in the international community, and this fact could create serious problems both for it and for the United States.

If both Peking and Taipei continue to insist that they will not be represented side by side as separate governments in the United Nations and if the member states simply vote to bring in Peking, the Nationalist government may have no choice but to withdraw. This development would certainly not be desirable from the United States' point of view, but if it takes place, the United States should continue unequivocally both its support of the United Nations and its guarantee of the security of Taiwan.

The search for some acceptable formula to bring Communist China into the United Nations may not produce immediate results. It might, in fact, result in a short-run situation in which there are no Chinese representatives sitting in that body. If such a situation occurs, the door must be kept open for future Chinese representation. To do otherwise would be to foreclose the possibilities either of making the United Nations a genuinely universal body or of bringing Communist China into a more normal relationship with the other members of the world community.

CHAPTER TWELVE

Taiwan:
Island of Contention

The island of Taiwan and its future constitute a problem of enormous complexity, for a variety of interests—including American, Chinese Nationalist, Chinese Communist, and Taiwanese—are tied up in it.

In the context of American policy in Asia and of United States relations with Communist China, the positions of the Nationalist government and the island of Taiwan are unique. They are unlike other governments and areas that the United States has supported in Asia in that the Chinese Nationalists, like the Chinese Communists, have consistently asserted that they constitute the government of all China and that Taiwan is not a country at all but simply a province of China. Since 1950, moreover, support of the government of the Republic of China and the defense of Taiwan have been foundation stones upon which the China policy of the United States has been built and have been looked upon as concrete and necessary symbols of the American determination to contain the Chinese Communists.

To Peking, Taiwan has been a prime symbol of American hostility and of what the Chinese Communists consider to be United States interference in Chinese domestic affairs. To the Nationalists, the island—their final stronghold—has been a base from which they continue to make their claim to be the legal government of all China and talk of a return to the mainland. The Taiwanese, who make up a majority of the population on the island, have their own interests and views, which have been largely obscured by the international forces that have converged on them.

240

They have simply endured a situation not of their own making and one of which a great many of them have not approved.

All these interests are affected by passions that inhibit quiet, sober analysis and make it difficult to disentangle the coils of a most intricate knot.

The American Interest

Taiwan, it will be recalled, came under United States protection at the time of and as a result of the Korean War, but by the end of that conflict, it had acquired a special place in American security policies in the western Pacific. As a further outgrowth of the Korean War, the Nationalist government acquired a political importance that its previous weakness and declining reputation had not foreshadowed.

Assessments of the military importance of Taiwan have varied over time and as between different observers. Some observers have viewed Taiwan as a possible base from which to launch an attack on the mainland. Others have regarded it primarily as a link in the overall American security position in the western Pacific and Asia. Still others have seen it simply as a strategically placed island that should not be allowed to fall into unfriendly hands.

During recent years, as was indicated before, the prospect that the Nationalist government will return to the mainland in the foreseeable future as a result of some type of amphibious military operation originating from Taiwan has become so remote that it cannot now be considered a serious possibility. Any return to the mainland is difficult to conceive, in fact, unless there were a major political upheaval in Communist China or a much broader military conflict in Asia which actively involved the United States and Communist China and in which Taiwan might also play a part. In the event of a major conflict, Taiwan could, of course, have an obvious military importance if the government and population supported the American effort.

While there is no evidence that Peking views Taiwan as a serious challenge or threat in military terms, the military power on

Taiwan does cause the Chinese Communists some concern and makes it necessary for them to maintain substantial forces in Fukien Province on the mainland coast opposite Taiwan. There is little evidence to date, however, that this has significantly reduced the Chinese Communists' military capabilities to pursue active policies elsewhere—in Korea, the Himalayan area, or Southeast Asia.

As was indicated before, one can only appraise the military importance of Taiwan to the United States intelligently by looking at Taiwan in the context of the overall security system and policies of the United States in the western Pacific and Asian area. Its strategic significance, in other words, lies in its relation to other elements in the American security system.

If the Chinese Communists were to establish control over Taiwan, they would thereby extend the range of their planes, ships, and submarines 100 miles eastward and would place their bases nearer to the major north-south sea lanes in Asia. There seems little doubt that this situation would trouble the Japanese, and it might cause real anxiety in the Philippines and other countries to the south which are fearful of Chinese intentions. Nevertheless, it is not clear to what extent the results, undesirable as they might seem, would upset the present overall strategic balance of forces in the area.

In viewing Taiwan, one must distinguish between the island's relevance to American security interests in Asia and its political significance to the United States as an island in the hands of a regime which claims jurisdiction over all China. Under existing conditions, the military and political considerations can be regarded as identical only if the island is viewed as a potential base from which to conduct military harassment against, or assaults on, the mainland—which is not the policy of the United States government. The possibility of pursuing any successful "roll-back" policy seems so remote and the usefulness of keeping up questionable fictions so dubious that the American interest in Taiwan and the Nationalist government should now be assessed in relation to other factors.

Continuing wholehearted, unqualified American support to the Nationalist government as the government of all China, rather than as the government of the island of Taiwan, could only be justified, in other words, if there was a reasonable prospect of its returning to the mainland or if it constituted a genuinely effective challenge to the legitimacy of the Communist government on the mainland. Neither of these conditions now exists. The United States, consequently, is today in the position of supporting a claim that is becoming more and more unrealistic with the passage of time, and it is pursuing a policy which, while it once represented a genuine hope, no longer reflects a real expectation.

Furthermore, the American policy of supporting the Nationalist government as the government of all China is not supported in any genuine way by many members of the international community, although some countries that do not agree with American policy still refrain from openly opposing it. At the same time, the desirability of permitting both the Chinese Nationalists and the Taiwanese on the island to lead a separate political existence, free from Communist control, has been increasingly recognized in the international community.

While United States policy should not be shaped by the views of other countries simply because of sentimental concern for their criticism, the lack of broad support for American policy toward China clearly is important, for in the long run that policy cannot be effectively pursued if the United States stands largely alone. On such issues as trade with Communist China, the representation of China in the United Nations, and the isolation of the Communists from the international community, for example, American policy has been slowly but steadily weakened by the decline in international support. As a result, today we face a situation very different from the one that was envisaged when we first undertook our commitments to give full support to the position of the Nationalist government.

Although American commitments clearly have created an obligation to continue to help protect the inhabitants of Taiwan from a forcible Communist takeover, it would be unwise to commit the United States indefinitely to the support of a legal claim that is today almost totally devoid of substance. Any re-examination or change of United States policy will, it is true, involve difficulties. The American position has been so distinctive and firm and the passions it has involved on the part of many have been so heated that any departures from past policy will involve problems—particularly risks that the changes may be interpreted as a sign of weakness—which could have consequences beyond the areas affected by the China problem itself. Obviously, if policy changes are made, the United States has an essential interest in insuring that the possible adverse effects on the confidence of other countries are minimized. But the undeniable risks and liabilities of changing policies must be weighed against those of attempting to maintain unrealistic policies that are steadily undermined by attrition.

American policy toward Taiwan during recent years and continuing conflict with Communist China, it should also be pointed out, have obscured the fact that the United States and the Chinese Nationalists, while sharing many interests, have pursued objectives which are by no means identical. The entire foreign policy of the Nationalists has been centered on one purpose: retaining recognition as the legal government of all China with a view to becoming once again, at some future time, the government of the whole country. For the United States, the problem has been different. While not indifferent to who governs China, the United States, of necessity, must concern itself with the foreign policies of whatever regime actually rules the bulk of the country, and it must—unless it is prepared to attempt to destroy the regime—adjust its relations to deal with that government, whoever controls it.

This divergence of interests between the United States and the government of the Republic of China has been apparent in a number of concrete situations. The Nationalists, for example, have refused to withdraw from the offshore islands despite American pressure that they do so in order to minimize the dangers of conflict in the Taiwan Strait. The United States, on its part, has made it amply clear that it will not support the return of the Nationalists to the mainland by force. Over time, moreover, the United States has made it increasingly clear that it sees no likelihood of the early demise of the People's Republic of China, and it has dealt and negotiated with representatives of the Peking government in various situations—to the dismay of the Nationalists, who feel that if they were to follow these examples they would in effect be denying their own legitimacy.

Thus, while not challenging the form and legality of the principle of a Nationalist return to the mainland, and in fact giving it legal support by continued recognition of the Nationalist government as the government of all China, the United States rejects the principle in practice, imposes what restraints it can on Taiwan, and tries to discourage the Nationalists from attempting to operate on the basis of the principle. As a result, credulity has become ever more strained and the reconciliation of hope and reality more difficult.

Would the collapse or overthrow of the Communist government on the China mainland fundamentally alter this situation? That is, would it then be in the interests of the United States to support the return of the Nationalists to the mainland? Even though there is no prospect that the Peking regime will collapse or be overthrown in the foreseeable future, the question needs to be posed.

It is obviously hazardous to speculate on a contingency which might arise under circumstances that no one can anticipate. However, it is worth noting some facts that are clearly relevant. The Nationalists, despite their greatly improved performance on Taiwan in recent years, were badly defeated and discredited when they left the mainland in 1949. It is not illogical to assume that the longer they have been separated from their homeland, the more difficult it has been to keep in touch with the situation there and the less knowledge the mainland population has had of them. There is no reliable evidence that Nationalist propaganda directed to the mainland has significantly influenced sentiment in their favor or that the hardships endured by the Chinese under Communist rule have made them turn to Chiang Kai-shek as a beacon of hope. The picture that the Chinese people on the mainland now have of the Nationalists must be a mixed one at best, and any image at all is probably becoming dimmer with the passage of time.

It is realistic to assume, in fact, that in the event of a major upheaval on the mainland, forces at work there, rather than external influence from Taiwan, would shape the future. The Nationalists would be remote in time, distance, and political empathy. Were the United States to plan on helping the Nationalists attempt to restore their power under such conditions, the result might be for the Americans to lose touch once again with Chinese realities. The desire to see changes in the nature of Chinese Communist rule, by either evolutionary or revolutionary means, is no excuse for continuing self-delusion that can only mislead ourselves and our friends.

Taiwan, as was indicated before, plays a major role in the conflict between the United States and the People's Republic of China, for the confrontation there is open and direct. The Seventh Fleet's policing of the Taiwan Strait not only restrains the Chinese Nationalists from the temptation of provoking a conflict that they might hope would return their regime to the mainland by force but prevents a Communist attack on the island.

In recent years, the Chinese Communists have insistently demanded the withdrawal of American protection from Taiwan as a precondition for any steps to improve relations between themselves and the United States. They maintain that their relationship with the "Chiang Kai-shek clique on Taiwan" is an internal Chinese question, and they scorn American demands that they renounce the use of force in their dealings with the Nationalists, even though at the same time they acknowledge that there exists, in fact, a dispute between China and the United States in the Taiwan region and that this is an international question.

The roots of the conflict between the United States and the People's Republic of China, however, are obviously much deeper than the controversy over the status of Taiwan alone, and even if the Taiwan issue were somehow resolved, the causes of the present antagonism would probably not quickly disappear. Nevertheless, it is difficult to see how any serious steps toward a reduction of tensions can be successful as long as the United States persists in recognizing the government on Taiwan as the legal government of all China.

The evidence suggests, therefore, that on the one hand continued American support of the Nationalist government as the government of all China corresponds neither to reality nor to essential American interests while on the other hand the United States does have a continuing responsibility for insuring that the population of the island does not come under Peking's control without its consent as well as a significant military interest in keeping the island of Taiwan out of Communist hands. This conclusion cannot be altered by any simple arguments that the issue is a domestic Chinese one or that the United States might just as well accept today a situation that it seemed prepared to accept in 1950.

Communist, Nationalist, and Taiwanese Interests

George Kennan has described the decision taken at the Cairo Conference in November 1943 to return Taiwan to China as a "thoughtless tossing to China of a heavily inhabited and strategically important island which had not belonged to it in recent decades," and he points out that the step was taken "before we had any idea of what the future China was going to be like, and without any consultation of the wishes of the inhabitants of the island. . . ." [1]

Whatever the wisdom of the decision, which was confirmed a year and a half later at Potsdam, both the Chinese Communists and the Chinese Nationalists have considered the action to be legal and binding, and the silence of the 1951 peace treaty with Japan concerning the future status of Taiwan—which implied that Taiwan's status is not yet settled—has not shaken their view. Moreover, they cite Chinese history as well as the agreements reached during the wartime conferences to support the validity of their position. For them, Taiwan is an integral part of China, wrongfully detached from it by the Japanese and rightfully rejoined to it as a result of Japan's defeat.

Therefore, as was stated earlier, both have strongly opposed all suggestions favoring the recognition of "two Chinas" (that is, one Chinese government based in Peking and the other based in Taipei) or of "one China and one Taiwan" (that is, a Chinese government based in Peking and a separate state of Taiwan). The view of Peking, simply stated, is that the province of Taiwan is regrettably but temporarily administered by members of the "Kuomintang clique" under Chiang Kai-shek, who, with American support, contest the authority of the central government in Peking. The view of the Nationalists is that the island is now, by force of unavoidable circumstances, the temporary seat of the national government until that government can re-establish itself on

[1] George Kennan, *Russia and the West Under Lenin and Stalin* (Boston: Little, Brown, 1960), p. 377.

the mainland. Both sides argue that the quarrel is essentially a domestic one and that no compromise is possible.

The offshore islands of Quemoy and Matsu, which are occupied by the Nationalists even though they are located only a few miles off the China coast, represent a special case and different problems. However, to both Peking and Taipei they are probably a symbol of the unity of Taiwan with the mainland since they were always a part of the mainland territory and were not joined to Taiwan during the half century of the latter's separation from China. That is, the Nationalists regard the offshore islands as a foothold on the mainland, while the Communists may have mixed feelings about recovering the offshore islands without also regaining control of Taiwan because they might thus weaken the link between Taiwan and the mainland and symbolically cast Taiwan adrift once again as an island with no connection to the mainland. Such symbolism, of course, might not deter the Communists if they felt they could actually occupy the islands. But since the crisis of 1958, Peking has not pressed to regain the offshore islands, and they have not been a major object of controversy, although one cannot ignore the possibility that they could again become a center of dangerous conflicts.

As was stated earlier, the attention of the Nationalist government on Taiwan has been focused above all on support of its claim to be the government of all China and its desire to return to the mainland,[2] and these objectives have in turn determined the nature of governmental structure and policies on the island, the allocation of resources between military and social purposes, and the government's foreign policy.

Persons from the mainland, who came to Taiwan after their defeat there and now comprise about 15 per cent of the island's population of 13 million, retain firm control over the governmental administration and public life of the island, although native Taiwanese have become increasingly prominent in local administration and in economic life. The mainlanders have kept

[2] A comprehensive examination of the present situation and recent developments on Taiwan will be contained in the forthcoming volume by Tillman Durdin in the Council on Foreign Relations series, *The United States and China in World Affairs.*

intact the forms of China's national political institutions, which operate on top of a Taiwanese provincial administration. Political controls have been firm and at times severe—even though they are much less harsh than controls on the mainland.

The economy of Taiwan, which had developed substantially under the Japanese, has prospered, and even though this progress has been due in part to American aid, the authorities are rightfully proud of what has been accomplished. Nevertheless, the regime has deliberately subordinated economic affairs, education, and social and cultural matters to political and military tasks and to the goal of returning to the mainland. It has made every effort to allocate resources so that the military forces would receive all they needed, it has tried to maintain a psychological climate that would forestall acceptance of the separation from the mainland as permanent, and it has been reluctant to give the domestic concerns of the island priority attention. These policies have provided a rationale for the mainlanders' continued monopoly of political power on Taiwan.

It is difficult to assess how real the hope of returning to the mainland now is, for the possibility of going back seems to diminish daily. Whatever their private beliefs may be, however, the Nationalists have not outwardly reconciled themselves to the idea of being simply the political leaders of an island, nor have they learned to accept as equals those over whom they now rule. Since they cannot count on the willingness of the United States to engage in major military conflict with the Communists simply to restore Nationalist rule on the mainland, they can now do little more than hope, with almost no hard evidence to sustain them, that the Peking government will collapse, or reveal weaknesses that they can effectively exploit, or become involved in a major war that would result in a Communist defeat.

Only a basic transformation of the outlook of the Kuomintang leadership would alter the premises upon which the authority and structure of the present government rest. At the moment, there seems little prospect that President Chiang Kai-shek can be persuaded to change his views, for they have been hardened during years of war and exile. On the basis of this consideration alone, therefore, it would seem likely that during his lifetime the

Nationalists will continue making every effort to maintain their existing policies and act as if the situation had not changed basically since 1949.

However, changes in the general posture of the United States in Asia and/or the policies it follows toward both the Communist and Nationalist governments could also profoundly affect the outlook of Taiwan's leaders. If, as seems likely, there is further attrition in international support for the Nationalists' claim to be the government of all China and the rightful representatives of China in the United Nations, this too will doubtless lead some Nationalist leaders to re-examine their position.

The passage of time, moreover, should bring to positions of power men with fewer ties with the mainland and deeper involvements on Taiwan. This development will undoubtedly have an impact on the perspectives of the leadership.

On the island of Taiwan itself, the Nationalists will probably continue to face a Taiwanese population that is dissatisfied in many respects with continued political domination by the mainlanders. A sharing of political power, however, would symbolize, in the eyes of many mainlanders, an acceptance of the idea of restriction to an island domain and an abandonment of national ambitions and the hope of returning to the mainland. Would this be the wiser choice, or would it be preferable to seek an accommodation with Peking, which today commands the levers of China's national destiny? This question is one that at least some Nationalist leaders on Taiwan may in time ask themselves.

The dilemmas that Nationalist leaders are likely to face in the future could be dramatic, and the probable outcome is obscure. If deprived by international developments of support for their claim to be the government of China, the Nationalists could try to keep the principle of China's unity alive in some form while they in fact reconciled themselves to their shrunken realm. It is also conceivable that in desperation they might launch an attack against the mainland in the hope that the United States would become involved and back them up. The risks in such a course would be great, though, and they would have to consider the prospect that their action might bring down their own government rather than that of the Communists. Instead of accepting the need to grant equality to the Taiwanese and to continue relying on American protection, some might prefer to come to terms with the Communists. But many would doubtless believe that a reduced international status is clearly preferable to rule by the Communists. Whatever the direction in which future events may move, it seems likely that the present situation cannot last indefinitely.

The position and interests of the Taiwanese in this situation should not be ignored, as they sometimes are. Despite their Chinese characteristics and origins, a half century of Japanese rule and geographical separation from the mainland have given them an outlook of their own. Most Taiwanese, in fact, are not enthusiastic about harboring a mainland government whose members they regard as strangers in many respects and whose administration reaches deep into the affairs of the island. The Taiwanese have bitter memories of the early days following the Nationalist takeover soon after World War II, when the new rulers were harsh and oppressive, and they resent many aspects of the tight control exercised by the Nationalist government today over the life of the island. These feelings are only partially offset by the advantages of economic prosperity and the increased participation of the Taiwanese in local political affairs in recent years. However, even though Nationalist rule is distasteful to many Taiwanese, opposition to the Communists on the mainland is even stronger.

In an era when countries far less populous, homogeneous, and experienced are demanding and receiving international recognition, it is not surprising, therefore, that voices for Taiwanese independence have also been raised. Indeed, it is probable that the Taiwanese majority, whose views have never been consulted, would, if given a choice, opt for an independent or autonomous government under Taiwanese leaders and backed by international support to protect the island against the danger of Communist attack. The Taiwanese independence movement itself, however, is not strong or united.

While most Taiwanese would simply like to see the mainlanders go away, the Taiwanese recognize that in actuality they are likely to remain. Therefore, the Taiwanese would like them to pay less attention to their ambition of returning to the mainland, which imposes such heavy political and military costs, and devote more of their energies to working on an equal basis with the Taiwanese for the benefit of the island's entire population.

As has previously been mentioned, the Chinese Communists look upon United States recognition of the Nationalist government and American protection of Taiwan as illegal interference in Chinese domestic affairs. Today, however, Peking—like the United States—confronts a situation in which reality is very different from theory or hopes, and many of the arguments used to criticize American policy can apply equally to the Chinese: facts should be faced, and situations recognized for what they are and not for what one would like them to be, by the Chinese as well as by the Americans.

While the People's Republic of China is steadily gaining increased international recognition, the international community in general, as has already been noted, now seems to be less disposed than it formerly was simply to turn the island of Taiwan over to Peking's control—because Taiwan's people as well as its government would clearly resist such a move and because the island has since 1949 established an international personality of its own and has a viable political structure and a prosperous economy. This fact has not, of course, prevented Peking from persistently reiterating its demands for the return of Taiwan or insisting that recognition of its claims to Taiwan is a condition for negotiations on other issues with the United States. It seems unlikely, however, that the Chinese Communists seriously expect the Americans simply to withdraw from the Taiwan area in the foreseeable future. Moreover, the offshore island crisis of 1958 must have shown the Communists that they are not now able, through threats of force, to compel the Americans to abandon their support of the Nationalists.

What the Chinese Communists are probably hoping for, in the long run, is a slow weakening of American resolve and a reduction of United States commitments in the Asian area as a whole —developments which, Peking would anticipate, might eventually demoralize the Nationalists and open the way to a political settlement that could unite Taiwan with the mainland. Indeed, the Communists have mixed hostility toward the Nationalists with appeals to their sense of Chinese unity and destiny and thus attempted to exploit a common pride in China and a distaste for foreign involvement in Chinese affairs. So far, the Nationalists have been little affected by such blandishments, but Peking obviously hopes that the Nationalists' frustration over their own impotence or resentfulness against the United States might one day change the situation.

In short, even though the Communists may recognize their present inability to regain Taiwan and solve the situation to their satisfaction, they may also hope that time is on their side. They may believe that they can afford to be patient, that eventually there will be an erosion of both American determination and Nationalist will, and that in the meantime they can try to obtain whatever political benefits possible out of the existing impasse. At the moment, certainly, Peking shows no indication of any willingness to bargain over the issue of Taiwan.

The Choices Ahead

The complications of this situation scarcely need to be underlined. The conflicting interests of the United States, the Chinese Nationalists, the Chinese Communists, and the Taiwanese cannot be fully reconciled, and whatever decisions are taken or whatever policies are pursued, there will be many difficult, irresolvable problems. So many interests and ambitions are at stake in an atmosphere of such great political tension that no one can presume to outline a course of action that will provide right and durable solutions.

If such is the case, it might well be asked why we need to do anything. Would it not be best simply to let matters remain as they are and allow future events to dictate our course of action? This course would be the easiest one but not the right one. While it is not unusual for there to be some gap between the foreign policy of a country and the international realities with which it is designed to deal, they cannot be allowed to diverge indefinitely until policy bears little relation to reality. In the case of Taiwan, time is running out as the claims of the Nationalists, supported by the United States, become less and less realistic and the international status of the government on Taiwan undergoes increasing challenge and erosion.

The best that the United States can hope to do in this situation is to set certain goals that do seem attainable and then begin moving toward them, even if it is impossible to know in advance all the steps that will have to be taken on the way or to predict all the twists and turns on the path. These goals must be determined primarily to achieve United States objectives and protect American interests, although every effort should be made to find common ground with others and to accommodate to the interests of others.

In regard to the Chinese Nationalists and Taiwan, the United States should move to obtain as wide an international consensus as possible on their right to continued, separate political life and existence, but it should abandon its effort to maintain the fiction that the Nationalist regime is the government of all China. Even though there is no foreseeable prospect that the Nationalist government will be able to extend its authority beyond Taiwan, there is good reason to believe that the continued existence of a non-Communist regime on Taiwan is not only desirable but possible. The United States should therefore continue its commitment to the people and government on Taiwan to protect them from any Communist attack that would bring them under mainland rule against their will, and it should recognize their present self-rule and jurisdiction over Taiwan.

Perhaps the argument that the United States should not have interfered in the Chinese civil war might have been valid in 1949, but the situation has changed. The United States now has both a moral obligation and a political interest in insuring that Taiwan does not come under mainland Communist control under existing conditions. There are also security considerations which argue in favor of this position, but they are not so crucial as to be overriding. The most important reasons are the moral and political ones.

While moving in the directions suggested, the United States should also make it clear that, without sacrificing its vital interests, it is willing to adjust its relations with the People's Republic of China and hopes ultimately to work out an acceptable *modus vivendi*. The long-run future of Taiwan need not be predetermined, so long as the commitment that the United States will defend the island against forcible Communist takeover and will support the principle of self-determination is maintained.

These steps can and should be taken by the United States on its own initiative. They would not necessarily involve any negotiations or agreements with the Peking government. Indeed, such negotiations would simply give the Communists endless opportunity for obstruction and would probably frustrate and embitter the Nationalists much more than unilateral American action. Nor would the steps depend on international action. However desirable, such action would be extremely difficult to obtain. The establishment of a United Nations trusteeship over Taiwan, for example, which some have suggested, would be most difficult to bring about and extremely complicated to try to put into effect. Any proposal for a trusteeship would arouse intense political passions, and it is difficult to see how it could be implemented in the face of the inevitable objections of the Nationalist government as well as the Chinese Communists.

While the United States can alter the basis of its relations with the government of the Republic of China and henceforth treat it as the government of Taiwan rather than the government of all China, it obviously cannot prescribe what form of government Taiwan should have or what claims it might itself assert over the mainland. The people and government on Taiwan are the only ones who can decide such matters. It seems possible, and desirable, however, that in time the leadership and government will include more Taiwanese elements. Nevertheless, it is difficult to predict whether the regime even then would identify itself wholly with Taiwan or would still look forward to eventual reunion with the mainland.

There are some corollaries, of course, to the policy of treating the Nationalist government as the government of Taiwan and not the government of all China. For example, although the United States should continue its military protection of Taiwan, it should limit its military-aid program to what is needed for defense and should continue to urge withdrawal from the offshore islands in order to reduce the possibilities of military clashes with the Communists. In addition, it should support the Nationalist government for membership in the United Nations as the government of Taiwan, as was suggested in the preceding chapter, and not as the government of all China.

Time will be required to implement policies such as these. The aim should be to proceed slowly, step by step, and to make constant adjustments in policy without losing sight of the ultimate objectives. At first, the Nationalist government might try to refuse to accept the consequences of American actions, and our relations with it might be strained for a period of time. Over the long run, however, it will doubtless adjust to reality, particularly if the United States clearly indicates its continued good will and continued commitment to defend Taiwan. In a sense, the basis of American relations with Taiwan would simply become similar to that which the 1952 peace treaty between the Japanese and the Nationalists established for Japan's relations with Taiwan. At that time, Japan recognized Nationalist sovereignty over "all the territories which are now, or hereafter may be," under Nationalist control.

At least some of the mainland elements on the island would adjust easily to the new circumstances, and others would argue that the govenrment must acquiesce in order to insure its continued viability. It seems likely, moreover, that the Taiwanese population would welcome the changes, although many would feel that they did not go far enough. For the new situation to produce basic changes in the relationships between these two groups, though, time and patience will be necessary.

All the adjustments which changes in American policy would entail might well be easier to effect after President Chiang Kai-shek no longer personally directs the affairs of the Nationalist government and defines its goals, for the passage of time is bound to reduce the mainland orientation of the government on Taiwan and to induce leaders there to face more realistically the requirements of the situation on the island itself. Nevertheless, we cannot delay our initiatives in the vague hope that time will solve the problem and that it will be easier to deal with later rather than now.

In view of Peking's present unwillingness to look favorably upon any change in American policy toward Taiwan short of total acceptance of its position, the Chinese Communists can be expected to denounce any changes in United States policy as further evidence of American "imperialism" and to claim that they confirm that the United States intends to dominate Taiwan. Peking would assert that American imperialism was simply taking a new form, and it would continue to demand the total end of Taiwan's separate status. In fact, however, there is little that the Chinese Communists could do except to try to persuade the Nationalists of American perfidy in the hope that the Nationalists would throw the Americans out and rejoin their Chinese brothers on the mainland. Peking might make attractive promises to the Nationalist leaders, but it seems unlikely that any large number of these leaders would decide that they would gain by falling in with such maneuvers.

Nor does it seem likely that the proposed changes in American policy toward Taiwan would immediately, or even soon, ease the way for an improvement in relations between the United States and the Chinese Communists, even though they would reduce the legal obstacles to American recognition of the Peking regime. In fact, in the short run the Communists' bitter opposition to such changes in policy might create new tensions. However, by creating a situation in which United States policy is closer to reality, the long-run effect could be to exert pressure on Peking to make adjustments in its policies too. In any case, the long-term problem of reducing tensions and working toward some kind of *modus vivendi* will depend on many issues having nothing to do with Taiwan.

The United States should attempt to enlist the support of other nations in its efforts to redefine its views on the Taiwan issue. Full consultation with and a broadened consensus among the principal countries sympathetic to a change in United States policy—countries such as Britain, Japan, France, and Canada, which can themselves influence the situation—could greatly strengthen these efforts and could increase their chances of success. Furthermore, many other countries which have been critical of aspects of United States policy and have long felt that is should be brought more into line both with reality and with the prevailing views of other nations would clearly welcome American moves of the sort suggested, and concerted action on our part should make it possible to bring about a broader consensus on issues relating to China in the United Nations, where, in the absence of some indication of a change in the American position, impatience with American policy might eventually reach such a point that it would leave the United States little room for negotiation. Many countries otherwise critical of United States policies toward China, for example, would certainly receive sympathetically evidence that the United States was definitely seeking a readjustment of its current policies, and at least some of them would probably be prepared to adjust their own policies in ways that would support the United States in the pursuit of its objectives.

Peking's closest Communist allies and other friends would certainly denounce the United States for not abandoning Taiwan entirely. A few countries in Asia, probably including those on China's periphery which feel most vulnerable and are strongly hostile to the Chinese Communists, might be fearful of the implications and possible consequences of changes in American policy for their own positions. Some might have misgivings as to whether American actions foreshadowed a general revision of United States policy in Asia and an overall reduction of its involvements and commitments. To offset these fears, it would be necessary not only to reassure these countries but also to underscore specifically the continued American commitment to defend Taiwan as long as the government and people of the island wish to have defensive support from the United States.

The risks of initiating new policies such as those suggested here are substantial, and not all of them are predictable. The new moves could result, for example, in serious discouragement and resentment among many of the Nationalists who cling to unrealistic hopes. Many, however, have already begun to adjust, at least privately, to the changes in reality in the past decade and a half. Conceivably, there might be a few who would argue in favor of a desperate attempt to return to the mainland despite American objections. It hardly seems likely that their views could prevail, though, if we made absolutely clear that they would receive no support for such an adventure. The majority would probably realize that the certain result would be a heavy loss of life and the probable disintegration of the Nationalist government. More likely than any military adventure against the mainland would be an effort to exert pressure on the United States through real or rumored negotiations between some Nationalist leaders and the Communists aimed at a political settlement of some sort. As was stated earlier, however, it is highly unlikely that the majority of Nationalist leaders would endorse any such settlement or that the Taiwanese majority on the island would willingly accept any arrangement whereby their fate would be decided without taking their wishes into account. And the continued interposition of American forces in the Taiwan Strait could doubtless prevent any agreement made between the Communists and a minority of Nationalist leaders from being put into effect. (In the unlikely event that the Nationalists and Communists were to reach an agreement which the majority of the Taiwanese also clearly supported, the United States should be prepared to disengage and withdraw its protection from the island. Whatever the military benefits to the United States of a continued American military presence on Taiwan, the American role would be vulnerable and fundamentally untenable if it was maintained over the objections of the principal parties concerned.)

One would like to point confidently to spectacular advantages certain to result from these proposed changes in American policy. However, the changes are desirable more to minimize the disadvantages in the present complex situation than to "solve" the basic problems, which clearly are not now soluble. One cannot but admit that the long-term outcome is uncertain and that there are short-term risks. Nevertheless, in a situation where the choice is between policy alternatives which all involve uncertainties and risks, the arguments for the changes proposed are strong.

The proposed changes in American policy should not be viewed as a "concession" to the Chinese Communists, who, in fact, would not be happy with them, but rather as a step toward the "unfreezing" of a situation that is not now to our advantage. It is essential to bring United States policy into line with existing realities before the isolation of the American position makes current policies even more untenable. Moreover, continued American recognition of the Nationalists as the government of China obstructs all attempts to normalize relations between Communist China and the international community, and this situation is un-

260

desirable, even though one cannot be optimistic at present that there can be any significant improvement in the immediate future in relations between the United States and the Peking government on terms compatible with basic United States interests.

Improvement of relations with the Chinese Communists will come, if it comes at all, only as the result of a series of many small steps backed by a genuine desire on both sides to seek some sort of accommodation. However, the proposed action regarding Taiwan might, in the long run, help lay the groundwork for such a development without endangering any essential interests of the United States or of the majority of the population on Taiwan.

CHAPTER THIRTEEN

A Summing Up

What, then, can be said in summary about the complex problems of American-Chinese relations? First of all, the shaping of United States policy toward China clearly requires more than a few decisions on particular foreign-policy issues. It must be fitted into an overall conception of world forces and of the relationship of the United States and China to them. That is, United States relations with China must be placed in historical perspective and analyzed in terms of existing conditions in Asia and the character of the international arena generally. We need to have a clear sense of direction and of purpose—of where we are going and how we expect to get there. And we must be prepared to pursue our goals with determination and patience and constantly adjust our policies to the realities of the world around us.

China today is many things. It is the heir to an ancient and great civilization, a culture which has nurtured men of talent and ideas that have had a great impact on the world. It is a Communist country which is undergoing a profound revolution and is dedicated to modernization, albeit by totalitarian methods that we deplore. It is a great power which is asserting its role in the world and is finding some echoes in other countries. As a Communist nation and a power demanding to be heard, China has adopted hostility to the United States as one means of achieving its ends—a hostility that has been intensified because we have opposed the claim of the Communist leadership to speak for China and because we have tried to block all their efforts to extend their influence throughout the world.

What we face is no passing phenomenon or disagreeable eddy in the flow of history. China's past and the political trends of the twentieth century have converged to create a new society that is making fresh demands on the world. Many of the policies Communist China is pursuing are alien to our own, but this fact does not mean that they will necessarily be short-lived.

There is no longer much mystery about these new doctrines or the problems that they aim to solve. Nor are the Chinese leaders magicians, for they, like others, have to cope with the recalcitrance of individuals and nations, of economic problems and human nature. They are not all wise or all fearful or even all bad, nor, as recent events show, are they invariably successful. We should treat them as skillful and determined antagonists but not as the diabolical incarnation of some new and strange evil. We have met and coped with quite similar problems in dealing with the Soviet Union, especially during Stalin's days, and we have at least managed to live with it without direct conflict for almost fifty years. Moreover, in full realization of the risks involved, we decided more than thirty years ago to establish diplomatic relations with Moscow.

It is not within the power of the United States to determine what sort of government or what form of society China will have, any more than the Chinese can shape the American future. The events of the past are already inscribed and cannot be erased. At the same time, a unified and modernizing Chinese mainland under authoritarian Communist rule and conscious of its historical role has a restless and menacing quality that can be neither ignored nor eliminated. The social, national, and technological revolution of the twentieth century has come to China, and the Chinese Communists are trying to assert the leadership of their country over others who for the first time are going through the same experience. Their success or lack of success will depend to a considerable extent on their performance at home, and no one knows what they will be able to achieve. It is likely, however, that for many years to come the United States will be faced by a China that is both Communist and ambitious, striving for modernization, and demanding a place of increased influence in the world, most particularly in Asia and the underdeveloped world.

The danger that Communist China constitutes for the United States and its friends is a very real one, and we will do ourselves a disservice if we ignore it. We will certainly not advance our interests, however, if we speak and behave as if the threat were greater than it is or if we exaggerate China's present power and influence and overlook its setbacks as well as its advances. There are now some, for example, who magnify China's accomplishments, overstress our setbacks, and make our friends uneasy. Still, China's strength and influence are real, and they should be appraised soberly.

China cannot be denied an important place in the world—a place which its history and talents have prepared it to assume and which the present Chinese leaders have pursued with vigor and considerable skill by maximizing the use of its limited resources. Many other nations have been readier than the United States to recognize the accomplishments of the Chinese Communist regime as well as the dangers it poses and the ideals underlying the Chinese revolution as well as the evils it involves. In the eyes of many, China has already taken its place among the major nations, even though it is viewed with a combination of apprehension and respect. The United States will have little support in the long run if it simply treats Communist China as a pariah among nations, cursed by a special brand that sets it apart from all others.

The intense hostility of Peking toward the United States, which has been and is today the principal target of Chinese attack, has discouraged any change in American attitudes. Even if the United States were determined to seek an improvement in relations more actively, the task would not be easy. The conflicts of interest are real and are envenomed on the Chinese side by a deliberately planned campaign of vilification. However, anger is not an effective response to this situation. Nor is mere "toughness" enough. What is required is firmness in defending and advancing American interests together with a recognition of legitimate Chinese interests and a demonstrated desire to seek accommodation on mutually acceptable terms if they can be found. Only with such a combination can we hope in the long run either to influence the Chinese leaders or to win the acceptance and support of many other nations for our policies.

Communism gives to China's attitudes an intensity and harshness that they would not otherwise have. Its doctrine, which leads the present Chinese leadership to seek, through struggle, to make the world over in the Communist model, allows little room for tolerance and conciliation. The disciplined militancy that has characterized the Chinese Communists may, of course, be tempered in time, but a regime that suppresses freedom and dissent at home and proclaims world-wide revolutionary ambitions is not a comfortable neighbor or an easy negotiating partner.

Nevertheless, we should not think that the regime is divorced from human experience and immune from the countless influences that shape the lives of nations. Communism is not a universal solvent capable of dispersing all other influences, and recent developments in the Communist nations demonstrate that they, like other nations, have their own special identities, individually shaped by the influences of their histories, geographical positions, and special interests.

We thus need to deal with Communist China, and with other Communist countries, within the broad context of a world moved by complex social forces and to recognize the varieties of Communist beliefs as well as the distinctive national policies that various Communist regimes pursue. Certainly, we should not ignore the Sino-Soviet split. Moreover, we can be sure that just as the relationships among Communist states have changed greatly in the recent past, they will not remain unchanging in the years ahead.

Instead of looking to the future with dogmatic views about the immutable nature of communism, therefore, the United States should maintain at all times a clear sense of changing realities and relationships. China now has and will continue to have its own place in this picture, as an important Asian and world power which neither owes nor commands automatic loyalty in the Communist world or elsewhere. Today it competes with the Soviet Union as well as the United States for influence and must use persuasion as well as power to achieve its objectives in relations with other nations, Communist and non-Communist.

The ambitions of the Chinese leaders to extend their country's influence and to spread communism have made themselves felt amid the turbulence of the postcolonial era in Asia and Africa. In some new nations, the Chinese Communists have found that anti-imperialism and racialism have created a sense of identification with their achievements and strengthened sympathy for their determination to command China's own destiny. Moreover, they, as well as other Communist regimes and parties, have sought everywhere to present communism as a national movement with local roots and inspired by concern for national welfare and independence.

Where the Chinese hand has been laid too heavily, however, it has generally been rejected, just as interference by other major powers has been repulsed. Throughout the less developed world, each nation has sought to balance the various pressures exerted on it and thus tried to use them to its own advantage. Economically weak, politically inexperienced, suspicious of most outside influences, and caught up in events they cannot control, these nations have been preoccupied above all with survival. China is, of necessity, a significant element in their calculations, a country whose presence many cannot ignore.

The United States' interests would certainly be gravely prejudiced if East Asia came under the domination of any hostile power. Although such a development might not immediately pose a direct threat to American security, it could upset the present balance of world order, damage the United States' prestige and reduce its influence, and endanger countries that look to the United States for support. On the other hand, the United States should not presume to act as policeman in every situation of unrest in Asia, and it should not strive to deny China a position of influence in the area.

The military danger from China cannot be overlooked, but it is not now the principal danger. For the present at least, the Chinese do not have the resources or, apparently, the inclination to undertake major military actions beyond their borders—particularly in the face of American strategic power and the presence on their continental borders of a Russia upon whose support they cannot count. The greatest danger results from the weakness and disunity of China's neighbors, which create vulnerabilities that the Chinese can attempt to exploit by a variety of means short of military intervention.

It is essential to deter possible Chinese aggression and check the expansion of Chinese influence, but the United States cannot rely solely on a policy of military containment to do so. As was just stated, the countries of the area are in danger not only from China but also from their own internal weaknesses and from the conflicts and tensions that divide them from each other. Effective leadership and time are needed for each to put its own house in order. Americans can help by providing many sorts of encouragement and assistance. The United States cannot, however, presume to put everyone's house in order. Nor can it hope simply to eliminate China's voice or to eradicate completely Communist influence in all its forms.

In Asia, as elsewhere, it clearly will be necessary to live with regimes of which we do not approve. Recognition of this fact should not deflect us, however, from doing what we can to promote the security and stability of the area and to support needed economic and social development. In this task, we should welcome the participation of all those who are prepared to do their share.

American objectives in Asia and the stability of the area will be difficult to achieve if the gulf between the United States and Communist China continues to be as wide as it has been. The Chinese Communists can be expected to continue opposing our presence in all forms, and some countries will see an advantage to themselves in playing off one protagonist against the other. The hostility that now exists creates conflicting pressures and divisive forces that contribute to the general state of tension and unrest.

It is not within the power of the United States alone to end the hostility that the Chinese feel toward us or to change their present compulsion to interfere in the affairs of other nations. The United States should, however, take whatever steps it can to remove existing obstacles to a more normal relationship with Communist China, and it should be prepared to change policies that no longer serve a useful purpose or correspond to the requirements of the present situation. We should permit, and even encourage, trade with Communist China, subject to the same restrictions on strategic goods that are applied to trade with other Communist countries. We should make a more vigorous effort to open up channels of contact with mainland China despite the fact that the government in Peking has yet to show any disposition to welcome such arrangements.

Even recognizing the likelihood that the Chinese Communists might reject out of hand any specific proposals we might now make to them, we should nevertheless search for new approaches.

We might, for example, consider putting forward a proposal indicating our desire to work out procedures for a more fruitful exchange of ideas, something better than the rather formal ambassadorial-level talks in Warsaw. We could offer to meet with them, at any time and at any mutually agreed place, to discuss how best to organize a series of meetings in which there would be no limiting agenda and in which, through private and confidential discussions, any and all problems in our relations might be considered.

While reaffirming the American commitment to protect Taiwan, we should no longer attempt to maintain the fiction that the Chinese Nationalist government is the government of all of China; and while we should insist on the right of self-determination for Taiwan, we should recognize that the future relationship of the island to the mainland cannot be accurately predetermined or predicted since it will depend on future political developments on the island and on the mainland, as well as in Asia generally. We should be prepared to recognize the government of the People's Republic of China as the government of China and to establish diplomatic relations with it if and when it becomes clear that our action would be reciprocated and would have some promise of yielding useful results.

As long as the United States recognizes the government on Taiwan as the government of China, we force ourselves to have only very limited and almost furtive dealings with the Peking government, and to support the Nationalists' claim to be the only legal Chinese government, we are also compelled to do our utmost to prevent the Chinese Communists from being accepted into the world community. This policy of isolating the Peking regime has steadily been undermined. In the United Nations, there is growing pressure for the seating of Communist China, and outside the United Nations, Peking has worked persistently to broaden the range of its international contacts, activities, and influence. The American position on this issue in the United Nations and other international institutions will be unable to survive for long the mounting pressures for change on the part of other nations. Even accepting the probability that Communist China might be a disrupting influence in the United Nations or other world bodies, the United States should be prepared to accept the full participation of the Chinese Communists in such international institutions in the belief that in the long run such participation may help to restrain them and moderate their behavior. At the same time, we should try to insure that Taiwan is not excluded from these bodies.

We should not continue to confuse a policy of trying to isolate Communist China, which has almost no real chance for success, with the necessary objective of limiting China's ambitions. We must continue to resist the efforts of the Chinese to upset the present world order by refashioning it to their own purposes, but the Peking government cannot and should not be excluded indefinitely from the normal channels of international contact.

Why, it may be asked, should not the United States use its overwhelming military strength to strike now to cripple or destroy China's power to challenge and upset the world balance? To answer that it should, one would have to have an almost unlimited confidence in the capacity of military weapons to solve political, economic, and social as well as military problems plus a contempt for China and the Chinese. Even if one assumed that a few well-placed bombs could easily knock out China's major industrial installations and its facilities for producing nuclear weapons, what then? Would the Russians stand by doing nothing? Would the Peking government collapse or mend its ways? Would communism in China or elsewhere disappear? Would the Chinese and American peoples soon renew their historic friendship? Would China's influence on the world scene be eradicated? While no categorical answers can be given even to questions of this sort, the probable answer to each of them is "no."

The United States is only gradually learning that for many international problems there are no simple solutions. There are still some who think that with our great power we should be able to settle matters once and for all and others who are equally certain that if only the United States would be "friendly," the Chinese Communists would certainly reciprocate. There is a fluctuating tendency to see the Chinese as being either on the threshold of actually establishing a world-wide Communist empire or on the verge of total collapse. One day, the Chinese leaders are pictured as rash and reckless, and the next, crafty and enigmatic.

American impatience and strong currents of political emotion often make it difficult to plan ahead and to manage our policy in a persevering but flexible way. The failure of American policy in China in the 1940s and the frustrations of the Korean War are still alive in American memories, even though their influence now appears to be receding. The hostility that the Chinese Communist leaders have shown for the United States and the lengths to which they have gone to indoctrinate the Chinese people with anti-American passion have angered us. Our emotions have been stirred by our opposition to Communist doctrine, and the Chinese have been particularly unsettling to us because they have re-affirmed the militancy of their dogma at a time when the Russians and many other Communists have appeared to become more reasonable. Our vexation has been compounded by our seeming inability to use our strength in simple and effective ways to reduce the threats to our interests which the Chinese have posed. We strongly oppose communism but have not always found it easy to separate the threat of communism from the problems posed by nationalism, social unrest, and other major forces at work in much of the world. We must learn to face the fact that while China's policy and Communist conspiracy both pose serious threats, neither alone is an adequate explanation for all the problems we face in Asia.

Matters have not been made any easier by the curtain that has separated us from the Chinese. The barriers have helped the Communist leaders to isolate the Chinese people from reality and poison their minds against the United States. We, too, have often been the victims of our own prejudices and have tended to think in stereotypes. We have deplored the narrow outlook of the Chinese leaders, but it has been difficult for us, living in a prosperous and stable America, to understand men trained in revolution and hardship and national movements born out of frustration and humiliation.

We should do what we can to overcome these barriers and view the Chinese in the full perspective of their historical past and present accomplishments. Neither ignorance nor anger is a prescription for effective policy making. A better understanding of the Chinese and of the environment in which they operate is essential if we are to achieve a satisfactory adjustment of our relations with them and successfully oppose their efforts to extend their revolutionary example throughout the world. What has happened in China has too many affinities with developments in many other areas of the world for us to regard it as a simple malignancy that can be neatly extirpated. Intense national sensitivity, hostility to outside interference, an impatient drive toward modernization, a tendency to expect the state to solve all problems, and a predisposition to subordinate the individual to national goals—these are characteristic of many of the social and national revolutions that are going on in numerous parts of the world. Therefore, we must try to understand the complexity of the developments both in China and in the world as a whole.

While we must exert every effort to limit the influence and extension of hostile forces, through diplomatic and economic as well as military action, we must also do what we can—difficult though these tasks will certainly be—to reduce the possibilities of conflict, to seek adjustment of contending interests, and to try to influence in a favorable way the outlook and behavior of our antagonists, including the Chinese Communists. In broad terms, our major goal should be to build a world in which there is both cooperation for the general welfare and toleration of a compatible diversity of different social and political systems. This will be an arduous task. And neither we nor the Communists will have things all our own way, for it is clear that neither we nor they can simply stamp out men and events in preconceived molds.

Although the United States and other nations will certainly have to show appreciation of China's legitimate concerns and interests in order to arrive at any sort of *modus vivendi* with it, developments in the rest of the world will ultimately and inevitably have an influence on the course of Communist China's policy and the evolution of China itself. Thus, if the United States in collaboration with other major nations is successful in its general efforts to build a viable and progressive world order, it will have done much to meet what is too narrowly called the China problem.

We must act simultaneously on many fronts to achieve our broad goals. Unless we are able to make some progress in our direct dealings with the Chinese Communists, though, we will continue to find ourselves frustrated in many other directions. Such progress, of course, does not depend on us alone. Nor does the urgency of the task mean that we should proceed with haste and without any regard for Chinese attitudes or actions. We cannot, however, afford to find excuses for inaction and simply hope that time will work in our favor. If we do, we are likely to find that pressures which we cannot control will shape our policy, and the possibilities for effective diplomacy may well diminish. In short, if we wait indefinitely to undertake the reappraisal that is already overdue, our ability to work effectively toward defined goals may diminish rather than increase.

Contentment with the present stalemate in relations with the Chinese is not statesmanship for the times. "Events," wrote former President Truman with regard to China, "are moving at a faster pace toward reshaping our world than man has heretofore experienced. In this kind of a world, any policy that falls back on a 'wait and see' attitude, or, 'we'll cross that bridge when we get to it' could spell trouble and possibly danger." [1]

We cannot be sure that efforts to reach a reasonable understanding with the Chinese Communists will succeed. The current prospects are not good. The present commitment of the Chinese leaders to a hostile attitude toward the United States is strong and will not be easily changed. But we must try. Until we take the initiative, affirm our leadership, and pursue our goals more vigorously but with greater prudence, patience, and understanding, we cannot know whether or not, over time, a better basis of relations, or at least a reduction in the present level of tension and hostility, can be achieved.

[1] *New York Journal-American*, September 29, 1963.

Index

Acheson, Dean, 107, 108–109, 110, 111, 113, 155–156
Africa, 189, 216
  and China, 1, 10, 15, 24, 43, 70–71, 74, 75, 76, 77, 137, 139, 140–141, 190
  and U.S., 139, 199
Afro-Asian nations
  and Communist China, 139, 190, 199, 229, 231–232, 234, 264–265; *see also* Communist China policy, newly independent states
  and U.N., 232, 234, 236
  and U.S., 139, 199, 200, 229, 236
Afro-Asian organizations, and Communist China, 50, 75, 139
Agriculture, 57, 183
Aid, economic
  Communist China
    to Pakistan, 36
  U.S.
    to Asia, 29, 31, 111, 142, 143, 201, 266
    to Communist China, 128, 209
    to Taiwan, 108, 249
  U.S.S.R.
    to Communist China, 57
Aid, military
  Communist China
    to Laos, 166
    to North Korea, 37
    to North Vietnam, 37, 166
  U.S.
    to Asia, 153 ff.
    to India, 160, 168
    to South Vietnam, 161

Aid, U.S., to Taiwan, 108, 112–113, 119, 145, 255
U.S.S.R.
  to Communist China, 86, 102, 162
  to India, 168
Aleutian Islands, 155
Algiers Conference of Afro-Asian states (1965), 50, 70
Ambassadorial meetings, U.S.-Chinese, 13, 97, 103, 124–125, 133, 202, 221, 267
American image
  in Asia; *see* Asian states, attitude toward U.S.
  in China, 6, 11, 18–20, 96–97, 149, 203, 269
Anti-colonialism, 47, 163, 199; *see also* Anti-imperialism
Anti-imperialism, 32, 47, 51, 178, 189
  and Chinese policy, 10, 15, 69, 77, 96, 163, 199, 232, 264
Anti-Westernism, 32, 33 ff., 45, 47; *see also* Anti-imperialism
  in China, 53, 71
ANZUS, 158
Arab states, 216
Armed forces
  Asian states, 153
  Communist China, 80–81, 83, 152–153; *see also* Military power, Communist China
Asia
  balance of power
    and U.S., 2, 5–6, 17, 22–25, 49–50, 187–188
  Chinese threat, 2, 144, 181, 188, 265

273

Churchill, Winston, 110
Civil war, Chinese, 42, 65, 72, 80
  U.S. intervention, 1, 7–9, 94, 96,
    106–107, 155, 219
Colonialism 22, 25
Comintern, 41
Communes, 57, 137
Communist China, 8
  economic development, 57–58, 61,
    137, 183
  foreign trade, 58, 208–209
    Asia, 38
    Japan, 30, 34, 75, 140
    U.S., 114, 120, 127, 130–131, 133,
      198, 208–211, 221, 266
    U.S.S.R., 57
    West, 58, 75, 133, 139, 140, 221
  image in U.S., 18–20, 202–203, 204
  Party dictatorship in, 19, 52–55, 58,
    61, 62
  regime's stability, 56, 62, 104
  and U.S. policy, 121–122, 129–
    130, 131, 134, 137, 148, 182–
    183, 216, 244
  revolutionary doctrine, 65–74, 167
  as tool of Moscow, 10, 13–14, 16,
    20, 72, 111, 117, 132, 134
  as world power, 56, 65, 90, 103–
    104, 184, 190, 261, 263, 264
Communist China, policy of
  accomplishments of, 17–18, 79–80,
    150, 181
  Africa, 1, 10, 15, 43, 70–71, 74, 75,
    76, 77, 137, 139, 140–141, 190
  Asia, 1, 10–18, 23–24, 42–45, 74, 76,
    89–90, 137, 139, 140–141, 150,
    162, 219–220, 262, 266
  Burma, 142
  "Intermediate zone," 75–76
  militant ideology in, 10–18, 33, 42–
    47, 62–63, 65–74, 76–77, 81,
    86, 90, 163, 183, 189, 190–191,
    263–264
  military factors in, 80–86, 161 ff.,
    265
  Near East, 15, 43, 190
  newly independent states, 10, 15,
    16, 43, 69–74, 75, 93, 96, 103,
    132, 137, 139, 140–141, 215,
    231–232, 262, 264–265
  nonofficial diplomacy, 77, 163, 190
  North Vietnam, 37, 84–85, 90, 127

Communist China, policy of, over-
  seas Chinese, 38–39
  Pakistan, 36, 75, 168
  Southeast Asia, 166–167, 168
  South Vietnam, 44, 77, 84–85, 90,
    127, 142, 166
  Taiwan, 11, 18, 77, 80, 84, 89–90, 98,
    99–101, 103, 125, 128, 143,
    152, 181, 219–220, 233, 247,
    252–253, 256–257
  traditional elements in, 10–18, 33,
    62–63, 65, 89–90, 183–184,
    190–191
  U.N., 2, 87, 90–93, 202, 224, 229–232
  U.S., 69, 73, 75–76, 82, 94–104, 162,
    219–220; *see also* U.S.-Chi-
    nese conflict
    conciliatory steps, 97–98, 124, 126
  U.S.S.R., 73–74, 75, 132, 154, 225;
    see also Sino-Soviet conflict
  Western Europe, 20, 132, 137, 190
Communist-led insurrections; *see also*
    Subversion
  in Asia, 18, 30, 43 ff., 142
  and Peking, 17–18, 42–44, 65–74, 86,
    142, 161, 163, 166–167
  and U.S., 14, 30–31, 160–161, 166–
    167, 169 ff.
  and U.S.S.R., 43, 66–67, 102
Communist movement, international,
    47, 134, 264; *see also* Sino-
    Soviet conflict
  plans for Asia, 40–47
  and Moscow, 23, 190, 192–193, 197
  and Peking, 2, 68, 75, 77, 190, 192–
    193, 215
Communist parties; *see also* Chinese
    Communist party
  Asian, 37–38, 46, 144
    and Moscow, 23, 40–41, 43, 46,
      145, 189
    and Peking, 39, 41–47, 75, 77, 79,
      145, 189
    and U.S., 188–189, 190–191
  Burmese, 36, 43
  Indian, 43, 46
  Indonesian, 26, 43, 45, 144
  Western European, 8
Communist threat
  Asia, 10 ff., 26, 40–47, 144, 189; *see
    also* Communist-led insur-
    rections; Subversion

COUNCIL ON FOREIGN RELATIONS

Officers and Directors

John J. McCloy, *Chairman of the Board*
Henry M. Wriston, *Honorary President*
Grayson Kirk, *President*
Frank Altschul, *Vice-President & Secretary*
David Rockefeller, *Vice-President*
Gabriel Hauge, *Treasurer*
George S. Franklin, Jr., *Executive Director*

Hamilton Fish Armstrong
Elliott V. Bell
William P. Bundy
William A. M. Burden
Arthur H. Dean
Douglas Dillon
Allen W. Dulles
Thomas K. Finletter
William C. Foster

Caryl P. Haskins
Joseph E. Johnson
Henry R. Labouisse
Walter H. Mallory
James A. Perkins
Philip D. Reed
Charles M. Spofford
Carroll L. Wilson

283

PUBLICATIONS

FOREIGN AFFAIRS (quarterly), edited by Hamilton Fish Armstrong.
THE UNITED STATES IN WORLD AFFAIRS (annual). Volumes for
1931, 1932 and 1933, by Walter Lippmann and William O.
Scroggs; for 1934–1935, 1936, 1937, 1938, 1939 and 1940, by
Whitney H. Shepardson and William O. Scroggs; for 1945–
1947, 1947–1948 and 1948–1949, by John C. Campbell; for
1949, 1950, 1951, 1952, 1953 and 1954, by Richard P. Stebbins;
for 1955, by Hollis W. Barber; for 1956, 1957, 1958, 1959,
1960, 1961, 1962 and 1963, by Richard P. Stebbins; for 1964,
by Jules Davids; for 1965 by Richard P. Stebbins.
DOCUMENTS ON AMERICAN FOREIGN RELATIONS (annual). Volume
for 1952 edited by Clarence W. Baier and Richard P. Stebbins; for 1953 and 1954 edited by Peter V. Curl; for 1955,
1956, 1957, 1958 and 1959 edited by Paul E. Zinner; for 1960,
1961, 1962 and 1963 edited by Richard P. Stebbins; for 1964
by Jules Davids; for 1965 by Richard P. Stebbins.
POLITICAL HANDBOOK AND ATLAS OF THE WORLD (annual), edited
by Walter H. Mallory.
ATLANTIC AGRICULTURAL UNITY: Is it Possible?, by John O.
Coppock (1966).
TEST BAN AND DISARMAMENT: The Path of Negotiation, by Ar-
thur H. Dean (1966).
COMMUNIST CHINA'S ECONOMIC GROWTH AND FOREIGN TRADE, by
Alexander Eckstein (1966).
POLICIES TOWARD CHINA: Views from Six Continents, edited by
A. M. Halpern (1966).
THE AMERICAN PEOPLE AND CHINA, by A. T. Steele (1966).
INTERNATIONAL POLITICAL COMMUNICATION, by W. Phillips
Davison (1965).
MONETARY REFORM FOR THE WORLD ECONOMY, by Robert V.
Roosa (1965).
AFRICAN BATTLELINE: American Policy Choices in Southern
Africa, by Waldemar A. Nielsen (1965).

NATO IN TRANSITION: The Future of the Altantic Alliance, by
Timothy W. Stanley (1965).

ALTERNATIVE TO PARTITION: For a Broader Conception of America's Role in Europe, by Zbigniew Brzezinski (1965).

THE TROUBLED PARTNERSHIP: A Re-Appraisal of the Atlantic
Alliance, by Henry A. Kissinger (1965).

REMNANTS OF EMPIRE: The United Nations and the End of
Colonialism, by David W. Wainhouse (1965).

THE EUROPEAN COMMUNITY AND AMERICAN TRADE: A Study in
Atlantic Economics and Policy, by Randall Hinshaw (1964).

THE FOURTH DIMENSION OF FOREIGN POLICY: Educational and
Cultural Affairs, by Phillip H. Coombs (1964).

AMERICAN AGENCIES INTERESTED IN INTERNATIONAL AFFAIRS (Fifth
Edition), compiled by Donald Wasson (1964).

JAPAN AND THE UNITED STATES IN WORLD TRADE, by Warren S.
Hunsberger (1964).

FOREIGN AFFAIRS BIBLIOGRAPHY, 1952–1962, by Henry L. Roberts
(1964).

THE DOLLAR IN WORLD AFFAIRS: An Essay in International Financial Policy, by Henry G. Aubrey (1964).

ON DEALING WITH THE COMMUNIST WORLD, by George F. Kennan (1964).

FOREIGN AID AND FOREIGN POLICY, by Edward S. Mason (1964).

THE SCIENTIFIC REVOLUTION AND WORLD POLITICS, by Caryl P.
Haskins (1964).

AFRICA: A Foreign Affairs Reader, edited by Philip W. Quigg
(1964).

THE PHILIPPINES AND THE UNITED STATES: Problems of Partnership, by George E. Taylor (1964).

SOUTHEAST ASIA IN UNITED STATES POLICY, by Russell H. Fifield
(1963).

UNESCO: ASSESSMENT AND PROMISE, by George N. Shuster
(1963).

THE PEACEFUL ATOM IN FOREIGN POLICY, by Arnold Kramish
(1963).

THE ARABS AND THE WORLD: Nasser's Arab Nationalist Policy, by
Charles D. Cremeans (1963).

TOWARD AN ATLANTIC COMMUNITY, by Christian A. Herter
(1963).

286

THE SOVIET UNION, 1922–1962: A Foreign Affairs Reader, edited by Philip E. Mosley (1963).

THE POLITICS OF FOREIGN AID: American Experience in Southeast Asia, by John D. Montgomery (1962).

SPEARHEADS OF DEMOCRACY: Labor in the Developing Countries, by George C. Lodge (1962).

LATIN AMERICA: Diplomacy and Reality, by Adolf A. Berle (1962).

THE ORGANIZATION OF AMERICAN STATES AND THE HEMISPHERE CRISIS, by John C. Dreier (1962).

THE UNITED NATIONS: Structure for Peace, by Ernest A. Gross (1962).

THE LONG POLAR WATCH: Canada and the Defense of North America, by Melvin Conant (1962).

ARMS AND POLITICS IN LATIN AMERICA (Revised Edition), by Edwin Lieuwen (1961).

THE FUTURE OF UNDERDEVELOPED COUNTRIES: Political Implications of Economic Development (Revised Edition), by Eugene Staley (1961).

SPAIN AND DEFENSE OF THE WEST: Ally and Liability, by Arthur P. Whitaker (1961).

SOCIAL CHANGE IN LATIN AMERICA TODAY: Its Implications for United States Policy, by Richard N. Adams, John P. Gillin, Allan R. Holmberg, Oscar Lewis, Richard W. Patch, and Charles W. Wagley (1961).

FOREIGN POLICY: THE NEXT PHASE: The 1960s (Revised Edition), by Thomas K. Finletter (1960).

DEFENSE OF THE MIDDLE EAST:Problems of American Policy (Revised Edition), by John C. Campbell (1960).

COMMUNIST CHINA AND ASIA: Challenge to American Policy, by A. Doak Barnett (1960).

FRANCE, TROUBLED ALLY: De Gaulle's Heritage and Prospects, by Edgar S. Furniss, Jr. (1960).

THE SCHUMAN PLAN: A Study in Economic Cooperation 1950–1959, by William Diebold, Jr. (1959).

SOVIET ECONOMIC AID: The New Aid and Trade Policy in Under developed Countries, by Joseph S. Berliner (1958).

NATO AND THE FUTURE OF EUROPE, by Ben T. Moore (1958).

INDIA AND AMERICA: A Study of Their Relations, by Phillips Talbot and S. L. Poplai (1958).

NUCLEAR WEAPONS AND FOREIGN POLICY, by Henry A. Kissinger (1957).

MOSCOW-PEKING AXIS: Strength and Strains, by Howard L. Boorman, Alexander Eckstein, Philip E. Mosley, and Benjamin Schwartz (1957).

RUSSIA AND AMERICA: Dangers and Prospects, by Henry L. Roberts (1956).